LEARNING FROM THE SIXTIES:

MEMOIR OF AN ORGANIZER

JOHN MAHER

CHARLES STREET PRESS

BOSTON

Library of Congress Control Number: 2011934449
ISBN: 978-0-9843733-1-4

Charles Street Press, P.O. Box 328, Charles Street Station, Boston, MA 02114
www.charlesstreetpress.com

Book and cover design: Joanne Legge

This book is dedicated to the next generation, and to those of my generation who struggled and in many cases gave their lives so that this world could be a better place for all our children.

For Joanne,
Keep up the great
work. All the best.

John

TABLE OF CONTENTS

ACKNOWLEDGMENTS

I would like to thank teachers at St. John's School and Harvard University, among them Max Mertz, Bob Moore, Stanley Hoffmann, Sandy Lakoff, and Barrington Moore, who opened my eyes to wider worlds. I would also like to thank my friends, colleagues, and comrades at Students for a Democratic Society, Vietnam Summer, the Boston Woven Hose, the Somerville and Boston Public Schools, Oxfam America, and Neighbor to Neighbor from whom I learned much and whose friendship and support made it possible for me to carry on.

This memoir relies primarily on memory, and letters, articles, speeches, and other documents found in my basement. But three published works were of enormous assistance in this effort. Kirkpatrick Sale's book *SDS* based on the archive he rescued when the Weathermen went underground provided a structure that helped organize and supplement my memories of the 1960s. Stanley Karnow's *Vietnam* provided similar help with my memories about how that war unfolded. Michael Zweig's *The Working Class Majority* is a must read for those who want to understand who the progressive movement needs to reach out to.

I have used real names of people except in a few instances. Any names that have been changed are noted with quotation marks the first time they are used.

The following were kind enough to read the manuscript in various stages of development and give me comments and suggestions: Penny Adams, Chris Affleck, Elayne Baker, Ann Bastian, Robbie Benner, Cynthia Bowyer, Cindy Buhl, Paul Buttenwieser, Jim Cronin, Steve Dembitzer, Herman Detering, Mimi Detering, Celia Duran, Tom Engelsing, Charlie Fenyvesi, Helen Garvey, Helen Geraghty, Allen Graubard, Colin Greer, Harris Gruman, Hope Haff, viii

Lee Halprin, Richard Healey, Emmy Homonoff, Alain Jehlen, Allison Kennedy, Jonathan Kozol, Dale Lasater, Garland Lasater, Mary Laub, Juan Leyton, Frinde Maher, Gregory Maher, Matt Maher, Sarah Maher, Bob McGill, Janet Moses, Erin Osborn. Prasannan Parthsarathi, Suzy Pearce, Betsy Reed, John Scanlan, Phyllis Seidel, Julie Thacker, Ike Williams, Katherine Yih, and Mark Zanger.

My deep thanks go to Linda Cox, my editor and publisher, who applied much energy, skill, and good taste to make this book happen.

I am especially grateful for the love and support of my wife, Ellen Sarkisian, who insisted I do a better job and patiently critiqued many drafts. Her wise advice improved the book immeasurably. I am grateful for this, and much more.

Despite all this help, errors undoubtedly remain, and the responsibility for them is mine alone.

INTRODUCTION

The sixties were a turbulent time in America, and I was there, in the thick of things, involved as an organizer for the New Left. In this book I try to tell honestly what happened and what I learned. I experienced directly many of the high points of the 1960s, like Vietnam Summer in 1967, and some of the low ones, like the chaotic demonstrations at the Democratic National Convention in Chicago in 1968 that provoked the backlash against the student anti-war movement. I started the decade of the 1960s graduating from Harvard College. I ended it working in a rubber plant on the other side of town and a world away from Harvard Yard.

Since the 1960s I have remained active as a public school teacher, an educator at an overseas aid and development organization, and as an organizer against U.S. policy in Central America. More recently I applied that experience from the 1960s to building a political organization led by low-income residents in working-class communities in Massachusetts. This memoir is an account of where I started, the roads I followed, what I learned.

In the 1950s critics of the way things were found themselves first marginalized and then destroyed. At the beginning of the 1960s, isolated voices of dissent at last become a roar. One hundred years of government-supported racist repression was brought out into the open and confronted by a Black-led civil rights movement. Millions of citizens and soldiers came together to oppose an unjust war in Vietnam. Throughout the country, people began to question the authorities whose judgments had been respected in the 1950s.

Democracy was in the air we breathed. "Let the People Decide" was a rallying cry for struggles of all kind. Within the civil rights and anti-war movements, women began the fight for equal treatment that would eventually transform the country. People who had been silenced and oppressed because of their race, gender, sexual orientation, poverty, or politics began to sense that a fuller life was possible. People who had grown up in seemingly separate worlds became friends and colleagues. A much more vibrant, diverse, democratic society was in the making.

Activists and organizers in the 1960s thought in terms of big and radical changes directly relevant to the lives of most Americans – an end to poverty, racism, the nuclear arms race between the United States and the Soviet Union, and building a truly democratic society here in the United States. They identified U.S. efforts at world domination as a major threat not only to other countries, but also to the aspirations of most Americans. For people in the movement, peace and justice at home were part of the same struggle.

I learned a great deal about the world through my friendship with Izzy Stone, Noam Chomsky, and Vlado Dedijer – their courage and commitment inspires me to this day. But as an organizer I started from scratch without much guidance from the previous generation of activists who had been defeated or demoralized. Sustained by grand visions and love for each other, we challenged authority in every aspect of life. Growing up in the 1950s in a country that seemed incapable of change, some of us saw our early victories in the 1960s as a sign that anything and everything was possible – now. Often bold, we also overreached. Sometimes we stopped listening, even to those from whom we had much to learn. When you read about our arrogance, remember how young we were.

In the 1980s, I asked a lawyer to request my FBI file. To my astonishment, it was 2,000 pages. I hadn't seen myself as accomplishing that much, and I was flattered. I had come a long way from my privileged upbringing in Houston, Texas.

This book is about what I learned in the 1960s and how I have applied this to my life as a teacher and an organizer. According to my friend the late Senator Paul Wellstone, progressives need to combine three things to become relevant to American politics: "a vision to inspire working people, grassroots organizing, and winning elections." We can and must become relevant again.

I

Growing Up in the Fifties

I TOOK TO POLITICS AT an early age. One day in the fall of 1952, a friend suggested it might be fun to wave "I like Ike" signs at the Stevenson rally the next afternoon at City Hall Plaza. Adlai Stevenson the Democrat and Dwight Eisenhower the Republican were running for president.

"Sure," I said. I was fourteen years old. I had thought about politics some, and I knew we all liked Ike. After all, it seemed that everyone at St. John's, my all-white private day school in Houston, Texas, liked Ike. Ike was from Texas originally; Stevenson was from some place up North. Ike had been a general, and Stevenson was an "egghead" with more education than common sense.

My mother admired Stevenson, but then she was an exception, always. Four years earlier I'd shown her the front-page newspaper picture of hecklers throwing rotten tomatoes at Henry Wallace, the 1948 presidential candidate backed by Communists, among others. I told her I thought Wallace was getting what he deserved. She shook her head – that picture had made her sad and angry, I could tell. I didn't tell her I was going to City Hall Plaza that afternoon.

When we arrived at the rear of the plaza, I saw Adlai Stevenson at the front, speaking from behind a raised podium, his head shining in the sun. Between Stevenson and me, I saw the backs of several thousand broad-shouldered workingmen in hard metal hats. They were standing there listening to him quietly and respectfully. I was surprised. I didn't think anybody except my mother supported Stevenson. We schoolboys stood at the back of the crowd and waved our "I like Ike" signs. Then a suntanned, tough-looking white man saw us out of the corner of his eye, and slowly turned around. He seemed seven feet tall as he towered over us. In a thick east Texas drawl he said, "Boy, you better get them signs outta here before I stick them up yo ass." Then he turned back to listen to his candidate. He didn't watch us leave – he didn't need to. I was scared silly. I ran as fast as I could to my friend's station wagon, the others close behind me. We sped away down the expressway to the safety of River Oaks, our well-to-do neighborhood. Those Texans with hard hats sure didn't like Ike, and that gave me more things to think about.

Growing up in the 1940s and 1950s, political organizing was far from my mind. Men worked at good jobs. Women were happy at home. Black people knew their place. Communist and socialist ideas were irrelevant, and their adherents in the United States isolated and discredited. The Soviet threat overseas had been contained by wise and firm policies enjoying bi-partisan support. Part of my growing up was learning to question these political certainties, and recognizing that the leaders I had respected did not want the same kind of world I did.

Early Conflict

My father was from a poor Irish American family. He had cut all ties with his parents, left New Orleans and come to Houston, then a boomtown, to make his fortune. When I was born, he was a salesman, then the owner of a small factory that bottled bleach and packaged other commodities. After the war, he bought a factory that made oil-well equipment.

My father expressed himself with pithy remarks and earthy stories. Someone he disliked wasn't just stupid; he was "too stupid to pour piss out of a boot with the directions written on the heel." Alternatively, if someone was lazy, "he was the laziest son of a bitch God ever died for." "Lower than whale shit" was reserved for someone who was entirely worthless. Some of my father's older sisters had married well and helped him attend college for a couple of years. But he was clearly not to the manner born.

A photo taken in his early thirties shows a tall, slender young man with red hair and clear sharp features shown in profile, elegant and dashing as he somewhat self-consciously smokes a cigarette. The man I remember as a child just a few years later already had a falling face and a paunch above his still-slender legs. It was if alcohol had already begun to wash his good looks down the drain. My father became a rich man, but he paid a high price for his success.

My mother was from a once powerful, still respected south Texas ranching family, the Lasaters. As a major landowner, my grandfather took his political obligations seriously. In 1912, he ran for governor of Texas on the Progressive Party ticket. He represented cattle producers in the National Food Administration during World War I. He sat in the state legislature much of his adult life. My soft-spoken mother sounded like a well-educated woman, and was: by tutors in her childhood; at Pine Manor Junior College and the University of Wisconsin when she was older. My mother was genteel, but she had also known hardship. She gave up an acting career to come home to the ranch and cook for her brothers after her father died and the Lasaters lost all of their money and most of their land.

Pictures of my mother taken in her teens in the late 1920s show a young woman with an oval face and long brown hair, very wholesome and pretty. Throughout her adult life, she was admired for her elegance, but pictures taken when I was little show a painfully thin woman with sharp features and an unhappy smile. Abandoning her career to come home after her father died and then marrying an alcoholic had cost her dearly.

My parents didn't get along. Early on I knew that there was a big difference between the American dream of family life and the life my family actually lived.

I was born in Houston, Texas, May 1, 1938. I grew up in a small redwood ranch house on West Lane that my parents had bought for $6,000 in 1940, with the help of my mother's mother. My brother Albert was born in 1942, my sister Mary in 1945. Sometimes this little house could barely contain us, and fights exploded into the back yard.

From my earliest memories, things did not seem right with the world. My mother was sick a lot, with headaches and other ailments. She would lie in a darkened room and cry. I didn't understand all that was going on, but I knew it wasn't good. There was a war in our house, and I took my mother's side. My father often drank, and when he did, my parents would argue, often about his drinking. When I was little I got knocked around. Life wasn't fair to children, I concluded, and when I grew up I would try to change things.

My mother's mother, Maya, was my protector and my source of hope. Maya lived in a large house on the modest amount of land in south Texas that had been saved from foreclosure. When as a child I visited Maya, my cousins and I would climb naked in the oak grove that shaded the ranch house. From Maya I learned to worship the gods of trees and streams and feel the spirits of people who had passed on. Emily Edwards, a close friend of my grandmother's, taught me how to paint and draw. Later she recalled that she, Maya, and Willie Best, the Black cook, would meditate together every day on the long porch of her house.

As my mother told the story, when my grandfather died in 1930, at the beginning of the Great Depression, Maya and her children had to sell almost all the land to pay off the banks. The beef cattle went for pennies a pound. Fortunately, the Mexican government offered to buy my grandfather's Jersey herd. The Mexican American families whose whole life had been caring for the herd loaded them onto cattle cars. When the train left, the people headed south, my mother told me, on foot along the tracks, back to Mexico, following the cattle they had cared for and that had fed them. My grandfather's empire crumbled to dust.

When I visited Maya, I also played with Mexican American children down around the barn. I didn't understand Spanish, but I was in awe of their strength and coordination. At lunchtime, my grandmother's maid rang a bell and I went up the hill to the big house to eat and take a siesta, while my playmates went home to small shacks. I was ashamed of myself and ashamed for my family. This wasn't right, and as the grandson of a man who had owned and ruled over much of the surrounding countryside, I grew up thinking I had the responsibility to make it right.

Maya's death in 1946 was the saddest moment of my life so far. She had had a stroke, and my mother had gone to San Antonio to be with her. One day, I'd heard, Maya had opened her eyes. That meant, I was told, that she was getting better. Then that evening my father told me Maya had died. "Why did she close her eyes again?" I cried. "Why didn't she try harder? Why has she left me all alone?" Then I walked and walked in a circle around our back yard, trying to figure out how to survive without her. I did survive, and Maya's spirit stayed with me. But I stopped painting and drawing – a decision I later regretted. I had to be tough.

In 1950 my brother Timothy was born. A new baby seemed like an omen for a more peaceful and harmonious future, but my home life continued to be turbulent. At one point in my early teens, I confronted my father while he was drunk and yelling at my mother and told him to get the hell out, or else. He left right away, but eventually he came back. I realized that if I wanted to be loved and have a home life, I had to get away from this family as fast as possible, and go off on my own. I spent much of my adolescence daydreaming about the perfect woman and the perfect love I hoped to find elsewhere.

Breaking Away

In June 1952 at age fourteen, I went with my mother and Maya's friend Emily Edwards to Mexico City to see the great murals of Diego Rivera, with whom Emily had worked in the 1920s. Rivera's mural at the Palacio Nacional depicts the flow of Mexico's history past and future – the flourishing life along the canals of Tenochtitlan, the capital of the Aztecs, followed by the brutal Spanish conquest of Mexico, the struggle of poor Mexican-Indian farmers for land and freedom, and the murder of revolutionary leaders by the army. Looking forward to a brighter future, Rivera's mural lays out the triumph of the revolution and the execution of rapacious capitalists and degenerate priests by the armed people.

The portraits Rivera draws along the way have stayed with me for a lifetime – Cortez, the leader of the Spaniards, an ugly, grotesque dwarf; the fat, soft, full-lipped priests; the thick-necked, cigar-smoking capitalists; and the calm, dark-skinned men and women who would in the end bring justice to Mexico. (Emily, a painter, and the great photographer Manuel Alvarez Bravo later published a book on Mexican murals, Painted Walls of Mexico.)

Revolutionary art and life were not far apart in Mexico in 1952. One day while we were in Mexico City, I heard there was going to be a Communist demonstration near our hotel. This I wanted to see. I snuck out of the hotel and headed for the Zocolo, the main square in Mexico City, then a lovely park, now paved over. Men were standing around, waving signs, and shouting slogans. Then the army arrived in trucks and placed machine guns in all four corners of the Zocolo. Behind me, a man whispered, in English, "Son, now is the time for you to get out of here."

I knew better than to break out and run. I had hunted quail and wild pigs in the thick mesquite and brush covering south Texas. When the game breaks from cover, you aim and fire instinctively. To the Mexican soldiers the demonstrators were fair game. So, I slowly shuffled to the edge of the crowd. Once out of the Zocolo and out of the line of vision of the soldiers, I ran all the way back to the hotel.

In Houston I was a skeptic in a community of regional, religious, and patriotic enthusiasts. As I entered high school, I came to dislike Houston more and more. I went to St. John's, a private day school that prepared students to go to college, even colleges in the East. But football was the sacred sport. The team was called the Rebels, and the mascot was a Confederate colonel.

Houston was a Southern city when it came to race and gender. All my friends in Houston had been white, though even then I did not accept the color line as the way things had to be. Adeline Lee, the Black maid in my parents' house, was a person I had always looked up to. She was, after all, much more reliable and responsible than my parents were. With a calm dignity, she kept our household together. Because she stood up to my father, he jokingly referred to her as a civil rights leader or the president of the local NAACP, which she was not. But what did I know? I thought that since Adeline was for civil rights, civil rights had to be a good thing.

In Texas, young men were expected to be tough and strong. In the summer we took hard, tough, dirty jobs to get stronger. My cousins worked on their family ranches. For two summers in high school I worked in the warehouse of my father's factory that made big and little "Christmas trees" with brightly colored valves and gauges that regulated the flow of oil and gas from the well. Every afternoon my father walked through the plant, waving his big hands and greeting the men with a booming voice. I kept my head down when he walked through – I found his gregariousness embarrassing, and God forbid I should have to say hello to him myself. But I studied him carefully. Personal leadership was one of the keys to his success as an entrepreneur.

My senior year in high school, Little Richard, the famous Black singer, came to town. His performance was wonderful – raucous and lewd. I can still remember him moving his hips back and forth holding the microphone between his legs. White and African American kids got all worked up together, but kept apart. When the African American kids started dancing, we white kids stayed in our seats. I wanted to cross the color line and move on to a new and better world, but I hadn't the slightest idea how to take the first step.

I worked hard in school because I knew that college was my ticket out. My grades were good. My U.S. History teacher told me that I got the highest score possible on the Advanced Placement Test that year. However, my interview with Harvard could have been a problem. The last football game of my senior year was on a Friday night. The interview was the morning after. Following longstanding Texas tradition, my teammates and I had spent the night drinking and carrying on. At about 2:00 a.m., I remember throwing up on the front lawn of a brothel in Sealy, a country town outside Houston.

I got home and tumbled into bed well after dawn. When the alarm rang at 8:00, I could barely crawl out of bed. Even after I brushed my teeth, I could smell the vomit in my throat. I arrived at school for the interview at 9:00 Saturday morning. There were three of us football players, paralyzed, one of our teachers, and the man from Harvard, nattily dressed in a seersucker suit with a white shirt and a bow tie. I was still too drunk to say a word. But the teacher explained to the man from Harvard that our horrible hangovers showed that we were young men of spirit. The man smiled and said Harvard would be happy to have us if we wanted to attend. On the way out, I wrung his hand and managed a smile, ecstatic that I had gotten through the interview without throwing up again and was headed for Harvard so far from home.

Later the man from Harvard explained to my father that they were eager to attract middle-class white boys from the South and Southwest so they wouldn't have to admit so many Jews from New York. This was how affirmative action worked in 1956.

I was accepted at Harvard and Yale. Yale offered me a small scholarship. Harvard was coed. The choice was easy.

Crossing the Color Line

At the beginning of the summer I worked six weeks in a copper mine. Then I sailed with my father to Europe. Away from Houston, I was less defensive and more relaxed, particularly since I knew I would never have to live in my parents' house again. He was proud of what his eldest son had accomplished, and eager to show me the world. On that summer trip my father and I had some good times together and got along. When I met a pretty New York girl on the ship, he indulged me by changing our itinerary so I could see her again in Austria at the Salzburg Festival. But first, after some business meetings in Germany, he took me to the French Riviera.

That first morning, I walked out to the beach in search of girls. I wanted to win a beautiful adoring young woman whose affection would be on display for the entire world to see. Spying a gorgeous young French woman sitting by herself on the beach, I sat down casually close to her and began to try to attract her attention.

I seemed to be making some headway when suddenly a dark- skinned young man sat down on the other side. He was African American, good-looking, athletic, and self-assured. He spoke French far better than I did. Quickly he became a rival for the young woman's interest. I continued my effort for a while, but after about an hour he walked away with the girl.

That afternoon, I ran into my rival and the young French woman at a run-down bar not far from the beach. When I looked at them, I probably had a grim expression on my face. Seeing her with him reminded me just how much I would have liked her to be with me. Responding to my obvious jealous interest in them, my rival came over and stood in front of me.

"Listen, Tex, I know it's tough losing a girl to a Black guy. If it would make you feel any better, we can go outside and fight."

In that era fighting over girls was what guys did. I quietly looked him over and assessed my odds. I was in good shape, but he was probably going to beat me. Then I thought to myself, "It's bad enough losing the girl. What's the sense of risking getting the shit beat out of me besides? The better man won the first time. I don't need to get whupped again."

"No, that's okay. Let me buy you a beer instead," I said with as much gallantry as I could muster. Impressing my rival had become much more important to me than impressing the young woman we might have fought over.

I bought him a beer. He went back to the girl. The next day I found out that he was traveling with his mother, the famous singer Lena Horne. No wonder he was so sophisticated – I had never had a chance.

So in the summer of 1956, when I was eighteen, I crossed the color line and found human beings just like me, for better or for worse, on the other side. I was determined never to go back. It was easy to cross the color line in France if you had a mind to do it. No one on that beach in France gave two sous whether the girl went off with the Black foreigner or the white one. And it made no difference if afterwards the two guys had a drink together. In the United States at that time, white people and Black rarely went to the same bars. In the United States a white woman walking off the beach in the company of a Black man could have caused a riot.

Coming to Harvard

When I arrived in Boston by train with a bag or two, I wanted to kiss the South Station platform, filthy as it was. I was safe. I had survived. I knew I brought some things with me from home that would serve me well, and now that I was out of the house I could acknowledge them. Both my parents were bright people who read and thought about the issues of the day. My father was a history buff. My mother was, like her mother, a pacifist and a liberal. From my mother I had learned the importance of duty and taking responsibility for a world my family had helped shape and govern. From my mother I also had a patrician sense of being the social equal of anyone.

My father was much more cynical about how the world turned. Hard work and a lot of luck got you to the top, not merit, and certainly not being a better person. Like many Texans of the generation of the Great Depression, when he saw a poor person his reaction was often, "I was lucky, and that poor son of a bitch wasn't." From my father I learned that you had to get out there and talk to people to make things happen. From my father I also learned that oppressed people (like the Irish) had a right to rebel. In front of his factory he flew a flag with the golden harp on an emerald background, the symbol of the country from where his ancestors came. "And if the KKK don't like it, they can come kiss my royal Irish ass."

Both my parents appreciated the wealth and power their position gave them. But my father's toughness and my mother's sense of duty were useful antidotes to the poisonous sense of entitlement of some of my classmates. They believed they were on top because they deserved to be, and that it would remain forever so.

From South Station I hurried to my dorm in the Harvard Yard, where the freshmen lived, to start my orientation to a new life. Holworthy Hall had been built with plain red bricks in 1818. "Can't get any better than this," I thought. When I walked into my room I met one of my roommates, who it turned out was from New Orleans, where my father grew up. We exchanged warm greetings. A quick glance at his record collection told me that his tastes in music were clearly more cultivated than mine.

Then he reached into a small bag and took out a folded Confederate flag and some thumbtacks. "Oh no," I thought, "don't tell me I've traveled 2,000 miles to put up with more of this Old South bullshit!" I had had enough "Dixie."

Then there was a rap at the door. In walked an African American student – a poet, valedictorian, and the captain of his high school football team, I later learned. He introduced himself and said he had just moved in upstairs. Then he looked up at the wall and saw the Confederate flag. "Take that fucking thing down," he said.

My roommate got back up on the chair, pulled out the tacks, and took the flag down. "Thank God!" I thought. He folded it up, put it away, and never mentioned the matter again.

In the U.S. in 1956, racial thinking and racism were everywhere. The color line was the law of the land, and ruled even in private institutions. I soon discovered that in my class at liberal Harvard, only ten or so of a thousand young men were Black, including foreign students from Nigeria and the West Indies.

Over the next few days, I found hundreds of ambitious young men and women, eager as I was to study, learn about the world, and put their pasts behind them. There were also the preppies, young men who had gone to private boarding schools and been wearing jackets and ties every school day since they were fourteen years old, or even before. Some of the preppies were brilliant, and amazingly knowledgeable and well educated. Others were simply entitled. Loudly, the entitled ones bragged about how little they went to class, showing little interest in what went on in the buildings named for their ancestors. Like me, they, too, had benefited from the affirmative action policies of the time.

The Hungarian Revolution

The Hungarian Revolution in the fall of 1956 and its suppression by the Soviets was a defining event in my young political life. I had come to Harvard a populist, a supporter of popular upheavals like the Irish and Mexican Revolutions. The fact that the Hungarian workers supported the revolution against Soviet domination told me which side I should be on.

The Hungarian Revolution caused a great deal of ferment on the Harvard campus. I felt I had to do something. Derek, a friend and classmate, and I decided to start the Harvard Freedom Council. We wanted to make contact with Eastern European students struggling to free their countries from Soviet domination. Our faculty advisor was Zbigniew Brzezinski, later President Carter's National Security Advisor. But the truth is the U.S. government had sold out the Hungarians, encouraging them to revolt, and then walking away when they did. There wasn't a damn thing we could do about that. We had one or two meetings before the organization faded away.

Brzezinski's mentor was Carl Friedrichs, the chair of the Government Department. Together they had written a book on the modern evil of totalitarianism. Based on the Nazi and Soviet examples, they saw totalitarianism as a political system based on party control of the armed forces, the economy, the media, the secret police, etc. Reviewing the book for a course, I had pointed out that many modern industrial states thought to be democracies, including the

United States, also had elements of totalitarianism. Our moneyed elite also had control over the government, the economy, the media, the army, and the police. Democracy was something we had to fight for, rather than assume we had.

Loyalty

My work with the Harvard Freedom Council and my election as a freshman rep to the Harvard Student Council brought me some attention. A top official of the National Student Association (who was later revealed as a CIA agent) stopped by to chat. One evening during my sophomore year, I was part of a small group that was invited to dinner with George Kennan, a hero to Harvard types who thought that U.S. foreign policy should be shaped by intellectuals who knew the languages and customs of other countries. As a Russian-speaking State Department officer with extensive experience in the Soviet Union, Kennan had written a memorandum in 1946, the famous "Long Telegram," calling for a new American policy to contain Soviet expansion in Eastern Europe. But in the fifties, Kennan seemed to be a voice of moderation that warned against the U.S. undermining its values and being consumed by anti-Communism.

Dinner was in a small, wood-paneled private dining room at Kirkland House, where I lived. Brzezinski was there too. During dinner Ambassador Kennan told some amusing anecdotes about the interaction between Roosevelt and Stalin at the Yalta Conference, where Kennan had been one of Roosevelt's advisors. "God, it's great to be an insider," I thought to myself.

After dinner, the discussion began. Early on, I raised a question that I thought the ambassador would be pleased to answer. After more than a year at Harvard, I had learned to speak pompously and in complete sentences. "Ambassador Kennan, locked as we are in a worldwide struggle against Soviet Communism, don't you think our position would be stronger if we distanced ourselves from colonial powers like Portugal, which is fighting such an oppressive war in Angola?"

His reply surprised me. "Like you I am very concerned with some of the excesses of Portuguese rule in Angola," he said. "But the Communists are active in Angola, and the Portuguese are a bulwark against the spread of Communism in the region. We cannot and must not abandon the Portuguese now."

I was surprised, but not silenced – a Harvard sophomore with a few drinks in his belly can be very persistent. "But sir," I said, "you and I know that the United States stands for freedom for peoples around the world. How are Africans going to believe in us when they see the U.S. arming the Portuguese colonialists? Don't you think that fostering a perception of us as hypocrites and liars is disastrous to our interests?"

Back and forth we went. Finally, I shut up.

When the great man left the room, the students and junior faculty fell upon the remaining bottles. No sooner was a fresh bottle of Rhine wine uncorked than Brzezinski fell upon me.

"You know," he said, "you're going to turn out to be a quisling." (Quisling meant traitor, named after Vidkun Quisling, a Norwegian military officer who had aided the Nazi conquest of his country.)

I reddened and rose from my chair, ready to punch him. Someone stepped between us. As I sat back down I thought, "Who does this son of a bitch think he is, questioning my patriotism?" I was proud of what my family had done to build the country and convinced that what I was doing was loyal to their tradition of public service. I had been insulted, but not intimidated.

The official from the National Student Association did not stop by a second time.

Friendship

My friend Derek and I had agreed to room together our sophomore year and host a Hungarian refugee. At the beginning of term my sophomore year Charlie Fenyvesi appeared. Charlie was short, sturdy, and olive-skinned, with a round head and a hooked nose. Looking at him there was no doubt that his ancestors had followed the banners of Attila the Great across the steppes of Asia and Eastern Europe to sack the city of Rome, finally settling on the banks of the Danube.

I was hoping for a real honest-to-god hero of the Hungarian Revolution to come grace our suite at Kirkland House. Charlie didn't seem like one of those and never claimed to be, though he had faced far greater dangers than I ever would. In fact, one of the most wonderful things about Charlie was that he was a person without pretense at a place and time when pretentiousness ruled.

When the Soviets invaded Hungary in the fall of 1956, Charlie was away at school in Debrecen in eastern Hungary near what was then the Soviet border. Hearing that the Russian tanks were coming, the students armed themselves and barricaded themselves in their school. Fortunately, the commander of the Soviet tanks entering Debrecen was a humane person. He parked his tank in front of the school and announced over a bullhorn that if the students gave up their arms they would be allowed to go home. They did, and he kept his word. Shortly after Charlie got home to Budapest, he left for the Austrian border and exile.

Charlie was one of only two males of his generation in his extended family to survive the Nazi murder of Hungary's Jews, and he had survived only through courage, discipline, false papers, and unbelievably good luck. Despite the horrors Hungary and Charlie's family had endured, Charlie had had a much more protected childhood than many of his hard-drinking, lonely, intensely neurotic Harvard classmates. Charlie was very smart, and he could take care of himself. He knew how to ask for what he needed, which was emotional support. Every evening before we turned in, he liked to have a little chat about the events of the day. I felt a little like I was tucking in a small child. Charlie didn't tell me about the horrible nightmares that inevitably came in the night. I tried to be supportive, but I could barely take care of myself. At that point in my life, the only parental emotion I had was guilt.

Harvard could be a very lonely place to grow up in. Campus life was riddled with groups, cliques, and clubs that provided some refuge from the often alienating and competitive academic grind.

Some sophomores were invited to join private off-campus final clubs. Final clubs served lunch on weekdays, dinner occasionally, and alcohol continuously. Looking on final clubs as potential refuges for drunks and snobs, I did nothing to indicate any interest in them. But to my surprise, two final clubs showed interest in me and invited me to parties and small dinners.

At first, I was inclined towards the Spee Club, to which then-Senator John Kennedy belonged. But one night out for dinner to a small café in downtown

Boston as a guest of the club one of the members began to brag about how in high school he had regularly gone "coon bashing," speeding through Black neighborhoods with a two-by-four out the window trying to knock down people walking in the narrow streets. I sure didn't want to make waves here, with my new friends. But the guy just wouldn't stop. I sat there quietly, listening while the rage grew inside me, all the more because this guy was assuming we were on the same side. When I'd had as much as I could stand, I called him a racist motherfucker and stormed out.

To the Spee Club's credit, the undergraduate president, a tall, serious fellow, apologized the next day for the member's behavior and asked me if I would still consider joining the club. Politely, I told him no.

Then there was the Fly Club. It was considered more prestigious than the Spee, but not at the pinnacle of the social hierarchy at Harvard, though Franklin Delano Roosevelt had been a member. Like the other final clubs it was predominately WASP, but its membership also included men from Asia and Latin America, as well as Europe. That internationalism was intriguing. The undergraduate members seemed worldly, bright, and fun. Who could not be impressed when an impeccably dressed Whitney Ellsworth took you out to dinner not once but twice and explained both times the secrets of French winemaking? I was intrigued, and impressed.

But as the day of decision approached, I still had reservations about joining a finals club. When some members of the Fly Club came by to chat, I decided to put them to the test. I reminded them that a friend of mine from Houston, who was Jewish, was also a candidate for membership in the club. "Look at it as a package deal," I said. "If you invite him to join, I'll join too, if you'll have me. If you don't invite him, I won't join." They smiled politely and went away. "That settles that," I thought.

Then came the morning when invitations to join the clubs were delivered at 7:00 sharp to the rooms of those chosen. Some sophisticated candidates got up early to receive their one or several invitations while smoking cigarettes in silk pajamas. I was sleeping soundly on the bottom bunk below Charlie when two club brothers-to-be dropped my invitation to join the Fly Club on my chest. I joined the next day, as did my friend from Houston.

Lunches at the Fly Club, with a glass of sherry, a sunlit dining room, clean linens, friends seated at a round table, and the conversations before, during, and after the meal were one of the real pleasures associated with my undergraduate life at Harvard. Gossip about professors, jokes about other clubs, Eisenhower, Khrushchev, Nasser, and Castro were all fair game for a pretty well-informed and worldly group.

My closest friend at the Fly Club was "Hussein," who became my roommate senior year. Hussein was handsome, well coordinated, and athletic, with light brown skin and a charming smile. Hussein was also a Muslim prince, a descendent of the Prophet, who wore lightly the cloak of fame. He was a good friend, brilliant student, a kind person, and a great conversationalist.

Belonging to a band of brothers was a great experience. But I was too interested in women for a men's club to be the center of my social life.

Love

I met Helen at a mixer at her dormitory at Radcliffe. She had a terrible cold, complete with a red nose and snotty handkerchief. But when I walked home after the dance I knew she was the most beautiful and intelligent woman I had ever met.

We made love soon afterwards, or attempted to. Making love on the bottom bunk in my room in Kirkland House, however, to someone who was making love back was different from what I had imagined, and much more challenging. I was unnerved. Thus, I could not perform at all, much less in the masterful fashion I thought men were supposed to. Nor did I have sense enough to relax and let my feelings for her lead me where they will. But my heart was hers, and I was almost certain the rest would come later. I asked her to forgive my failure and to be patient. The next time she was very gentle, and we made love. She was eighteen years old and I was twenty.

I adored her. When we were apart, I daydreamed about her constantly, doting over her brown hair, big blue eyes, full lips, and soft cheeks. Mentally, I caressed the little scarlike marks on her hips. When we were together and went across the street for coffee after studying for a few hours at Widener

Library, I found the smell of her damp trench coat, her lavender body powder, and her body itself intoxicating.

Having Charlie as a roommate was great for us, especially when Saturday night came. If he could get his hands on some pepperoni sausage, he was gone for an evening feast with his pals, leaving the room to Helen and me. Since we couldn't keep our hands off each other for very long, we also made love wherever we could find a little privacy, at night on the grass, or in a forest in the snow. Eventually, we rented a room near Central Square.

We had many things in common. We were both Irish Americans. We both came from crazy families. We were both blessed with mothers who had tried to make an independent life. We were sick of what we saw as passionless middle-class conformity, but we both believed in loyalty and hard work, in addition to love.

Helen's favorite play was Shakespeare's *Tempest*. Like Miranda, she was looking for a brave new world, while I trailed after her. Really, we were like Hansel and Gretel, lost in the woods. Sometimes after making love, we would sink into sadness and depression, unable to cut the cables that anchored us to the past.

At college, I felt guilty over abandoning my sister and brothers, above all my youngest brother, Timothy, to crazy parents. Unfortunately, my parents' marriage had continued to be an unhappy one. After I left for college they had built a huge house whose silence could not conceal their misery. Later, when my father stopped drinking, my mother became an alcoholic herself.

Helen and I had come together both burning to be free of middle-class conformity of the fifties and our own crazy families. And burn we did for two years, alternating passion, misery, ecstasy, and depression. Looking back it is clear I didn't have what it took then to sustain a relationship of this intensity. It was love I wanted, but I couldn't handle it. When I felt bad, I didn't know how to talk about what I felt. I came to realize that for self-protection since my childhood I had come to deal with human beings from behind a mask. Helen was trying to tear the mask away, but underneath it, I was still a frightened and angry child. Making love brought us together, but my fear of togetherness pulled us apart. The breakup, reconciliation, and final breakup our senior year devastated me.

I was exhausted as well as brokenhearted. I had hoped to break free of my past but I was still stuck there. Smoking, drinking, and hard work had also taken their toll. I was alone and depressed and remained so for two years afterwards.

In June of 1960, I graduated with honors from Harvard College. I felt that I had learned some important things, but I had enough humility and common sense to recognize that without my parents' money I would not be where I was. I felt duty bound to repay a debt to those who hadn't had the resources to make it as far as I had. The first step I decided was to study and travel abroad for a year to understand something more about the world. Some friends including Hussein asked me if I would like to join them on a trip to the Soviet Union and Eastern Europe right after graduation. I was a little scared, but I jumped at the chance. I believed that if the United States were to fulfill its mission as a great power, Americans had to understand the Soviet Union and its people and devise a rational approach that reduced the risk of war.

II

Education of a Radical:
Traveling Around the Soviet Union,
Living in France, 1960-1961

WE WERE SIX MEN, INCLUDING Hussein and myself, and two women traveling in two leased Fiats. We left Helsinki in the morning and headed for the Soviet frontier. We were among the first Americans to be allowed to travel in the Soviet Union on our own, without guides, though we followed a set itinerary worked out with Intourist, the government travel agency. An hour or so after we crossed the border into the Soviet Union in early July 1960, we were totally, hopelessly lost, and low on gas. Through the dark, empty pine forests we drove, increasingly conscious of the need to be in Leningrad by evening, as we had been instructed. There, we imagined, the hotel rooms we had paid for in advance awaited us.

Suddenly we saw a large wooden building by the side of the road. We pulled into the driveway. One of us knocked on the door.

Out the door came pouring my worst nightmare, a dozen young, short, tough-looking soldiers with Slavic and Asian features, carrying burp guns. What we thought was a farmhouse was actually a barracks. The Soviet soldiers milling around and scratching their heads were just as stunned as we were. Eight foreigners in two small cars had just appeared out of the forest.

I was worried. In all the movies I had seen these men with burp guns were ruthless killers. What would they do to us if they found out that one of us was the daughter of a prominent CIA official? We were not in a big city where Western diplomats could protect us, but on the frontier, at a military base, without permission, in the middle of nowhere. How easily our peaceful intentions might be mistaken.

Out came our passports and Intourist vouchers. Our one Russian speaker went quickly into overdrive explaining that we were students from the U.S. on a mission to bring greater peace and understanding between peoples, unfortunately lost in the forest, and requiring their kind assistance to get to Leningrad, where our arrival was eagerly awaited by the responsible officials of Intourist.

Miraculously, they believed our story, poured gas into our tanks, and gave us directions. We piled back into the cars. As we headed down the driveway to the road, our world turned suddenly upside down again. Two young soldiers who had smiled shyly a moment ago suddenly jumped in front of our cars and stuck out their hands to signal stop. We had to obey. It was like a scene from a spy movie: a sudden phone call from a sinister superior alerts the border guards, who bar the hero's escape from East Berlin. Though Stalin was dead, denounced by Nikita Khrushchev, and buried at last, I really was scared.

Moments later two soldiers came running from behind the barracks with bouquets of red and blue flowers that they passed through the open car windows to the two women in our party. Then the soldiers waved us on. I was close to tears.

The conventional wisdom in the U.S. was that Soviet leaders were hell-bent on world domination, and that only American nuclear superiority stood in their way. In that same scenario the Soviet people were often portrayed as brainwashed automatons ready to kill and die at their rulers' behest. The leaders of the Soviet Union seemed to me a ruthless but cautious lot, concerned not with world domination but with protecting their positions and their empire in Eastern Europe. But what did the Soviet people think, and what kinds of lives did they lead?

Nothing worked smoothly in the Soviet Union. Due to bureaucratic ineptitude, the hotels on our itinerary never had reservations for us. No one was ever expecting us when we arrived. Traveling in such a world, you must depend on the kindness of strangers. When we arrived without reservations, someone would always find us rooms and honor our vouchers.

Fifteen years after the end of World War II, the Soviet Union was still a wreck. What we saw from the car window was that the fields were brown and disorderly and the cattle thin. New buildings were ugly and poorly constructed. Between Moscow and Leningrad was a two-lane highway with more potholes than most county roads in Texas. We had to ford small streams.

Soviet people regarded our little shoebox Fiats as technological marvels. They would stand out in the middle of the empty highway transfixed in amazement as our cars came nearer. Sometimes we had to slow down and honk to get them out of the way. Coming out of a museum in Kiev, we saw two thousand people in the Main Square. I thought it was a demonstration, or perhaps a fair, but the attraction, it turned out, was our two small cars.

Beneath the rigid order imposed by the state, there was a world of conflict and chaos mediated largely by family and personal relations. Most, but not all, of the people we met in the Soviet Union were wonderful, constantly reminding us that they wanted to live in peace. Like the young soldiers, they showed again and again their humanity to the visitors from another world.

However, hustlers were a constant problem in the major cities. Because few consumer goods were available in the shops, we were constantly hassled by black marketers, particularly in Moscow, looking to buy dollars, the shirts off our backs, and the blue jeans off our butts. Then we got lucky – we met a group of Russian students who decided to show us around the capital. They took us everywhere, the big tourist sites, and their modest homes, and never asked for anything.

The day we left Moscow, we put all our spare high-prestige trade goods, button-down shirts, blue jeans, ballpoint pens – the works, into a box for our friends. In front of the old and distinguished Leningradskaya Hotel where we had been staying, we stood with our Russian friends in a circle, facing each other, while our one Russian speaker made the presentation. As soon as he had begun his little speech, we were surrounded by police who hustled us off to a nearby station. All of us, American tourists and their Russian friends, had been arrested as black marketers.

The police station where they took us was dark and dingy. The police were rough but seemed uncertain and disorganized. We had fallen into the hands of the regular cops, not the all-knowing, all-powerful secret police. I was shocked at the utter contempt with which the police treated our Russian friends. Their leader protested. He reminded them that he was, after all, a reserve lieutenant in the Red Army; his word of honor meant something. But the police laughed in his face, in front of us, calling him a Yid and Jew boy. After a while, they told the Americans we could go, but we refused to leave the station until our friends were released also. In the end, they released us all.

We were relieved to be out on the street again, but sad and angry for our friends. In three days, we would be across the border, but they were like criminals for being kind to us.

It wasn't just the effects of the war or even Communism that had made the Soviet Union physically so ugly and depressing. The buildings built since the war were falling down. The countryside seemed barren. When we crossed the Polish frontier, we went from brown to luscious green fields filled with fat horses. Warsaw was becoming again a beautiful city. Even the modern apartment buildings there had style, each apartment with its own balcony displaying flower pots. But Poland had suffered the same war, and now too had Communist government.

Paris at War

I had arrived in Paris in the late summer of 1960 to begin post-graduate studies in political science, focusing on the struggle for independence in France's colonies in West Africa. France had waged a series of colonial wars since the end of World War II, first in Indochina and then in Algeria. Now there was also a war on the streets of Paris. Since World War II, hundreds of thousands of Algerian workers had moved to Paris and its suburbs to take dirty, difficult, and low-paid jobs. Since the fight for independence from France broke out in November 1954, these Algerians living in France had provided money and recruits to the Algerian National Liberation Front (FLN). Police stations were fortified with sand bags against attack by the FLN. At night, anyone walking around the working-class districts where Algerians lived could be stopped at submachine gunpoint and interrogated by the police. I learned to keep my U. S. passport at the ready. And late at night, you could hear shooting echoing all across the city. Who knew what the dawn would bring?

As a sophomore, I had taken a course on French politics with Professor Stanley Hoffmann. I was totally engaged from the first day. Unlike the American experience, French political history seemed to be defined by struggles over a number of basic issues. Also, Professor Hoffmann was the clearest thinker I had met. I wanted to continue to study France and if possible live in Paris, the cultural capital of the Western world. Professor Hoffmann had recommended me to l'Institut d'Études Politiques, "Science Po," where a good portion of the French political elite was formed. He was doing research at Science Po the same year I was a student there. Stanley was brilliant, but impatient. I feared disappointing him, which I felt I often did.

Several months before I came to Paris I'd written my undergraduate thesis on Pierre Mendes-France, the French premier who had had the political courage in 1954 to negotiate an end to the first Indochina War. Due to what I regarded as the anti-Communist phobia of the Eisenhower administration, the United States had been subverting the peace agreements signed in Geneva, attempting to set up the southern part of Vietnam as a separate country allied with the United States, rather than with the Soviet Union. Not for a second did I think that U.S. intervention in Vietnam was anything more than an obvious mistake that would soon be corrected.

I had high expectations for my country. I saw the United States as a leader of an expanding free world, soon, I thought, to put aside the anti-Communist obsession that had led us to overthrow democracies and support colonial regimes. I believed that my country, having renounced colonialism and empire building, would endure as a great power for centuries to come. At home, I foresaw an end to racial segregation and a more rational economic system, which would distribute the benefits of our dynamic capitalism much more widely. I felt that the conscience of the country was on the verge of a great awakening.

I had voted for John F. Kennedy in November 1960. In the euphoria after the election, many students shared my feeling that a new era had begun, and the world was opening up to us. In our minds, we downplayed the extent to which Kennedy was bound to the past – much of his political success had been bought by his father's wealth acquired through bootlegging and stock-market manipulation. Rather, we saw his public service as washing away whatever transgressions getting rich had required. Now, in the new era, old prejudices would be reexamined and talent rewarded, including of course our own. Harvard men of that time were particularly susceptible to wishful thinking that aligned the good of humankind with our own welfare.

To the Tomb of Baudelaire

As luck would have it, my beloved Helen had come to Paris too. No sooner had I arrived in Paris than I went to her lodgings in the Montparnasse district, consumed with anticipation and anxiety. Feeling the sweat through my shirt and the anxiety on my breath, I arrived at the downstairs door of the apartment where she had rented a room.

Her landlady informed me that she had stepped out. No matter. In a vision as clear as that early fall day, I envisioned her in the Montparnasse Cemetery, at the tomb of Baudelaire, whose poems we had often read together. That I could see her now, that I knew exactly where she was at this very moment was a sign that our souls were still joined together and that she loved me despite our breakup in the spring. My hopes rose. Right then, there was nothing I would not have given for us to be together again.

I asked for directions. Yes, the cemetery was nearby, as I had imagined. I ran to find her there. Turning a corner in the cemetery I looked up an allée between the tombstones. There she was. What I wanted so much to happen had come to pass.

But she was not alone. She was there with her new boyfriend Steve, short, dark-haired, and pudgy, as befits someone whose major sports were playing pinball machines and poker. I had hoped she had left him behind in Cambridge. Trying to be a sensible, modern, adult human being, I made every effort to conceal my sadness and sense of betrayal as the three of us walked from the cemetery back down to the street. I knew I was in for a hard year.

Visiting the Brothel on Scissors Street

The war in Algeria and the war in Paris were continually discussed in every circle I traveled in, as were the peace negotiations between the French government and the Algerians that had recently begun in Evian, Switzerland. A key question was, Did the Algerian negotiators, big officials who had been in exile in Egypt, really speak for all the fighters, particularly those in Paris? Only the Paris leadership of the FLN could answer that one. One of my acquaintances, an aspiring journalist, told me that if he could interview the Paris leadership of the FLN, his career would be assured. I told him I would have no problems arranging such an interview, and bet him a good dinner I could make it happen.

At first I had wondered how the Algerians paid for the guns, ammunition, and living expenses for the militants. It's hard to hold a day job if you're out all night shooting up police stations. Could the FLN squeeze all the cash they needed out of the Algerian day laborers? Every day I walked from where I lived at 33 rue de Seine above the Librairie Fischbacher down Boulevard St. Germain to Science Po, I passed by a brothel masquerading as a restaurant on the rue de Ciseaux (Scissors Street). Often I noticed Algerian pimps and tough guys outside. One day it came to me that whoever the owners were on paper, this brothel had to be an important financial asset of the FLN, an asset they had to watch over very carefully.

One evening the aspiring journalist and I presented ourselves at the brothel door. An Algerian waiter led us to a table in the dining room of the brothel, and the conversation began:

"We have a number of beauties over there. Please make your choice and I'm sure you will be satisfied," he said, pointing to a group of tired, worn-out, and utterly nondescript women sitting in chairs along one side of the room.

"We haven't come here for women. My friend here is a distinguished young journalist and intimate of the Kennedy family," I lied, "who wishes to interview the leadership of the FLN regarding the negotiations at Evian."

"We have nothing to do with politics here. You must make your choice or leave."

We didn't leave, so the maître d' came over, dressed in a nice suit, as a maître d' should be. I pitched him as I had the waiter, to no avail.

"This is a brothel. We have nothing to do with politics. But I hear an English accent. Perhaps you would prefer a boy. We have some very nice boys there," he said, pointing to a door behind which they were presumably hidden.

"We came here neither for your girls nor for your boys, but because my friend here is a distinguished young journalist and intimate of the Kennedy family," I lied again, "who wishes to interview the leadership of your movement regarding the negotiations at Evian. This is a priceless opportunity for the Paris leadership of the FLN at this crucial juncture to make its views known to the U.S. public and the world." Then I looked him directly in the eye. "Surely you don't want to be responsible for missing this opportunity?"

Everyone knew that FLN leaders were hard and unforgiving when it came to dealing with the mistakes of their subordinates. He walked away, puzzled and annoyed. But we were allowed to stay. Minutes later, a gift bottle of cheap champagne arrived at the table. I knew we were on.

Then they arrived: two thin, tough-looking Algerian guys with rifles poking out from under dirty raincoats, to arrange an interview to take place at a later time.

As soon as they arrived, I got up to leave. I was adventurous, but not crazy. I was neither a distinguished journalist nor an intimate of the Kennedy family. In fact, I wasn't even a journalist. Unprotected, I wanted no information that might tempt the French police to torture me.

As I left, the maître d' smiled and shook my hand.

"You have good taste, young man. I would never touch the syphilitic lesbians who work here," he said with great disdain.

The aspiring journalist got his story, and I got my good dinner, along with a few things to think about. I supported the right of Algerians to be free of the

French, but I was unnerved to hear the women whose work was financing the revolution so insulted. Colonial regimes were clearly not the only source of cruelty in the world.

Where My Studies Took Me

When I arrived in Paris, I knew very little about Africa. I was drawn to Africa because I saw it as a place where, with the end of colonialism, humanity could begin to build just and free societies. Knowing little, I filled in the large unknowns with what I wanted to believe.

I decided to focus my research on French West Africa, where the former colonies were taking steps to become more independent of France. A topic in this area provided me with many opportunities to declaim against French colonialism and encouraged in me a patriotic self-righteousness that must have been very annoying to my French classmates.

Paris was a great place to study Africa, especially, of course, French-speaking Africa. Many African students and scholars of Africa lived in Paris. Paris was a ferment of magazines, newspapers, lectures, and political events happening on a daily basis. Making friends with African students was also an excellent way to learn about Africa.

After Kennedy's victory, I was particularly eager to try to represent the best of my country to my new African friends. Initially, like many American students studying abroad, I was suspected of being a CIA agent. At the time I didn't know that the CIA controlled the U.S. National Student Association, so I was a bit put off to have my integrity questioned. In the end the students believed my indignant denials, and I was accepted.

I met Souleymane Diarra from Mali at one of the many meetings I attended that fall. He was tall and handsome, with very dark skin. Like many other African students, he gave off an air of dignity and elegance, dressed usually in a carefully pressed brown suit and tie. He spoke French carefully and eloquently, with a beautiful West African accent. Around him, I often felt I was his opposite – poorly dressed, disorganized, and undisciplined. But we shared a love of politics and a vision of democratic socialism. To me it was clear that on his return he would play a leadership role in the development of his country and go on to do great things. I hoped that I could find a way to join him in this great endeavor of our generation.

Like many French students, the African students lived in the Cité Universitaire on the outskirts of Paris, where the government had built dormitories and cafeterias after the war. I spent a lot of time with Souleymane there. The rooms were small and crowded but the atmosphere was wonderful if discussions were what you wanted. It was clear to me and to them that students like him would become the next generation of leaders on their return to their home countries. I identified with them because I had very similar expectations of myself when I returned to my own country. I was certain that together we would build a better world.

Racism in France

I learned a great deal about racism in France from my African friends like Souleymane. To many in France, the people in their African colonies were savages. But those who were learning the language and culture of France were *évolués*, evolving towards becoming more civilized human beings, and, eventually, French.

French colonial authorities pursued a policy of cultural assimilation, often with an amazing lack of sensitivity. An example that was both funny and infuriating to my African friends was the required history text in France's African colonies. On the first page was a picture of a fierce, blue-eyed warrior with a golden moustache. The first sentence began: "Nos ancêtres les gaulois" ("Our ancestors the Gauls"). The colonial authorities in Africa did not expect their students to become white, but they did demand that they become French. Forgetting their own ancestors and revering the Gauls was one step in this direction. Africans opted for independence rather than assimilation for many reasons, not the least of which was because the authorities did not recognize their histories and customs as a legitimate part of human civilization.

In the United States being white was what mattered. In most parts of the U.S., the authorities actively patrolled the color line to prevent "light-skinned" Blacks from passing into white society. Renouncing your culture was a tremendous price Africans living in the French Empire had to pay for acceptance, but for African Americans even that option was closed.

Cultural arrogance poisoned French society the way racism poisoned our own. In the 1960s, cultural arrogance brought down the French Empire. Today cultural arrogance threatens to alienate France's large Muslim population.

People from many nations gathered in Paris and traveled throughout France. Hosts to people from around the world, the French in the 1960s often remained self-centered, provincial, and incurious about the ways of others. In this respect, they were very much like Americans.

An Eager Recruit

I learned many useful things in France, including how to think about political conflict and ways to organize to win. Like workers, students in France were represented by a union and entitled to benefits. Foreign students had the same benefits as the French students – a library card to the Bibliothèque Nationale, for example, a decent meal with wine in any student cafeteria for less than ten cents, and the right to vote for the leadership of the student union. In the fall of 1960, a crucial election was held at each school in the university system including Science Po to decide whether the students would be represented by the anti-war National Union of French Students (UNEF), or by a pro-government union. The campaign was hard fought.

A pro-UNEF student at Science Po began to discuss the issues with the foreigners. One by one, he approached us before the election and explained what was at stake. He was friendly, persistent, and persuasive, a model organizer I would later realize. From him I learned that you won big campaigns by recruiting people face to face, one at a time. For me a vote for UNEF was a vote against the Algerian War and against French colonialism, so I was easy to persuade to vote for UNEF.

I also went to student anti-war demonstrations and marches. The French understand the public theater of street demonstrations better than anyone else I know about – the lore of how to do street demonstrations well must be passed down from generation to generation in France. No demonstration in France was complete without banners and signs of many colors. No demonstration in France was complete without clever chants. Everything is choreographed in a way certain to impress the bystander and hearten the participant.

Early one evening I went to a demonstration with Helen and her boyfriend Steve. With several thousand others, mainly students, we marched along the Left Bank of the Seine chanting slogans against the war. First, the regular police assaulted the front of our column. Then, as we fell back along the quay above the river, we were ambushed by the special riot police, tough Corsican guys wearing combat helmets, who surged out from the side streets swinging their rifle butts.

We started to run, but Helen, who had gained weight, was no longer as fleet of foot as before. Steve, energized by panic, took off running as fast as he could, heading up the quay to safety, giving no thought to the fate of my former beloved, now his. Why had she left me, who would happily die defending her, for a coward who cared so little? A disheveled drunk lying on the sidewalk nearby got up to complain that his nap had been disturbed. A rifle butt to the face dropped him to the ground, his head covered with blood. I grabbed Helen and pulled her into a laundry shop while the violence surged past.

After our march was ambushed, I understood why the students always called for the Communists to join them. The police did not attack us when the brawny autoworkers from the suburbs showed up with their bicycle helmets and big clubs. When it came to the Communists, the police were almost always very circumspect.

Everyone who could read between the lines of the censored press knew that both sides pursued the Algerian War with uncommon ferocity. Where Algerians were concerned, the rules of war and the laws of France were rarely followed. Violent confrontations built on conflicts going back sometimes centuries echoed up and down the streets of Paris in 1960. Confrontations like these were foreign to me, but important to understand. The French accepted the idea that because people had different interests and different values, there would always be conflict between classes, countries, and cultures. Political struggle for the French was not a symptom of social disease, but a fact of life. Across the ocean, excepting a few soft rumbles, my own country slumbered like a dormant volcano.

The Murder of Patrice Lumumba

The murder of Patrice Lumumba, a former schoolteacher newly elected president of the Congo, in February 1961 was a brutal awakening for my African friends and me. Sitting in a dark movie theater night after night, watching the newsreels in horror, we witnessed each step in his passion: betrayal, overthrow, flight from Leopoldville, capture, and cruel execution in Katanga Province by the soldiers of Moise Tshombe. At each step on his path to martyrdom, I hoped that somehow he would escape the evil plotters and prevail. Like people all over the world we witnessed the last minutes of his life – bound in the back of a pickup truck, mercilessly beaten by his captors.

In the late nineteenth century, King Leopold of Belgium had held the Congo as his personal property. When his genocidal crimes were revealed in the European press of the time, the Belgian state took over as ruler of the Congo. Both the king and the Belgian government brutalized the population and extracted the vast mineral wealth of the country. Belgium did not even put in place the physical and the educational infrastructure that France was to leave behind in her African colonies.

That free elections were held in the Congo despite all the obstacles of poverty, lack of education, and experience in democracy was evidence that progress could follow on the departure of the Europeans. Lumumba was a hero to the African students and to many of the rest of us. For me he seemed to be both a man of the people and a modernizer who would be a natural ally of the United States in the struggle to eliminate colonialism and backwardness.

To some his murder showed the horrible lengths to which the Western imperialists would go to hold on to their former colonies. To others it was a sign that with the departure of the Europeans, Africa was descending once more into unspeakable barbarism, perhaps even cannibalism. A cartoon in a left-wing magazine captured the racism stirred up by the event:

Tshombe is at the dinner table quizzing his major Congolese allies.

"Do you like Lumumba?"

"Yes!"

"Well then, have some more," says Tshombe passing the platter.

In fact, the U.S. and the colonial powers were still calling the shots, and it was they who decided that Lumumba must die.

On February 18, after Lumumba's death, I went to a protest meeting organized by the French Communist Party (PCF). The public meetings of the PCF seemed to be as much about ritual as they were about facts. When I remember that meeting, the constant repetition of the party's name, in speeches and in chants, "le Parti Communist Français," still rings in my ears. In addition to the constant repetition of the party's name, the ritual featured blaming the CIA for all the ills of the world.

The Communists accused the CIA of collaborating with French and Belgian colonial interests in Lumumba's murder. We know now that, though he may have been killed by others, Eisenhower ordered the CIA to eliminate Lumumba. (See Tim Weiner, *Legacy of Ashes: The History of the CIA*, pp.162-163.) I was skeptical at the time of the Communist criticism of the U.S., but the meeting did raise some questions about the U.S. government's role in his death, questions that didn't go away. Could it be that my country's support of anti-colonial struggles was merely a ploy to conceal the ambitions of our own ruling elite, who like the old colonialists wanted access to Africa's resources on their own terms? With the murder of Lumumba it began to dawn on me that the path to freedom might be rocky and dangerous.

Communism in France

The French Communist Party (PCF) was as French as pommes frites, despite its isolation in parliament by the Cold War and by their own pig-headed support of the Soviet Union. France was an American right-winger's paranoid fantasy realized – Communists were everywhere, above all in the factories and workplaces.

Since Communism was a fact of life in France, the French had a more tolerant and realistic view of foreign Communists. The French government fought the Communist-led Viet Minh because they wanted to keep Vietnam in the French Empire, not because most French politicians were true believers in the worldwide crusade against Communism. The French government used Crusader language of good versus evil when they came to Washington to lobby the U.S. government to pay for their war to keep their colony. They succeeded – we were paying for the French War in Vietnam long before we were foolish enough to make it our own.

However, when the French Army was defeated at Dien Bien Phu in the highlands of Vietnam and the war was lost, they dropped the Crusader rhetoric and made a deal with the Viet Minh to save what could be saved. They reminded themselves that the Communist leader Ho Chi Minh was not such a bad fellow after all, seeing that he had lived in France, spoke French quite well, and had served as sous chef to the great Escoffier.

An Exchange of Views

At about the time of Lumumba's murder, a pleasant-looking fellow began to appear at many Africa-related events. He wore an ugly, ill-fitting suit and spoke French with a Russian accent – the Soviets had decided to court the African students in Paris. While he was polite to me, he was unfailingly critical of the United States. Most disturbing of all, he spread a vicious rumor that the U.S. was about to invade Cuba. One day after some sharp disagreements on this and other topics, he suggested that we meet for lunch for a further exchange of views.

Sounded like a good idea to me. I felt that I was getting the better of the argument. My view of the Soviets had been formed by the Soviet invasion of Hungary, my studies at Harvard, as well as the trip to the Soviet Union after I had graduated. Lunch was an opportunity to understand how a Soviet official viewed the world, and, who knows, convince at least one of them that they should change their policies that fed the Cold War.

We met, this Soviet diplomat and I, at various Vietnamese restaurants on the Left Bank. The dining rooms were typically dark and not crowded, which afforded us a certain amount of privacy. The atmosphere between us was friendly. I did most of the talking. I admitted that racism was still an ongoing problem in the U.S., but soon to be solved I was sure by President Kennedy. The Soviet invasion of Hungary in 1956 and the Berlin Wall that was being built as we spoke were definitely embarrassments for his side. He did not try to defend the Soviet invasion of Hungary. But he did uphold the party line on the Berlin Wall – a temporary measure, he said, to staunch the hemorrhage of talent from East Germany so that the economy could be stabilized and collapse prevented.

When we discussed the alleged preparations the United States was making to invade Cuba, he seemed to accept my assurances that such an invasion was unthinkable. After all, as a recent Harvard graduate I was practically an insider. I had studied with Arthur Schlesinger Jr., and I was familiar with the work of many of the leading intellectuals who had moved from Cambridge to Washington to run the country. Surely, he was misinformed. "Perhaps," he said. "Perhaps." My confidence grew with every meeting.

An Exchange of Views Turns Serious

One morning in early April I read in the French newspaper *Le Monde* that a United States-backed invasion of Cuba had begun at the Bay of Pigs. I was angry and frightened. I had had very high hopes for the Kennedy administration. They were after all the new generation of which I felt myself a part. But clearly, the anti-Communist phobia of the Eisenhower years had found a home there.

I knew there were thousands of lives and important issues at stake in the invasion, but I also took it personally. Adlai Stevenson's pathetic performance at the UN made me even more ashamed. Initially, he heatedly denied U.S. involvement. The next day he was revealed as a foolish errand boy whom the real insiders had left totally in the dark. The Bay of Pigs invasion had made a mockery of my campaign to present a better picture of America. I felt betrayed and humiliated in front of my African and French friends. I felt that I too had been made a fool of.

I could only stay in bed so long, and after a couple of days, I was out and about. When my Russian friend called, we set up another restaurant rendezvous. When we met, it was clear to us both that the balance of power had shifted in the relationship. But rather than ridiculing my naïve assertions of the previous weeks, he took another tack.

"Very important changes have taken place in U.S. policy since the last election," he said looking at me carefully. "We in the Soviet Union need to understand these changes. Because of your connections and education, you can give us a better understanding of them. And, as you know, better understanding strengthens the chances for world peace."

"I don't know any secrets, but I'd be happy to answer any questions you might have," I replied, "and tell you all I know if it would strengthen your understanding of the United States."

"Actually," he said, moving to the crunch part of the meeting, "I would like to ask you to do this a different way. As you have said, you know Arthur Schlesinger Jr. personally and have studied with him. He is a key advisor to President Kennedy. What I would like you to do is write a brief memo on his thoughts and philosophy for me to take back to study at our embassy and discuss with my colleagues. After a few days I will return the memo to you so that your security will in no way be compromised."

Always cautious, I told him I would think about his proposal and get back to him soon.

I was less of an insider than I had pretended. Actually, Arthur Schlesinger Jr. and I were not exactly on intimate terms. In 1957, as a freshman, I had been admitted to his course on American intellectual history. Each lecture was polished and sophisticated. This was what I'd come to Harvard for!

When it came time to write a paper, I took up Woodrow Wilson's New Democracy, about which Professor Schlesinger had written so favorably. I praised Wilson's insights and accomplishments. In the end, however, I suggested that New Democracy might have gone further had Wilson put markets aside and "restored man as the measure of all things."

When I got the paper back, I saw that the graduate student grading it had liked the paper and had given it an A-. Then with a pencil the great man himself had lightly crossed out the A- and written in a B+ beside it with the comment "an interesting effort, young man." I took no more courses from Arthur Schlesinger Jr.

Regarding the memo about Professor Schlesinger, there was really nothing to think about; regardless of how well I knew him I would never have written it. The fate of the Hungarian leaders was proof enough that the Soviets' word of honor meant nothing. If I had written such a memo for them, they would have photographed it. Later they could blackmail me if I didn't go along with whatever they demanded. I would be compromised for life, and unable to be a real leader in my own country. I was learning to be careful.

I was furious at the thought that anyone might think I was naïve enough to fall for such a stupid trick. I never spoke to my Russian friend again.

Adieu

I did not know when I left Paris in 1961 that I would never see most of my African friends again. Then it seemed we would be friends and allies in building a better world for the rest of our lives. I felt certain that I would be visiting them in their homelands in a couple of years after I had finished graduate school in the U.S.

I had been drawn to their company partly because I saw Africa as a place where humanity could begin again to build just societies outside the framework of the Cold War. Fifty years later so many hopes have been dashed. Even as its resources are stolen and its people exploited, Africa is widely regarded as a basket case, surviving only on foreign aid. Actually, the Cold War and other conflicts had played out in a most ruthless fashion in Africa. Patrice Lumumba was merely the first in a series of martyrs.

In 1962, after I returned to Cambridge, my Malian friend from Paris, Souleymane Diarra, visited Houston, Texas, on a mission for his government. It was still a segregated Southern city. He visited my parents' house and was the first Black person to stay there as a guest. That they were so pleased to receive him was a tribute to his great dignity and savoir faire, but also the rising status of Africa as a new economic and political frontier in the minds of many Americans, including my parents.

To me my African friends were not only symbols of the possibility of a new and better world, but real people, intelligent, charming, and determined. Whatever became of them? Were they devoured in the great maw of war? Are the dreams we shared gone like the snows of yesteryear?

In 1969 Mamadou Dia, president of Mali, a principled socialist of the old school who had defied the French the way no other African leader dared, was overthrown in a CIA-sponsored coup. What happened to Souleymane when his president was overthrown? When I was in Mali in 1986 on a mission for a U.S. economic development agency, it was still ruled by the military. I made discreet inquiries, but nothing more, for fear of putting him in danger should he still be living there.

III

My First Campaign

I CAME BACK TO THE U.S. to go to graduate school. The country I returned to in the late summer of 1961 was beginning to throw off the long sleep of the 1950s. Young people, in particular, were on the move. Even before I had left for Europe, the new Black student-led Civil Rights Movement had begun with sit-ins at the lunch counters in the South. Hundreds of years of racist repression and broken promises were being challenged. In Latin America the U.S. hegemony was also being challenged. In 1959, Fidel Castro, barely thirty, had spoken to thousands of students in Harvard Stadium and then moved on to an unprecedented stay in a Harlem hotel while he was addressing the United Nations. By the time I returned from Europe in 1961, the 1960s were in full swing.

I had no nostalgia for the political certainties of the 1950s. With Fidel Castro and Che Guevara, revolution was no longer associated with Soviet oppression, or boring, Stalinist hacks. But I was no revolutionary – I still thought that change was certain to come about in the American way, gradually and peace-fully, as people of goodwill came to recognize that change was necessary to fulfill our potential as a just and fair society.

The early sixties were a time when young people like me were certain that their choices could have an effect on the world. I applied to the Harvard

Business School and the Harvard Law School. The Law School could prepare me for a career in government in the United States. The Business School, I thought, could teach me the secrets of American capitalism. This knowledge would be something of value I could bring with me when I went to live and work in Tanzania or Mali where the governments seemed committed to building a more just economic and social order. I chose the Business School. I was not alone in my idealism, soon young Americans in the thousands would be going abroad to participate in the Peace Corps.

I had planned to spend a week or two at home in Texas before heading back up to Cambridge for school. A late August hurricane hit Houston and delayed my departure. I arrived a couple of days late and never really caught up.

Looking over the transcript I am amazed that I passed all six courses the first semester. Going to the Business School was based on a big misunderstanding on my part. Their mission at the time was to train men (at that time their doors were closed to women) to run small and medium-sized U.S. companies, not impart practical knowledge to young radicals headed for poor countries overseas. The students were smart and driven, and unlike me, prepared to put in eight to twelve hours a day outside of class sharpening their skills and learning the trade of making money. I was prepared to work hard, but I had a different agenda in mind. The "B" school and I were an odd couple whose relationship had to end. I applied to the Graduate School of Arts and Sciences as a special student and was accepted. I transferred fast before flunking out.

The folk music scene had come to town while I was away. I had always loved listening to folk songs like "Red River Valley" and "You Are My Sunshine," songs of longing and lost love. Now Joan Baez was singing "All My Trials" and "Donna Donna" at the Club 47 on Mt. Auburn Street. Joan entranced me, as she did hundreds of other young men around Cambridge. I was thrilled when one day she asked me to come to her house in Belmont for afternoon tea. At the appointed hour I arrived in my little sports car, bounded up the stairs and into the parlor. Sitting around the table were three Baez sisters, Mimi and Pauline as well as Joan. After Joan poured the tea, the sisters lit into me. It seemed as if Joan had invited me to a pig roast rather than a tea, with me the "B" school student cast in the role of pig to be roasted. Fending off all three Baez sisters at once wasn't easy, but I held my own, so we became friends. I continued to hang out with them at the post-concert parties.

Richard Farina and Bob Dylan brought a more political edge to the folk scene with songs like "Birmingham Sunday" and "With God on Our Side." My brother Albert and a friend of his worked for a time as Dylan's bodyguards, responsible mainly for safeguarding his stash. Later Albert and Bob had a falling out over the love of the lovely Suze Rotolo. But young people in Cambridge in the early 1960s seemed blessed. They could do whatever they wanted and no one would get hurt. Sometimes I felt old already at twenty-three and out of it.

When I transferred to the Graduate School of Arts and Sciences, I took Professor Hoffmann's seminar on World Politics and World Order. In the seminar the question for me came to be: How does the world survive two antagonistic superpowers facing each other armed to the teeth with nuclear weapons? The logic of the balance of terror seemed on the surface to preclude war between the United States and the Soviet Union: one side didn't dare attack the other because if it did in the end the attacker would die too. Since the potential attacker was rational and could predict this outcome in advance, the attack would never come.

The balance of terror seemed stable in a perfectly rational world, but in the real world people make miscalculations and mistakes. Many of the scenarios we examined in the seminar had the quality of "they do this, we do that, they do another thing, and then, oops, we blow up the world." Professor Hoffmann was, as always, analytical, scholarly, and dispassionate. But I was angry as it sank in that gamblers in very high places were staking my life and hundreds of millions of others on a game of chance where we could lose everything, forever. Plans to spend a lifetime building a better world seemed irrelevant if a small group of irresponsible leaders could blow it all up in a day. This had to change.

Hughes for Senate

Then an opportunity to do something about the nuclear arms race came my way. H. Stuart Hughes, a Harvard professor, decided in the spring of 1962 to run for U.S. Senate from Massachusetts as an Independent, one of the first political campaigns of the growing nuclear disarmament movement. Fortunately,

I had enough money from my parents to live on so that I could devote myself to a job that paid nothing. I volunteered for the Hughes campaign with the enthusiasm of a crusader. I never finished the paper I was writing for Professor Hoffmann's seminar.

President Kennedy was still king in Cambridge, in my mind and in the minds of many others. Teddy Kennedy, the president's brother, was running in the Democratic primary against Eddie McCormack, and there was a prominent Republican in the race too. Winning was clearly a long shot, but if we could demonstrate support for our position we would be better able to pressure the Kennedy administration from the outside.

Back in September 1961, Teddy Kennedy, one of his friends from Houston, my father, and I had shared a ride headed north in my father's private plane. My father was actively involved at that time in taking over companies he considered undervalued, restructuring them, firing the managers he considered incompetent, and selling the companies at a profit. My father was a proud Irish American and like Joe Kennedy, Teddy's father, a bit of a buccaneer besides.

Teddy and his friend were going to West Virginia for some political event where Teddy was to speak, while I was headed for business school. I spoke to him at great length about the administration's mistaken reliance on military means to rid the hemisphere of the Communist threat, when regional economic development and respect for human rights had a greater chance of success.

Teddy was polite, but clearly he had a lot on his mind, and foreign policy wasn't one of them. As the booze flowed freely, he turned his attention to the task at hand, adapting a St. Patrick's Day speech he happened to find in his coat pocket to the needs of a West Virginia audience he was speaking to that evening. My father, no leftist or even liberal, was nonetheless proud of my efforts. I was, after all, the eldest son. "I saw Teddy put that card with your name and number on it in his ass pocket," he said; "that's a sure sign he plans to call you." But the call never came.

The Hughes for Senate office was a few rooms overlooking what is now called JFK Street in Cambridge. Marty Peretz, a fellow graduate student then on the left (now publisher of *The New Republic*), took me to the office to sign me up as a volunteer. The candidate's wife was a beautiful French woman who was wearing short shorts that day. Seeing her clinched the deal for me. But at that point, the campaign consisted of a lot of conversation and not much action. Clearly, that had to change, too.

To get on the November ballot as an Independent candidate for U.S. Senate in Massachusetts in 1962 required a total of 72,514 voter signatures, validated by the election officials in each town, and turned into the secretary of state's office in Boston by a certain day in July. The response was good, but I remember most of all the stairwells and the sweat.

We met the deadline with signatures to spare. But with Stuart Hughes on the ballot, we could no longer appeal to voters to support our right to be heard; we had to win their votes on the issues. And we had to win enough votes to become a measurable political force after the election. Everyone in the campaign agreed that to do well we had to expand beyond the base of the traditional peace movement. When I looked at the demographics, it was clear to me that we needed more working-class supporters if we were to become a serious political force in Massachusetts. After all, working-class people were the majority of the population, and they had a lot to lose from war – their lives – and the most to gain from an economy focused on meeting human needs.

To be effective, I felt, the campaign had to acknowledge that there were two crises in the United States, not just the possibility of nuclear war but also the reality of poverty right here right now. That there was poverty a plenty I knew well, not just from the data but also from going door to door to get signatures. But reaching out to the working class required the campaign to view the twin crises as an opportunity – expand the program beyond peace and talk about what a peacetime economy could be like for the working class, with higher wages and more public funding for things like housing and education.

Expanding the program to include economic demands was not popular with everyone in the campaign. Some of the well-to-do people saw the danger of nuclear war as the only issue worth talking about. After all, nuclear war wasn't good for workers either, so why dilute the program with extraneous issues? It was hard for them to realize that workers already faced serious problems in their lives. For workers the possibility of nuclear war was just one more damn thing. That working people might have other priorities besides preventing nuclear war was hard to understand for those whose lives were comfortable now and would be likely to remain so, if nuclear war didn't spoil it for them.

Eventually I persuaded the campaign to embrace a progressive economic program. With a program, I went out looking for the workers to support it. As the conventional wisdom required, I went around to the union officials who were gatekeepers to the labor movement in Massachusetts. "Run for Senate against the president's brother? You gotta be kidding!" was as much encouragement as I got from the social democratic gatekeeper of the labor movement in Boston.

I decided to try to find a way to bring the ideas of the campaign directly to workers, with or without the gatekeepers. First, I went back to the census data showing a major concentration of working people in southeastern Massachusetts. Then I sat down with a burned-out ex-Communist labor organizer and wrote a leaflet titled, at his suggestion, "What Is to Be Done," after Lenin's manifesto. Jerry Grossman, the new campaign manager, groaned but said okay. With my new title of labor organizer for the Hughes for Senate Campaign and a car trunk filled with literature to pass out at the factory gates, I hit the road. My first campaign had begun.

Looking for the Russian Submarine

Harvard Square and New Bedford sixty miles to the southeast were hardly on the same planet. Driving into the city, I saw the office of the *New Bedford Standard Times* and decided to stop and announce the arrival of the Hughes for Senate Campaign to southeastern Massachusetts. I asked to speak with the editor and was shown into a large office on the second floor where a crusty old Yankee with a bow tie and close-cropped hair rose from behind his desk to shake hands.

I started pitching the campaign, stressing our national interest in a negotiated end to the arms race. As I was speaking, he got up from his chair and went to his large window looking out over the harbor.

"I'm just looking for the fuckin' Russian submarine that let you off here," he said.

"I came by land," I said as I went to the window and pointed out my little sports car in the parking lot. As my nerves settled I went back to making the case that negotiated disarmament was in the national interest, adding the anti-Communist clincher: "Don't you think our system of free enterprise can defeat Soviet Communism without resorting to nuclear weapons?"

Fifteen minutes or so into the conversation his attitude seemed to shift from total hostility to grudging respect.

"Listen here, young fella, you're right about a few things you've said, and dead wrong about most. The fact is I feel sorry for you because no one around here is going to buy this nonsense, except of course a few softheaded liberals like"– he gave me a name. "And then of course there's that comsymp"– he gave me another name – "and that hopeless sonovabitch"– yet a third name.

"Excuse me, sir, how do you spell that?"

He spelled out the third name and gave me about ten names total. Overjoyed, I thanked him for his time, left, and headed for a payphone to set up appointments with the contacts he had given me.

The editor clearly didn't think much of the people whose names he gave me. But his enemies were my core group. They were most amused when they heard who had given me their names. After a few days of calls and visits, I had pulled together the New Bedford Hughes for Senate Committee.

Building the Campaign

On my list were Arnold Dubin and Nick Roussos from the International Ladies Garment Workers Union (ILG). The ILG in New Bedford was heir to a noble tradition of labor militancy going back to the first and second decades of the twentieth century, when women workers in the textile mills had led strikes inspiring workers all over the world. Their hymn "Bread and Roses" inspires labor activists to this day.

But there was a world of difference between 1915 and 1962. By 1962, many of the big mills had moved down South to find low wages and avoid unions. The clothing manufacturers remaining in southeastern Massachusetts were squeezed hard by the wage competition from the mills in the South. For the most part, they turned around and squeezed the workers as much as they could get away with. For the ILG it was a dirty, ugly defensive war to protect the livelihoods of thousands of low-wage women workers who lived in New Bedford and Fall River.

Arnold Dubin was the regional director of the ILG. He was tall, thin, balding, and serious, somewhat formal and courtly in manner, weighed down by the awesome responsibilities resting on his shoulders – to protect his people who would be destitute without the union. Nick Roussos was dark-haired, medium-sized, and strong, a tough guy who was capable of giving the bosses who squeezed too hard a nasty surprise or two.

I learned a lot from Nick and Arnold. I learned to share their contempt for the diamond-ringed "pork choppers" who were then flourishing as leaders of many labor unions, getting fat off big salaries and larger expense accounts while their members struggled to survive. I also learned how to deal with the anti-Communism and anti-unionism that pervaded popular culture. When things got rough we could always sing, to the tune of "I Don't Want Your Millions, Mister," an old American labor song, the right-wing knock off "I Don't Want Your Union, Mister," including verses like this:

> *I don't want your union, mister,*
> *You can keep your working class.*
> *Take your Lenin, take your Trotsky,*
> *Stick that red flag up your ass.*

If you took unions seriously in the early 1960s, it was either learn how to laugh or leave in despair.

Nick and his wife, Jo, put me up in an extra room in their house in New Bedford and provided the nurture necessary to keep me going. Arnold gave me a desk in the ILG office, and every day I went out to leaflet factories and talk to workers when they arrived and left work. Over time, I think they came to admire my commitment and energy. By leafleting, I felt I was having some impact on public opinion. However, sustained conversations were very difficult at the factory gate. According to the *Standard Times*, Communists and comsymps were everywhere and dangerous. Talking to a stranger, who might be some kind of Communist, right out where the boss could see you, was a risk most workers didn't want to chance.

But one day about noon, as Nick and Arnold were leaving for lunch, Nick pointed to the open office safe in the ILG office.

"You know that in that safe is the list you've been asking about, with the name, address, and phone number of every shop steward in New Bedford."

Unions as a matter of policy never give out contact information about their membership. But on the table by the safe was a stack of three-by-five cards and a pencil.

"We'll be back in a couple of hours."

I knew this was my big chance, but I was also scared. With the list in hand, I had to deal with my fears. I knew from my experience in France that you recruit people to a campaign one at a time. Building the campaign meant visiting people as a guest in their homes. I wasn't sure I could pull it off. Would the workers accept me? Could I accept them? As I thought about my feelings, I was ashamed to admit that many years of elite education had made me look down on people with less education than I had. I had gotten along well with the workers in the warehouse and in a copper mine where I spent my high school summers. But my contact with them had only been on the job. Then came Harvard. The consistent message there was that we were the chosen ones, selfless, intelligent, and sensitive, surrounded in the larger society by less fortunate people we could either pity or despise, but never regard as equals.

In the evenings after leafleting the factories, I made calls to set up visits with a shop steward or two for the following day, applying the lessons about the need for personal one-on-one contact I had learned from the French anti-war organizers. At Harvard I had been schooled in the conventional wisdom that only college-educated people could respond to new and big ideas. But I found that the conventional wisdom was dead wrong. The shop stewards were interested in the campaign's domestic and foreign policy agenda. These grassroots leaders brought their own experience and critical intelligence to the conversation. My apprehension melted, and my confidence in my ability to do this work grew. In addition to learning a lot, I began to recruit volunteers to do things like distributing campaign materials to their friends, neighbors, and fellow workers. I felt like we were beginning to build a real organization.

The Kennedy mystique was very strong in Massachusetts, but the Kennedy mystique did not dominate the conversation when I was sitting around a shop steward's living room talking about the issues. Of course, I did not attack the president directly or personally; instead, I pointed out how different policies could lead to different and better outcomes for workers. There is something about being a guest face to face with people in their own living room: if the TV set is off, you and your message are the center of attention. If you make sense, people will work with you, regardless of mystique. Organizers build movements through one-on-one discussion.

One day I was leafleting a screw-machine shop where the workers seemed particularly aware of the issues. One of the workers with whom I was chatting suggested I go see the director of the union. He pointed to a tiny outbuilding close to the factory. I walked in and introduced myself to a tall, strong-looking, dark-haired man in his early forties sitting behind a battered desk. When he introduced himself as Doug Perry, I realized who he was. His name did not appear on my list of union officials. Nick and Arnold had referred to him once or twice, but had never actually laid eyes on him.

Doug Perry was the district director of the United Electrical Workers Union (UE). The UE had been thrown out of the Congress of Industrial Organizations (CIO) in 1948 when it refused to purge the Communists from its ranks. There was a lot of cheap talk about Communists in the newspapers, but Doug Perry was the real thing. I had no particular soft spot for Communists, but I was a little in awe of my audience as I pitched the campaign to him. His response was very straightforward. He thought it was about time for independent politics. He would help. Then he stood up, shook hands, and said good-bye. I was too shy and inexperienced to ask him what he planned to do, much less how it might fit in to an overall plan for the area. Not that that would have made any difference. At that time, fear of associating with Communists was so strong that I could never have integrated him and the UE with the rest of the campaign.

Many Communists had made the mistake of trying to hide their political beliefs and commitments. Doug survived because he never tried to hide. Because he was so honest and straightforward, the workers in his shop trusted him, and because they trusted him, they stuck by him, even when the local press and state government portrayed him as a dangerous subversive. The best the anti-Communists could do was to try to isolate him from the rest of the labor movement; there was no way they could get rid of him.

At the end of the summer, I received a wonderful compliment: Arnold offered me a job with the ILG. I turned him down because I wasn't ready yet to give up on graduate school as the path to greater understanding, and because I was dead tired. About a week after I left New Bedford, I learned that Teddy Kennedy had won the endorsement of the ILG by only one vote. Since the ILG was considered a pillar of the Democratic Party in the region, I considered this a great victory for the campaign and for myself.

Unfortunately, there were many things about organizing I didn't understand yet. My first lesson came about a month after I had left New Bedford when I returned with Stuart Hughes for a public meeting of the campaign. Very few people were there. In fact, it was a bust. Doug Perry was the only local pillar of the campaign who brought real numbers to the meeting. The middle-class people whom I had recruited were now all scared because of the attacks on the campaign in the papers. The Kennedy organization had started to crack the whip around the labor leaders who had shown interest in the campaign as well. The shop stewards I had visited in their homes weren't there either.

But I had really messed up, too. When I went back to graduate school, I had no idea that my departure would create a vacuum. My ignorance was both naïve and self-serving. In retrospect I had been a campaign mobilizer, not an organizer and I hadn't even left behind a group of people with clear responsibilities for managing the local campaign. I had no framework in which to assess or develop the skills of the shop stewards and other grassroots labor contacts I had recruited. When I left, I put my volunteer network in the hands of a minister who had agreed to chair the campaign but who knew even less than I did about how to keep this branch of the organization working and growing. He had done virtually nothing, so that branch had fallen off the tree. The meeting was a learning experience, a painful one.

The Cuban Missile Crisis

I heard President Kennedy's initial speech on a car radio on the way to an evening off-campus class on speed-reading, then a fad that the president himself had encouraged. He announced that U.S. spy planes had discovered and photographed Soviet missiles in Cuba aimed presumably at the United States. He demanded that the missiles be withdrawn immediately and warned that a U.S. fleet was deploying to enforce an embargo on Cuba. The grim scenario seemed to be right out of Stanley Hoffmann's seminar that had propelled me into the campaign. I turned the car around and headed home. With civilization on the edge of destruction, going to a speed-reading class seemed a waste of time.

As the nation soon found out, Soviet freighters were already on their way to Cuba. If they didn't stop, and the U.S. tried to enforce the embargo, a military confrontation between the two main nuclear powers would ensue, the outcome of which could be catastrophic.

The Cuban Missile Crisis was a real test of Stuart Hughes and the campaign. The next evening the campaign gathered to decide how to respond. Disagreeing with a president when the country could be on the verge of war was a recipe for political disaster if politics meant votes gathered. However, Stuart thought that in politics ideas mattered, and that intellectual integrity was more important than votes in an election.

The meeting went on for some time. The statement that emerged, "Hughes Peace Plan for Cuba," was a measured, but powerful call for an international effort under UN auspices to deal with all foreign nuclear bases, not just the ones that were upsetting the United States at that moment:

> "When we think of the panic we feel when we contemplate Soviet offensive potential in Cuba, we should also remember that for years we have maintained almost 100 bases around the Soviet Union. A permanent UN commission should be given the responsibility to inspect and control the threat of war from foreign nuclear bases anywhere in the world, and to prevent the future spread of nuclear weapons." (Quoted in Jerome Grossman, *Relentless Liberal*, pp. 109-110.)

A few days later, the Soviet agreement to withdraw the missiles from Cuba resolved the crisis.

Besides fear, the most powerful emotion I felt at the time was anger at the hypocrisy of the Kennedy administration. They refused to acknowledge that we had been encircling the Soviet Union with missiles for years. What Castro and Khrushchev were giving us was a very unpleasant dose of our own medicine. Instead of recognizing foreign missile bases as a threat to both countries, our government chose to pretend that we were the only aggrieved party.

At the time it was portrayed that Kennedy and Khrushchev had gone eyeball to eyeball, and Khrushchev had blinked; the missiles had been withdrawn because of the administration's firmness and determination, rather than some demeaning deal. What actually happened was close to what the campaign had advocated, though we didn't know it at the time. In addition to promising not to invade Cuba, the administration withdrew the U.S. missiles from Turkey a year after the Soviets withdrew their missiles from Cuba.

We later learned that the president and his brother Robert Kennedy, the attorney general, both recognized that to remove a threat from our doorstep we had to remove a threat from the Soviet borders. The Kennedy brothers made the deal that spared the world a nuclear holocaust despite bad advice from the Pentagon and their top advisors. Unfortunately, what remained in the public mind was the idea that the U.S. need not negotiate when the administration says that national security is at stake.

Ten Thousand Men of Harvard

Everyone active in the Hughes for Senate Campaign knew that to criticize the president's policies on brink of war, in the president's home state no less, guaranteed electoral defeat, a vote below even our previous modest expectations. Election night Marty Peretz gave a "victory" party. I drank steadily and copiously as we listened to the returns. When the count got close to 10,000 for Hughes, Mark Mirsky, whose father was a "real" politician in the state legislature, taunted me with verses of the song "Ten Thousand Men of Harvard," as if to say only the Harvard crowd voted for Stuart Hughes. I drank even more.

By the next morning, Hughes had about 50,000 votes, or 2.3 percent of the total. It was a real defeat, but I did not feel crushed. Despite the difficult and unpopular position criticizing the president we took at the end of the campaign, the peace movement was much stronger in November than it had been in May.

ღ ღ ღ

What I Learned from the Hughes Campaign

- To build a grassroots campaign:
  - Focus on winning the active support of the people who have the most to gain from its success.
  - Have confidence in people's ability to respond rationally to the case you are presenting.
  - Get the message and the key facts down cold to be able to present the campaign's positions in a clear and interesting way.
  - Press hard to do the work that needs to be done, above all to bring in new people. If you work hard, allies will help you and even enemies might.
- The most effective way to recruit people to a campaign is face to face, person to person.
- Never let a gatekeeper tell you whether you can speak to the people directly. People that you persuade can vouch for you the same way a formal gatekeeper would.
- To consolidate the gains of a campaign requires the skills of an organizer to build the local group and develop new leaders.

The Assassination of President Kennedy

The news came through that the president had been shot on November 22, 1963, in Dallas, about thirteen months after the end of the Cuban Missile Crisis. I was stunned. Like everyone else I hoped against hope that he would survive.

The day before the president's assassination, my brother Albert, my future brother-in-law Levi Laub, and Phil Luce, a friend of theirs, had come to Cambridge to speak at Harvard about their travels to Cuba in defiance of the state department's travel ban. For this they faced ten years in federal prison. Seeing Cuba and facing prison had radicalized my brother. Through him, I was coming to see more of the other side of Camelot.

After the news broke I went to a coffee shop in Harvard Square where Albert was having a late breakfast. In my hand was the *Boston Globe* with the headline "Kennedy to Dump Johnson." "Well, they got that one wrong," Al said, "Johnson just dumped Kennedy."

Terrible news or no, I had work to do, so I took off to the Boston University African Studies Center to finish some research I'd begun in France. On the way, the radio announced that the president was dead, and the program continued by playing Beethoven's Sixth Symphony, which I will forever associate with that sad moment. Arriving at the library, I was initially surprised at how the staff there was paralyzed by grief. After a few minutes, I realized that this day was not a day for research.

My brother and his friends' delegations were organized by the Progressive Labor Movement in an effort called the Student Committee for Travel to Cuba. They visited Cuba and came back to report the "truth" about Cuba to whoever would listen, including the audience at Harvard where they spoke on November 21. The Progressive Labor Movement was a self-proclaimed Communist organization that had split from the more conservative Communist Party of the United States, adhering at that time to the Chinese Communist Party's critique that the Communist Party of the Soviet Union had sold out to the West, and that "peaceful coexistence" was a sham. When Albert got off the plane in New York on his return from Cuba, a reporter asked him if he was a "Chinese Communist." In a slow Texas drawl he replied, "Do ah look Chahnese?"

At the time, I found my brother's bravado embarrassing, calculated to offend rather than convince the public. I also was put off by his enthusiasm for Fidel and the Cuban government. The notion that Castro was uniquely qualified to make all the important decisions for the Cuban people was absurd. Without democracy, I felt, the best one could hope from the Cuban experiment was left-wing charity work that infantilized the Cuban people.

The main purpose of the State Department ban on travel to Cuba, it seemed to me, was to control the flow of information to the American public. Controlling information from Cuba meant that Americans could remain ignorant of the positive aspects of the Cuban Revolution, as well as the ugly and illegal means our government was using to bring it down. The Bay of Pigs Invasion had failed. To resolve the Cuban Missile Crisis, the U.S. government had to commit to not invading Cuba. Thus, the Kennedy administration had been limited to subversion, terrorism, and assassination as means to rid themselves of the revolutionary government and restore law and order to Latin America. Kennedy's policies made a bad situation worse. Didn't he realize that if the only choice offered the Cuban people was between Fidel and American domination, Fidel was bound to win?

A stupid policy towards Cuba required repression at home to succeed. I remember reading Albert's indictment and being surprised that a well-known Cambridge liberal lawyer, who had become an assistant attorney general, signed it. "You no good son of a bitch," I thought, "how do you sleep at night?" My brother for all his bravado was just a kid with some big ideas, not a terrorist, yet he faced ten years in prison for traveling to Cuba. The FBI played rough, following him from place to place and tapping his phone regularly. My brother did not hold up well under the constant pressure, and he became more argumentative and paranoid as time went on. Albert and some of his comrades had started using heroin as a tranquilizer, to which he became addicted and which was in some measure responsible for his death by suicide thirteen years later.

Throughout the afternoon, most people I knew assumed that the president had been the victim of a right-wing plot. The anger was deep. I remember commiserating with a friend, an Irish immigrant, the superintendent of Kirkland House where I had lived as an undergraduate. "The fucking Dallas rednecks have killed our chief, the first of our race to attain high office," he said. I agreed. This was not the time to discuss policy differences I might have with the Kennedy administration.

Late in the day, the story shifted. Lee Harvey Oswald, the presumed assassin, was not a right-wing nut, but a left-wing one, associated with the Fair Play for Cuba Committee. At that time the sectarian rivalries among left-wing groups assured that there was no connection between the Fair Play for Cuba Committee of Lee Harvey Oswald and the Student Committee for Travel to Cuba of Albert,

Levi, and Phil. But was the FBI going to make subtle distinctions when the roundup came?

That evening Albert, Levi, Phil, Marty Peretz, and I went for dinner at Mother Anna's in the North End of Boston. We sat down at a table and ordered. The usually crowded restaurant was deserted, and the more we talked about the situation the more depressed we became. We hurried through our meal and then practically ran back to the car. The next day they went back to New York City. Several months after we were together in Cambridge, Phil Luce of the Student Committee for Travel to Cuba denounced his comrades in an article in *The Saturday Evening Post* and disappeared. To this day, I have no idea whether he succumbed to the constant pressure of harassment, or had been an informer all along. In 1964, a federal judge ruled in favor of the defendants on the travel ban to Cuba.

Like most students at Harvard, I spent the weekend of the funeral glued to the TV. My attitude towards the Kennedy administration was very different from those proud and hopeful days in Paris right after the election – the Bay of Pigs Invasion, the Cuban Missile Crisis, the travel ban, and now Vietnam all tarnished the hopes for a better world through the new president. Also, I was Irish, just like the Kennedys. They were fucking with my brother, and that made it personal. I felt I knew too much to share without reservations the nation's grief.

Would John Kennedy, with his greater knowledge of foreign affairs and the confidence he gained in the Cuban Missile Crisis, have caged his hawks and chicken hawks and spared our country and Vietnam the horror that began in 1965? We will never know.

In the spring of 1964, I began casting about for a course of action. Since 1961 when I had left the Harvard Business School, I had spent two-and-a-half years studying politics, economics, and economic history. I had vague ideas about getting a PhD, but had had enough of graduate school. I was too unsure of myself to take off, go to Africa, and make a life there, as I had planned to do earlier. I had learned from the Hughes campaign that grassroots organizing was a rough row to hoe. Then a great opportunity came along.

IV

The Short-Lived Hope
of the Johnson Years

GAR ALPEROVITZ, THE WASHINGTON DIRECTOR for Senator Gaylord
Nelson from Wisconsin, asked me to come to Washington to research and write
the first draft of a critique of the president's War on Poverty. The senator and
his staff would then rewrite it and publish it as a book with the senator as the
author. The book was not to be an attack on the new president, but a construc-
tive critique urging him to go further than he otherwise might in ending poverty
in this country, which was then the wealthiest nation on earth. I was ready to
put to work in the real world the things I had learned in school.

Washington, D.C., had a small-town feel. It was a company town – everyone
worked in the same business, if not for the same employer. Outside of politics,
news about politics, or gossip about politics, people in Washington typically
didn't have a lot to talk about. But in the summer of 1964, Washington was the
place to be.

Liberal Washington, aside from a few snobs and Kennedy irreconcilables,
was cautiously optimistic about Lyndon Johnson. I came to agree, with a little
bit more emphasis on the caution. When the president announced his War on
Poverty, I felt the call, came to Washington, and settled in.

HUAC Also Comes to Town

That summer my brother Albert was hauled before the House Un-American Activities Committee (HUAC) hearings in Washington. Of course I was in the audience. Al denied nothing.

"So you were at the illegal anti-war demonstration in New York City?"

"Yes, sir. I was there when the policemen charged in on horseback."

"So what did you do then, Mr. Maher?"

"Well sir, you know what happens when you hit a horse right in the nose like this?" Al demonstrates a straight punch angled upward.

"Of course I do, son. It stops them cold. So what did you do?" The questioner and another congressman from the Southwest leaned over the dais in genuine interest.

"Well, I hit him right in the nose and he stopped so sudden that the cop fell right off him. Then I ran."

"Good going. Think I'd a done the same thing," said the congressman, forgetting that Albert was the enemy.

The pattern had been that when people were subpoenaed to appear before HUAC they did one of two things: either they spilled their guts and implicated their former political associates, or they took refuge behind the Fifth Amendment to the Constitution that protects against self-incrimination. Either way, leftists came out looking like cowardly conspirators with a lot to hide.

Al and his pals played the game differently. Standing there in rumpled clothes they proclaimed their Communism to the members of the committee and the audience. They read the party manifesto into the public record, and then kept talking, and talking. The members of the committee were stunned. Worse, the spectators at the hearings began to laugh at the committee. HUAC was politically useful only so long as it could get dissenters to grovel. When witnesses started to make fun of the committee, the show stopped and HUAC faded from the public view.

In a company town, news travels fast. I was worried that Senator Nelson might be upset with a researcher whose brother was a self-confessed Communist who disrupted the proceedings of HUAC. The senator was curious and amused, but not a bit concerned, at least as near as I could tell. In fact, Gaylord, as we called him after hours, had several discussions on his own initiative with Albert. In one discussion, at a hotel bar in Cambridge, Albert went out of his way to antagonize the senator. Instead of pulling rank to end the discussion, Gaylord challenged Albert to continue the discussion outside and so he could punch him in the nose. With difficulty, I persuaded Gaylord that a fistfight between a Communist hothead and a U.S. senator might create a scandal even in Cambridge.

Freedom Summer

Three civil rights workers were murdered at the beginning of the summer of 1964, and hundreds of civil rights workers remaining in Mississippi were in constant danger. The Ku Klux Klan and other racist organizations responsible were ugly, violent bastards with strong support among whites in their communities. They were terrorists, and they had me terrified. I knew that non-violent organizing in Mississippi required more courage than I had.

The FBI and most of the Justice Department had long supported the illegal status quo in the South. They couldn't care less about protecting civil rights workers from attacks by racist terrorist groups like the Klan. I worried about the civil rights workers I knew. Their courage helped me put in perspective the small role I was playing from the safety of Washington. I did what I could to support Freedom Summer. Constant pressure on the government was vital to their survival. I visited congressional offices, sent letters, and spoke with whomever I could.

I. F. Stone

One day I went for lunch in the Senate cafeteria, famous for its delicious navy bean soup, where I saw a short man with coke-bottle glasses eating off by himself. Not only was he eating alone, but also the whole corner of the cafeteria where he sat appeared to have been evacuated. No one in official Washington wanted to be seen with Izzy Stone. I asked if I could join him, and we became fast friends.

My brother had turned me on to reading *I. F. Stone's Weekly*, an extraordinary publication that relied primarily on sources from within the government, like the Congressional Record and other federal publications, to ferret out high-level malfeasance. Izzy Stone, the sole editorial employee of the *Weekly*, was a legend, but no one I knew had ever met him.

Izzy was a real independent journalist, a person without a party line who was not at all shy to criticize the party line of others, left, right, and center. People attached to the status quo hated him, but he was also a problem for the existing left. He had nothing but scorn for leftists who talked big and couldn't deliver. At that time, many leftists avoided him as much as the right-wingers did. To me he was a role model, and I treasured our dinners when we ate spicy Korean food, drank beer, and took apart the governments of the world.

The Tonkin Gulf Incident

In early August, I was well into my project of attempting to lay out what a real war on poverty might look like when the real war in Southeast Asia exploded on the front pages. On Sunday, August 2, three North Vietnamese patrol boats off the coast of North Vietnam attacked the destroyer *U.S.S. Maddox*. Four U.S. aircraft from the carrier *Ticonderoga* had come to the assistance of the *Maddox*. One of the patrol boats had been sunk, and the other two damaged. One of the U.S. airplanes had been damaged, but no Americans had been hurt. Clearly, something was up. The next day the papers carried reports of a second assault on the destroyers *Maddox* and *Turner Joy*.

Gaylord Nelson's staff included Gar Alperovitz, Bill Spring, and John Berg. We sat around the office and tried to pick the administration's story apart. The Communist leader Ho Chi Minh was no fool. Why would he order an unprovoked attack by his tiny navy on the biggest naval power in the world?

On August 4, President Johnson announced to key Democratic members of Congress that the North Vietnamese had attacked two U.S. destroyers, that the U.S. was going to retaliate, and that he would ask the U.S. Congress for a resolution of support. On August 5, President Johnson sent the resolution to Congress. The Tonkin Gulf Resolution enlarged the president's powers to wage war in Vietnam to protect U.S. forces and to shore up our client state there. The president was asking Congress for a blank check.

On August 6, my friends and I got a break. A sentence or two in the *Washington Post* suggested that before the first attack the *Maddox* had been involved in covert raids by South Vietnamese commandos against North Vietnam. Now we knew that Lyndon Johnson had been lying about the first attack being "unprovoked."

We swung into action and began to pull together as much information as we could about what had really happened in the Tonkin Gulf. Other senators, like Wayne Morse of Oregon, had their own doubts and sources of information. (See Stanley Karnow, *Vietnam: A History*, p. 391.) After a briefing by Gar on what we had uncovered, Senator Nelson prepared an amendment calling for efforts to avoid direct U.S. military involvement. At that time, our soldiers were serving only as advisors to the South Vietnamese army, not as combat troops.

August 7 was the day of the big showdown. I remember seeing Senator Nelson stand up on the Senate floor and pose questions to Senator Fulbright, a liberal senator from Arkansas, head of the Senate Foreign Relations Committee, who was the lead sponsor of the Tonkin Gulf Resolution. In response to Nelson's inquiries, Fulbright stated that he had it on the "word of honor" of the secretary of state that this resolution would not be used to justify direct U.S. military involvement in Vietnam. Apparently satisfied, Senator Nelson sat down. His amendment was withdrawn.

I was stunned. The word of honor of the secretary of state! It seemed to me that these men had no honor, so what could their word of honor possibly mean? But I decided to keep my dissatisfaction to myself rather than confront Senator Nelson directly. After all, I was low on the office totem pole.

We actually did win a victory that day, despite the fact that the resolution passed with little dissent. Senator Nelson's questions and Senator Fulbright's reply made it clear that the intent of Congress in passing the Tonkin Gulf Resolution was not to authorize sending U.S. troops to fight the war in Vietnam. This exchange between senators provided the basis to later challenges in the courts and elsewhere to the president's authority to wage the war.

At the time I knew that the Johnson administration had lied about the circumstances surrounding the first incident, but I had no idea that the second incident in the Tonkin Gulf, so vividly reported by *Time*, *Life*, and *Newsweek*, had never taken place. The leader of the U.S. air squadron that had come to assist the *Maddox* and the *Turner Joy* had reported on returning to the carrier Ticonderoga: "Not a one. No boats, no boat wakes, no ricochets off boats, no boat gunfire, no torpedo wakes – nothing but black sea and American firepower." (Karnow, p. 386) According to the pilot who was best placed to see what was going on, the combination of fog, confusion, and malfunctioning equipment had led U.S. ships to invent an enemy that was not there. But his report was disregarded.

At the time, we guessed that the incidents were merely an excuse to get authorization from Congress to send troops to Vietnam. In fact, we know now that Johnson's staff began to draft the resolution five months before the incident. (Karnow, p. 360) One force driving U.S. policy towards the direct involvement was the fear that our Vietnamese allies might negotiate an agreement to end the war, thus depriving the U.S. of an opportunity to demonstrate the overwhelming power of U.S. military strength. So much for the "word of honor" of the secretary of state and the Johnson administration.

First Draft

A senator's office is a great place to be doing economic policy research. The Library of Congress had the reports and books I needed. Although I was an intern, I had a nice sunny cubicle to work in and the run of the place. When I needed some additional data, a simple call usually sufficed:

"Senator Nelson would like to know the correlation between the rate of unemployment and the rate of poverty since World War 1."

"Yes sir, we'll get the data to you right away. Is tomorrow noon soon enough?"

Throughout the summer, I had worked away on the project, largely on my own. In the early fall of 1964 I began to pull together my research on poverty in the United States into the first draft of a book. My strategy was not to criticize the programs the Johnson administration was presenting, but to talk about policies that might really work.

One-fifth of American families in 1962, more than thirty million persons, had money incomes below $3,000 per year. Ending poverty by work was the American way.

Unemployment, particularly during the 1920s and 1930s, had been associated with the rise of Fascism and Communism. In the aftermath of World War II, the issue of unemployment was addressed forcefully in many parts of the world. The European capitalist democracies had made legislative and even constitutional commitments to full employment as a right of citizens. In the United States, a similar Full Employment Act was passed in 1946. The difference in practice was that in Europe in the late 1950s and early 1960s, full employment was the cornerstone of economic policy, while in the United States the Full Employment Act of 1946 was a dead letter.

If jobs are the American way, what was the problem with getting full employment policies implemented in the United States? European democracies made full employment work not only having private or public sector jobs available for those who needed them, but ensuring that the unemployed received the relevant job training to make them employable and, if necessary, relocation assistance to get where the jobs were. It also meant that some public authority measured and made projections concerning every aspect of economic life – investment, production, consumption, and employment so that economic policy makers could predict what kind of workers would be necessary where. From these projections came plans on how the goals for production, investment, consumption, and employment would be achieved.

In Western Europe governments typically got private sector cooperation to carry out economic plans by tax, loan, or foreign exchange incentives, rather than by direct orders as in Soviet-style command economies. Economic cooperation and planning was essential part of Western Europe's dramatic economic growth after the war. For the United States to have full employment policies, and thus an effective war on poverty, we too would have to have an accountable public authority that planned.

When I presented my draft to Gar Alperovitz and Bill Spring, Senator Nelson's senior staff, in the late fall, I could tell from their expressions that it had more political problems than they had counted on. In Europe, the interest groups fought hard about what the priorities of the plan should be, but there wasn't much dispute about the need for public economic planning. In the United States businesses planned, but public economic planning was associated with wartime austerity, Godless Communism, or both.

The draft was done. As I packed my bags to leave Washington, I still believed that the coming period might be one of reform, one where I might be able to play a significant role. In terms of my critique of the War on Poverty, I knew that a lot of work, salesmanship, and luck would be required before the book would see the light of day. I planned to return to Washington soon to make it happen.

A Trip to Oxford

I left Washington in the late fall to go to Oxford, England, to visit a young woman. I had met Frances Aldrich, Frinde, at a party in Boston given by Hussein and others in the late spring for Jay Rockefeller who had just returned from a long sojourn in Asia. There I saw this young woman with gleaming black hair, full red lips, blue eyes, tan skin, a round face, flat chest and stomach, and gently curving hips. She looked Slavic, or perhaps black Irish. "Intriguing," I thought. We fell back from the crowd, too elegant for us, and talked. As it turned out, she was a New England WASP, a distant cousin of the guest of honor.

A few days later, I saw Frinde in Harvard Square. She waved jauntily, and I caught up with her. Soon we were dating. By the time I got around to figuring out I really liked her, it was May, only a few weeks before she graduated from Radcliffe, and a couple of months before I had to go to Washington. We had a brief but intense romance in Cambridge and then traveled around together some.

One day Frinde and I went with a dozen or so other people to the beautiful Victorian summer home of Corliss Lamont, a major donor to leftist causes, up the Hudson from New York City. Bob Dylan and Joan Baez were also on this excursion. In the late afternoon, someone discovered that we had missed the last train back and would have to spend the night there. No problem we were told, there were two bedrooms, and the rest could retire to sleeping bags on the living room floor. Joan was quick on her feet, and so was I. Our eyes locked for an instant. Quick as a flash I grabbed Frinde's hand and pulled her into the downstairs bedroom, while Joan grabbed Bob Dylan's and ran upstairs. Romance had its privileges.

I was busy that summer. But in retrospect, that house party happened in a quiet and peaceful time, before the war began. Soon I would have no time for folk concerts or house parties.

In July, Frinde and I parted when she went with her family to travel in Scandinavia before going to Oxford for a post-graduate year. I moved to Washington, and we continued to correspond, more ardently with each letter, as the fall progressed. By the end of the fall, romance had become love, and I couldn't wait to see her.

Since I was going abroad, my brother Albert gave me some pictures and articles concerning the U.S. anti-war movement to deliver to a Viet Minh representative in Paris. I was reluctant to undertake this mission as it could be seen as subversive, and I was trying to get a job in Washington. Also, I was not very impressed with my brother's comrades in the Progressive Labor Movement. It seemed to me these odd characters were so detached from reality they couldn't do much in the real world to aid the Vietnamese.

In the end, my sense of duty overrode my ambition. I agreed to deliver the packet to the Viet Minh because it was my brother who asked me and because as far out as they were, at the moment these American Communists for all their faults were the best friends the Vietnamese had.

Once I reluctantly agreed to deliver the material to the Viet Minh representative, I proceeded immediately to broaden the mission. Ever since the Tonkin Gulf Incident, I had been reading the papers carefully about Vietnam, particularly the *Washington Post*. Judging by the quantity and quality of the trial balloons that sailed past, I had concluded that the Johnson administration was preparing to resume bombing the North sometime after the presidential election in November 1964. Should I warn the Viet Minh? Would that be spying for the Communists?

I decided I had a moral obligation to warn them, and that it would not be spying since my only source of information was the newspapers. I would do the right thing, fervently hoping that nothing would come of it. The Viet Minh had to know already what was going on. After all, they had to have much better sources of information than I did.

Frinde was living in Oxford with a group of American young women who were very friendly and good company. But Oxford and their digs were cold and dreary, and I didn't want to spend our vacation there. I wanted to see France again, my second homeland.

On the Street of the Fishing Cat

Immediately after we arrived in Paris and checked into a small hotel, we went to the Viet Minh office on the rue du Chat qui Pêche, the Street of the Fishing Cat, down by the left bank of the Seine. I wanted to deliver my brother's materials and get this business with the Viet Minh over as soon as possible.

We walked into a small, second-floor office, and I introduced us in French to a slender Vietnamese man in his late thirties sitting behind a desk. I was nervous and he appeared a bit taken aback when two Americans walked in unannounced. Nguyen Kien who appeared to be the person in charge was polite but reserved at first. He became more relaxed and friendly when I passed him the packet of information on the U.S. anti-war movement. Then he asked us to sit down.

Once I was seated, I took a deep breath and proceeded to deliver in as measured a tone as possible my warning about an imminent U.S. attack. To my surprise he disagreed. Then he proceeded to challenge my understanding of American politics. Mr. Kien did not speak English, at least with us, but he was clearly keeping abreast of the American press, which he quoted extensively in French to support his argument.

"You misunderstand the profound nature of the split in the U.S. ruling class over foreign policy and whether to go to war," Mr. Kien said. "President Johnson represents the faction of your ruling class that wants to deal with the internal contradictions in the United States, the conflict between capitalists and workers, and Black and white, with a reform agenda. That reform agenda cannot be carried out if there was a war." He paused and then went on, "What you read in the newspapers is bluster to divert the right wing. What in fact is going to happen in 1965 is a complicated struggle involving conflict and negotiations that will lead ultimately to a compromise between capitalist and Communist approaches and the reunification of Vietnam."

At first, I didn't buy his argument. We went round and round in a friendly but combative fashion. But Mr. Kien was very persuasive and well informed. After several hours of discussion, he had won me over.

The conversation had been too intense for me to translate much for Frinde's benefit. When we left, we walked around while I explained to her what had happened. Then we went to a restaurant to eat dinner and drink some wine. Not long after we sat down, Mr. Kien came in with a woman and sat down across the room. He did not appear to have noticed us. Immediately they fell into deep conversation, obviously in English. Was she a girlfriend? If they were a couple, they were an odd one, he thin, dark, and good-looking, and she heavy-set, plain, earnest-looking, and unmistakably English.

I was a little drunk as we got up to leave. I went over to wring his hand and thank him again for sharing his insights. When I came to his table, he blushed. His embarrassment was so obvious that I thanked him quickly and fled the restaurant, feeling that I had crossed some boundary that I should have recognized, but didn't.

Frinde and I spent a few days in Paris and a few days traveling around France. Much of the time I spent trying to persuade her to come back to the United States so we could spend time together. I had a terrible head cold the whole time we were traveling in France. When we got back to England, Frinde agreed to leave Oxford. My head cleared immediately. After a brief sojourn in England, I left for the United States, while Frinde stayed on to wind down her affairs.

Mr. Kien was right – President Johnson had to choose between reform and war. He was wrong when he thought President Johnson would make the rational choice.

V

Building the Student
Anti-War Movement, 1965

THE VIET CONG ATTACKED A U.S. base near Pleiku in the central highlands of South Vietnam on the night of February 6, 1965. In retaliation, the United States began bombing North Vietnam, significantly escalating the war. The Johnson administration had long planned this escalation; the attack on Pleiku had merely provided the pretext. (Karnow, p. 428) I was taken totally by surprise. When I heard the news that the bombing of the North had begun, Frinde and I were lying in bed in the apartment of my sister, Mary, and her boyfriend, Levi Laub, in New York City.

I had written my undergraduate thesis on Pierre Mendes-France, the French premier who had negotiated their withdrawal from Vietnam in 1954 after eight years of war. I knew something about the Vietnamese resistance to foreign domination. I knew this adventure would end badly for the United States. Immediately I felt that the period of reform, the hope of the Johnson years, was over. I felt totally isolated and helpless. I stayed in bed.

On returning from France I had decided to go back to Washington to finish drafting Senator Nelson's book analyzing the War on Poverty, hoping that it would be published and influence the shape of the national poverty program. But why go back to Washington now?

Major world events like the Bay of Pigs Invasion and the Cuban Missile Crisis had shaken me. But during the Cuban Missile Crisis, the Hughes for Senate Campaign at least provided some structure for collective action. Two days after the bombing began I got up with a course of action in mind – instead of going to Washington, I would go back to Cambridge, where I knew people, and join the anti-war movement. Frinde's parents lived in Marblehead, Massachusetts, and she had roots in Cambridge also. Instead of a career in public service, I would fashion a new career as an organizer. Because I had money from my parents, I could afford to make this choice without sacrificing my hopes for a family with children and living a decent life.

Events moved swiftly. On February 11, Operation Flaming Dart, supposedly in retaliation to the Viet Cong attack on Pleiku, was replaced by Operation Rolling Thunder, bombing that would continue for three years. On March 8, troops came ashore at Da Nang, South Vietnam, the first U.S. soldiers to be sent directly into combat since Korea. The fat was in the fire. In the short term I was wrong about the war bringing domestic reform to a close – immigration reform, Medicare, and the Voting Rights Act were still to come. By the end of the year, however, as the catastrophe unfolded, the war began to consume everything.

Frinde decided to work with the SDS community-organizing project in Boston's Roxbury neighborhood. I decided to work with the May 2nd Movement (M2M), which had been initiated by Progressive Labor on May 2, 1964.

Progressive Labor and my brother Albert's involvement in M2M had put me off them. But SDS seemed to have plenty of activists – they didn't need one more. What SDS and the movement seemed to lack was sufficient information and analysis to be able to stand up to the pro-war intellectuals on the one hand and win over the undecided citizens on the other. Some graduate students who belonged to M2M had studied Vietnam and come up with some important insights that could help us make our case to the American people.

In February 1965, the State Department had issued a "White Paper" titled *Aggression from the North: The Record of North Vietnam's Campaign to Conquer South Vietnam*, which laid out the administration's case for war. The title told it all – North Vietnam had invaded the South in response to its growing prosperity, which had made a peaceful takeover of the South by the North Vietnamese Communists impossible. (Marvin Gettleman, *Vietnam: History, Documents, and Opinions*, pp. 324-357) *I.F. Stone's Weekly* immediately pointed out that a close reading showed that the data in the document did not support the assertion that the bulk of the enemy soldiers and equipment came from the North. Surprisingly few weapons captured were manufactured in Communist countries. Also only six of the infiltrators cited in the White Paper of the many thousands referred to were actually born in the North. (I.F. Stone, "A Reply to the White Paper," cited in Gettleman, pp. 357-363)

A key part of the real story was what the M2M group had uncovered. During the war against the French, the Viet Minh had taken land from the largely pro-French landlords and given it to farmers with little or no land. The pro-U.S. government under Diem had brought the landlords back. Now in South Vietnam, farmers under U. S.-backed land reform (highly touted in this country) were not given land; they were forced to buy land back from the landlords, land which the Viet Minh had given them. ("The Significance of the White Paper," Harvard-Radcliffe, May 2 Committee, 1965)

Many Americans thought fighting Communism was the right thing to do, but I thought they could understand that sending our boys to fight in a faraway country on the wrong side of the land question was asking for real trouble. If we could help them understand that the war in the South was being carried out by people from the South who wanted their land back and their country reunited and free from foreign interference, maybe the majority of Americans would change their mind. International agreements like ideological differences were abstractions most people found confusing. There is nothing abstract about land.

My Radio Debut

Soon after I arrived in the Boston area, I was invited on a big talk radio to debate Gordon Hall, Boston's expert on "extremist groups," who wrote for the *Boston Herald*, in addition to regular radio gigs. His message was that dissenters were basically Communist infiltrators, who manufactured issues and operated in bad faith. "For those committed to the total overhaul of American society, it can be fairly said, that if crises did not exist, they would have to be invented." (Gordon Hall, "The Story behind Those Vietnam Demonstrations: Boston's Radical Student Left," *Boston Sunday Herald*, May 23, 1965)

I asked around about Hall. People told me that he had no compunction about pretending to be an expert whatever the issue was, denying any facts that supported his opponent. Lying can work. It had worked against Malcolm X, I heard. When Hall flat out denied the existence of pervasive racism in the United States, Malcolm had lost his temper and let his presentation dissolve into angry accusations. This angry outburst probably reinforced the image of Malcolm X as a Black extremist driven mainly by irrational hatred rather than concern for real issues.

I prepared for the radio show with Hall like a final exam. I tried to anticipate the different ways he might try to defend the war, and made sure that I had a counter-argument prepared for every point he might try to make. I reviewed materials and made outlines. I resolved to stick to the facts and keep my cool. If Hall pointed out there were Communists in M2M, as I was sure he would, I was going to point out that these Communists, like my brother, were very public, no infiltrators here. Then I would move on.

I arrived at the radio station dressed in a suit and tie, with documents stuffed in my pockets, including, of course, the State Department White Paper on Vietnam. Hall was big, round, well dressed, and scholarly looking. Hall's sidekick, a young man named Barry, reputed to be of great wealth, accompanied him. He was a smaller version of his mentor. Seen together they looked a little like Batman and Robin in civilian clothes. To my surprise, there was a third participant, Peter, a representative of the Young Socialist Alliance (YSA), a Trotskyist student organization. Our host and the three debaters sat around a table in a small room, each with his own microphone. Barry sat in the back, behind Hall, and smiled.

I let Peter start because he was more experienced and had debated Hall before. But Peter made himself the perfect foil for Hall. First he insisted on using an alias, when Hall knew his real name. Round one: Hall had unmasked the infiltrator. Then Hall lured him into a longwinded effort to establish his credibility by distinguishing Trotsky's brand of Communism from Stalin and the Soviet variety. The show was supposed to be about U.S. government policy in Vietnam, but Peter allowed himself and the YSA to be put on trial.

When my turn came, I stuck to my plan and made the case for U.S. withdrawal from Vietnam. Hall kept quiet until I got to the internal inconsistencies in the State Department White Paper on Vietnam, claiming an invasion from the North with almost no real evidence to back it up. Then he took the bait. "You're just making those numbers up in a typical left-wing fashion," he said. "The case the State Department makes for North Vietnamese aggression causing the war is consistent from beginning to end."

"Have you read the document?" I asked him.

"Of course," he said.

Then I knew I had him hooked good. "Here's one for Malcolm," I thought. Then I pulled out the White Paper and asked the host to read the highlighted passage to the radio audience where the State Department acknowledged that almost all the Viet Cong fighting us were from the South. He did. Hall melted. Barry stopped smiling. After the show was over, the host told me he would like me to come back soon, without Gordon Hall.

Soon after, I did go on the show again. One caller seemed particularly hostile and aggressive, accusing me of being a left-wing liar. The host covered the microphone with his hand and said, "That's Gordon Hall, disguising his voice. He's done that before." So I said, on the air, "Talk about liars, let me tell you the story about how Gordon Hall lied the last time he was on this show." "That's not relevant," said the caller, choking on his words. I couldn't wait to tell the story.

Another media opportunity came up when the head of the Massachusetts Veterans of Foreign Wars (VFW) proclaimed that all the students demonstrating against the war should be horsewhipped. Liking nothing better than a good dogfight, another of the big talk shows invited me on with him.

I walked into the anteroom of the studio, all neatly dressed in coat and tie. About a minute later a man on the other side of the room said nervously to the man beside him, "Where is he?" Clearly, he was expecting "him" to have long dirty hair with a reefer dangling out of his mouth. I went over and politely introduced myself to the head of the Massachusetts VFW. When the show started he began, "Our boys are out there dying for their country. They need and deserve our support. Americans who don't support our boys are traitors."

I began with "I couldn't agree with you more," and went on to say that the problem wasn't our boys, or the demonstrators either, but the politicians who put our boys in mortal danger without leveling with the American people about what is going on. "That's right," he said, "it's those damn politicians." I went ahead and made my case that supporting our boys meant bringing them home, and for the rest of the show we sang in perfect harmony.

Another big step towards legitimizing our position came when Alan Gilbert from M2M was able to hold his own in a debate at Harvard with McGeorge Bundy, former dean of the faculty and then national security advisor to President Johnson. That McGeorge Bundy was being forced to come back to shore up his base at Harvard was already a sign that the anti-war movement was gaining ground there. That M2M's views had to be included in the panel that discussed the U.S. policy in Vietnam with this most prestigious and well informed of administration spokespeople made it even clearer.

When Alan asserted that reverse land reform, which had taken land from the farmers and given it back to the landlords, was an important cause of the conflict, Bundy was clearly caught off guard. When he did respond, it was to dismiss the whole argument out of hand. It was nonsense, he said, but cited no facts to back up his position. Everyone in the lecture hall noticed this lack of evidence. More people recognized that we were serious and knew a thing or two.

Young Christian Students

I knew nothing about the many progressive visionaries in the Roman Catholic Church. Luckily, one day I ran into Rory Ellinger, coordinator of the Young Christian Students. Meeting Rory changed everything. After spending some time with him, I realized that, with the help of YCS, I might be able to reach out to Catholic students. Outreach to students in the smaller public and Catholic colleges also made sense because SDS was focused on the elite campuses, and I wanted to influence SDS, not compete with it for recruits.

Many soldiers and politicians, and not just from Massachusetts, were from an Irish Catholic background. Irish Catholics were a key constituency for the anti-war movement, but they were often a tough bunch to reach. At that time, there was no War on Communism the Roman Catholic hierarchy wouldn't enthusiastically support. Worse, since many of the hard-core Vietnamese anti-Communists were Roman Catholic, the hierarchy had all the more reason to support U.S. intervention in Vietnam.

As an immigrant group subjected to a great deal of discrimination, militant anti-Communism had been a way for Catholics of Irish descent to establish their patriotism. Anti-Communism was the daily fare at many Catholic schools and colleges. FBI agents were recruited from these same institutions. Though my free-thinking father was from an Irish Catholic background, like many young college radicals I thought Catholics were a monolithic group hostile and intolerant to our point of view.

YCS was a Catholic student group inspired by the example of Dorothy Day. Much of their work was with homeless alcoholic men, among the poorest group in the cities. For myself I felt that I'd had enough of obnoxious Irish American drunks to last a lifetime. But quickly I came to admire the patience and devotion with which the YCS students worked with them. Moreover, like Dorothy Day herself, the young activists of YCS were not afraid to take on the war as a moral issue. Turning up at a Catholic college with anti-war leaflets seemed to me like a good way to get beat up. Their willingness to take the issue of the war to Catholic schools and colleges made them among the bravest of the brave as far as I was concerned, almost as brave as the civil rights workers in the South.

Rory and I hit it off from the beginning, but we were quite a pair. People could not believe that the leader of a Catholic student organization could actually be a friend with and work with a Harvard leftist from an organization with *Communists* in it. Our relationship worked because I admired them and felt I had to help them succeed at all costs. I was determined to earn their trust, and keep it. That meant letting them define how far left we could go at any given moment. Rory trusted me, and the YCS members trusted Rory.

What I had to offer was a straightforward, low-key way to talk about the war, which I had developed on the talk shows. After a few presentations to the group, they wanted me to speak at their schools. I was apprehensive, but these were offers I could not refuse. When I spoke at a school like Boston State College, the majority of the audience was going to be hostile, that was a given. Because I was sponsored by YCS, I could probably count on a few minutes before the hotheads would become physically threatening. In that narrow window of time, I had to raise enough interesting questions – Why are the Vietnamese fighting us? What's the best way to support our boys? – in a way sympathetic enough for the audience to continue the dialogue rather than run me off.

Turning a Corner

People remember the sixties as a period of massive demonstrations. The truth is that in the spring of 1965, the turnout was tiny, and most visible off-campus anti-war work was pretty tough. If M2M or SDS called for a rally at the Boston Common near the main subway station at Park Street, a turnout of one or two dozen for our side was considered good. On the other side, there would be the self-described "Polish freedom fighter" who turned up without fail to bellow at the demonstrators, tough and menacing Cuban exiles, well-dressed college students from Young Americans for Freedom, plus assorted other right-wingers including Gordon Hall, Barry, and the Boston Police Red Squad taking pictures. It was hard work standing there with a microphone with half the people in front of you telling you to go fuck yourself. After a while, even the most optimistic organizers began to feel a demoralizing sense of futility and isolation.

Then we began to turn a corner. By early April the teach-in movement began. Students and faculty all over the country came together in all-night sessions to learn about the war. I had kept in touch and developed friendly relations with the SDSers at Harvard. Students for a Democratic Society (SDS) was the major anti-war organization in the Boston area. Tocsin, the Harvard-Radcliffe peace group, had continued to grow after the Hughes for Senate Campaign and was now a chapter of SDS. SDS had smaller affiliates at Brandeis, Boston University, and Tufts, and several dozen other chapters around the country. In late December 1964, even before the bombing of "North" Vietnam began, SDS had called for a national March on Washington to End the War for April 17, 1965.

SDS, though largely white, was closely allied with the Student Nonviolent Coordinating Committee (SNCC) and the Northern Student Movement. In addition, in the summer of 1964, about 125 SDS volunteers had gone to live in poor communities in Newark, Chicago, Cleveland, Philadelphia, and several other cities of the North to organize an interracial movement of the poor to fight for economic justice. (See Kirkpatrick Sale, SDS, p.115.)

The SDS mission was stated on every membership card:

> "It maintains a *vision* of a democratic society, where at all levels the people have control of the decisions which affect them and the resources on which they depend. It seeks a *relevance* through the continual focus on realities and on the programs necessary to affect change at the most basic levels of economic, political and social organization. It feels the *urgency* to put forth a radical, democratic program counterposed to authoritarian movements both of communism and the domestic right." (Quoted in Sale, p. 56)

Reports from Boston and around the country indicated that the march that had originally aimed at bringing 3,000 people to Washington could actually bring 20,000 to 30,000. If this happened, it would dwarf all previous anti-war efforts and be a tremendous boost to our visibility and morale. The M2M activists at Harvard decided to put their energy into building the SDS march by going door to door in the dorms.

I had another reason to be interested in the March on Washington. Education was our most important weapon against the war. Most support for the war was based on ignorance, ignorance of what was happening in Vietnam and ignorance about what the war would mean for the lives of most people in this country. The fact was that in the spring of 1965 relatively few anti-war activists knew enough about the issues to act as educators, to rebut publicly the administration assertions about Vietnam, or to understand the deep-rooted nature of the policies that had brought us there. The information and analysis had to get out so that instead of hundreds we would have thousands and tens of thousands of grassroots educators, all around the country.

M2M had the information and SDS had the activists. If we had a pamphlet that clearly made the case, then the activists could look it over on the way home on the bus and start using it the next day.

I was determined to make this happen. I turned to Progressive Labor, which like most left-wing sects had its own press. I said we should print 20,000 copies. They said 2,000. After all, the largest anti-Vietnam War demonstration to date, organized by the three major Marxist sects in New York City, Progressive Labor, Young Socialist Alliance, and the DuBois Clubs, on May 2, 1964, had drawn 2,000 people. How could a bunch of "liberals" in SDS do any better than that? I got tired of arguing, so I said I would pay to have 20,000 printed and delivered to Washington on the morning of April 17.

The SDS March on Washington

I arrived in Washington on the morning of April 17. When I walked over to the White House, I saw a huge picket line on the sidewalk outside the fence. The White House itself seemed far away across the green lawn beyond. The picket line was mainly white; some were older middle-class people and the majority students. But the marshals were mainly SNCC organizers who had come up from the South. The marshals clapped their hands and chanted, like the Southern civil rights demonstrators I had seen on television. Gradually the people picketing began to absorb the energy of the marshals and pick up the chants. Soon everyone was booming their opposition to the war at the top of their lungs. I was surprised and moved that the SNCC cadre had taken the time from the life-and-death struggle in the South to join a demonstration against the war in Washington, D.C. as well as the fact that white demonstrators were accepting the leadership of the Black marshals. After so many years of racial division, seeing such unity brought tears to my eyes.

Then I went to the place where the pamphlets were to be delivered. As the buses continued to unload, about 25,000 demonstrators streamed by me to the amphitheater where the rally was held. I waited for the pamphlets to arrive, and waited, and waited, torn between ecstasy over the success of the march and fury over the stupid incompetence of the New York comrades who couldn't get anywhere on time if their worthless lives depended on it.

Finally, they arrived, looking hung-over, unwashed, and bedraggled.

"Hey man, sorry. I forgot to set the alarm, and then we broke down on the turnpike."

"Where are the 20,000 pamphlets?" I asked.

"Well, we printed 20,000, but we left 18,000 at the office. Didn't want to waste any. Hey man, there are a lot of people here!"

"No shit, you fucking asshole," I thought to myself as I started passing out the pamphlets.

By the time I had finished, I had missed I.F. Stone, Senator Ernest Gruening from Alaska, and the other speakers. When I arrived, Paul Potter, president of SDS, had begun speaking. I was surprised at how thin and tired he was, as he stood there, older looking and more careworn than I expected a student leader just out of college to be. He spoke clearly and carefully, slowly moving his out-stretched arms as he addressed the audience on one side of the podium and then on the other. Paul gave the best speech I had ever heard:

> "We must name that system. We must name it, describe it, analyze it, understand it and change it. For it is only when that system is changed and brought under control that there can be any hope for stopping the forces that create a war in Vietnam today or a murder in the South tomorrow or all the incalculable, innumerable more subtle atrocities that are worked on people all over – all the time."
> (Quoted in Todd Gitlin, *The Sixties: Years of Hope, Days of Rage*, p.184)

In his speech Potter laid out the agenda for not only his generation of Americans, but every generation since. Then he went on to talk more specifi-cally of the relationship between the Vietnamese and ourselves:

> "... [I]n a strange way the people of Vietnam and the people of this demonstration are united in much more than a common concern that the war be ended. In both countries there are people struggling to build a movement that has the power to change their condition. The system that frustrates these movements is the same. All our

lives, our destinies, our very hope to live, depend on our ability to overcome that system." (Gitlin, p.184)

Unlike the left-wing sectarians, Potter did not name the system, nor did he lay out a blueprint for changing it. Asking hard questions but rejecting dogmatic answers drew me towards SDS and away from Progressive Labor.

Meeting the Leaders

Right after the march, I went to the Institute for Policy Studies, a progressive think tank in Washington, for a conference on the future direction of the movement. I was expecting academics. Instead I found myself in the same room with some of the most important leaders of the New Left – Bob Moses and Cleve Sellers from SNCC, Tom Hayden and Ritchie Rothstein from SDS, and a delegation from the Southern Student Organizing Committee (SSOC), a white student group allied with SNCC in the South. I was overwhelmed.

Tom Hayden, plainly dressed in cotton pants and shirt, with close-cropped hair, looked the part of a neighborhood organizer, someone not anxious to call attention to himself. But like Bob Moses, the leader of the Mississippi Summer Project, he was by then a legend. In 1962 Tom Hayden had drafted the Port Huron Statement of Students for a Democratic Society, which was the founding manifesto of the New Left in the United States, carving out territory between the compromised liberals who couldn't hold their ground and the dogmatists of the Old Left, both Communists and socialists, who wouldn't move with the times.

By 1964, more than 20,000 copies of the Port Huron Statement had been distributed by SDS. Two things made the document unique. One was the "thoroughgoing critique of the American system in all its aspects – political parties, big businesses, labor unions, the military industrial complex, the arms race, nuclear stockpiling, racial discrimination – coupled with a series of suggested reforms...." (Sale, p. 50) The other was the break with Cold War orthodoxy. (For the complete text see James Miller, *Democracy in the Streets*, p. 329ff.)

Tom had also initiated the Economic Research and Action Projects in which hundreds of students had gone into the ghettos of a dozen cities "to improve the lot of the poor by direct action and 'community unions.'" (Sale, p. 8 and Chapter 7)

I was new, untested, from a little left-wing group, and I had stumbled into an important discussion that had begun long before I had arrived. The others had been working together for several years and had some serious issues to resolve among themselves, particularly in light of the expected right-wing counterattack against the Civil Rights Movement in the South. When Bob Moses challenged the Southern Student Organizing Committee with "When push comes to shove, what are you going to do?" I thanked God I wasn't the one trying to organize whites in the South to support the Civil Rights Movement. I listened and said little.

There was a sense that the leadership believed that each step forward for the movement added to their responsibilities and put them more on the line. It gave me pause to see charismatic leaders much more knowledgeable than I so consumed with anxiety the day following such a great victory.

For all our faults the movement was becoming my family – close friends, I hoped, and comrades for the rest of my life. Paul Potter came to Cambridge after he left the presidency of SDS. He too joined my circle of friends and heroes. A sense of duty had brought me to the anti-war movement. What kept me going was feeling part of a "beloved community" of organizers working together to build a better world, bound together by love and trust that covered not just our political lives, but our personal lives as well. I believed that a moral compass guided each one of us and that we would follow this path to the end, regardless.

The U.S. Invades the Dominican Republic

On Wednesday, April 28, 1965, the U.S. Marines were ordered ashore in the Dominican Republic, ostensibly to evacuate American citizens from the capital, Santo Domingo. (Tad Szulc, *Dominican Diary*, p. vii) A rebellion had begun in Santo Domingo Saturday, April 24, led by Lieutenant Colonel Francisco Caamano Deno. The rebels, including many civilians, were fighting to restore the elected president, Juan Bosch, whom the military had overthrown in a coup in September 1963, as well to restore the 1963 constitution under which the election had been held. (Szulc, p. 3)

The anti-Vietnam War movement responded as best we could. We held teach-ins and rallies. Informed opinion throughout the country was very disturbed, forcing the Johnson administration to change its rhetoric at least for a while and make one half-hearted attempt to reach a compromise with Dominican democracy and constitutionalism.

In the weeks that followed the invasion, the U.S. military presence grew from 400 to 22,000 soldiers and marines. As the crisis unfolded it became clear that the U.S. was there to ensure that the forces fighting to restore democracy and the Dominican constitution were defeated. Dozens of U.S. soldiers died in the conflict and thousands of Dominicans were killed, both in the fighting and in the repression that followed. In the end the rebel movement was crushed, coaxed to surrender with promises that were never kept.

The Johnson administration again lied regularly to the American people, about why we were there and what we were doing. They attributed the rebellion first to local Communists and then to the "Sino-Soviet bloc." (Szulc, p. 290) Because this crisis had suddenly erupted close at home, and because of the excellent reporting by journalists like Tad Szulc of the *New York Times*, the lies put out one day were unmasked within the week.

In 1965, one could still argue that Vietnam was a mistake. What after all did American decision-makers know about Vietnam, a French colony so far away? However, the Dominican invasion so close to home was pure viciousness. For weeks the rebels held out in the old part of Santo Domingo. Although I am not a religious person, I prayed to God every day to protect Colonel Caamano.

I identified with Colonel Caamano. I saw him as a humane and open person determined at all costs to make his country more democratic and egalitarian. Although he was many times more courageous than I was ever called upon to be, at thirty-two years old in 1965, he was a member of my generation, not a father figure, but an older brother.

Getting Ready to Go Underground

A few weeks after the invasion of the Dominican Republic, my brother Albert and a friend came back from New York and invited me to a secret meeting.

I was keyed up and ready to conspire. Sitting around someone's bare living room, they told me that Progressive Labor in New York was alerting the leading comrades to prepare to go underground. Going underground, they explained, meant not only hiding somewhere where the police couldn't find us, but also being able to reestablish contact with our comrades from the new location and continuing to do useful work. I was flattered that PL had included me in the inner circle of reliable and indispensable people.

It seemed to me that a government effort to lock us up then when the anti-war movement was still small was a real possibility. There was already a legal basis for internment – legally, subversives could be interned during a state of national emergency. President Truman had proclaimed a state of national emergency during the Korean War, and this proclamation was still in effect in 1965. I knew that the internment camps were set up in several western states and ready to be filled. I also felt that, if I were Lyndon Johnson, I would be seriously thinking about interning the leaders of the anti-war movement right then before we became more powerful.

Our duty was to educate Americans about what was really happening in Vietnam and how U.S. imperialism, if unchecked, would ultimately destroy our country. If we continued to do our work, and did it properly, then we would win, I believed. However, if the existing leadership were scooped up and interned, then our victory would come more slowly and many more Americans would die in the war. Figuring out how to avoid the roundup and how to keep on working under more oppressive conditions was the prudent, common sense thing to do. I knew my phone was tapped, so there was certain urgency to the discussion.

Of course, many activists at the time thought their phones were tapped. It was a badge of honor, an affirmation that the government thought you were doing important stuff. Perhaps all our suspicions were correct. In the early fall, I was meeting one morning at my house with Sam Bowles and some other radical economists when the phone rang. When I picked it up there was a click from deep inside the receiver, then the previous conversation around the kitchen table where the phone was began to be played back. I passed the receiver around, and we all had a good laugh. After that, I never discussed anything near a phone, much less on one, if I didn't want to share the conversation with the FBI.

One way I diffused the surveillance-related tension in our lives was to imagine the amount of household trivia the spies had to wade through to find out there was nothing illegal we were doing anyway. Frinde and her mother were both great talkers, and when they got going on the phone I loved to imagine our stalkers crammed in a closed van, sipping stale coffee, and breaking wind as the chat went on.

In the 1980s, I asked a lawyer to request my FBI file. It was 2,000 pages. I told my lawyer I wasn't sure I'd accomplished quite that much. I was flattered, but surprised. My lawyer explained that I was obviously on the list to be interned. A lot of the file was routine checkups, where was I living and where was I working, so when the order came through they could find me quickly.

Several days after our meeting, Albert and his friend disappeared, without a trace, without a word. As near as I could tell they didn't go underground, they just took off. No one seemed to know where they were, and it would be months before I heard a word from either of them. Later the friend reappeared and resumed an active and important role in the movement. Albert was never active in the movement again. We were all scared, but for Albert isolation led to paranoia, and paranoia to an inability to function.

Albert went back to Houston to work for our father, who could be a cruel and demanding taskmaster. One day you were a hero, the next a damn fool. To escape the stress, Albert dove deeper into drugs. After things didn't work out with my father, he moved to New Mexico. We corresponded occasionally, but after he left Cambridge I had little to do with him.

After consulting with some of the graduate student members who were still around, I proposed to SDS that we work jointly on research and action for the summer. One of the products of this first joint effort of which I was most proud was the *Vietnam Study Guide and Annotated Bibliography* by Stephen J. Rosenthal, printed and distributed all over the country by SDS. I felt by then that the May 2nd Movement had fulfilled its function of educating the movement, and it was time for me to move on. By the early fall I was an SDS organizer.

🐦 🐦 🐦

What I Learned as a Spokesperson for the Anti-War Movement

- Organizers and leaders need to know the issues cold.
- Make your basic presentation brief and interesting. The more you know about an issue the easier it is to do this.
- Use the media.
- Don't avoid big public debates, but carefully prepare.
- Never write off potential constituencies, particularly ones you really need.
- Acknowledge the legitimate concerns of the people you're trying to reach out to.
- Don't act belligerent towards people who have simply been misled.
- Don't allow yourself to be stereotyped.
- Tides turn. When things are difficult and only small-scale activities are possible, make sure you know what you are going to do when the possibility of large-scale activity opens up.
- Isolation and paranoia are a vicious circle. Don't allow yourself to become isolated from ordinary people.
- Always keep the larger movement in mind. Don't let organizational jealousy interfere with your judgment about what it takes to make the movement stronger.

VI

Becoming an SDS Organizer, 1965-66

ONE MORNING IN THE SUMMER of 1965, Frinde and I had taken some LSD, a powerful hallucinogen popular at the time. One tab seemed to have no effect, so we each took a second one. A few minutes later, we rocketed into space and orbited. We spent the rest of the morning hallucinating, watching chariot races on top of a light fixture, for example, and the man in a print on the wall change expressions rapidly back and forth from smile to frown.

Then I heard a knock at the door. When I opened it, there was a slender red-headed man in his early thirties standing there. He asked for me and then introduced himself, Carl Oglesby, the new president of Students for a Democratic Society. I was stunned as well as stoned, speechless with embarrassment at meeting a movement leader for the first time, or anyone else for that matter, in this condition. I apologized and explained to Carl as best I could what was going on. "Well, I'll be damned," he said softly, with a Midwest accent, amused to find two of his activists incoherent so early in the day. Carl quickly put us at our ease.

By noon it was hot. We walked from our apartment down Oxford Street to a spot under a large, leafy tree in Harvard Yard, where we sat down to talk unrecorded. Carl told us about his recent trip to Southeast Asia, the high point of which was his trip to South Vietnam. After checking into his hotel in Saigon (now Ho Chi Minh City), he took a cab out to the countryside. A few kilometers from the center of the city, the Viet Cong stopped him at a checkpoint and took him away to meet with leaders of the National Liberation Front. "I think they knew who I was and where I was going from the minute I landed in Saigon," Carl said. Clearly, the Viet Cong operated effectively, everywhere, even under the very noses of the enemy.

After listening to Carl for a while, any lingering doubts I had about the direction of SDS were gone. He clearly was not afraid to take on the whole host of lies and myths that had led us into Vietnam. Moreover, he was a real intellectual, as smart and well spoken as the previous leadership had been. I volunteered to help him build SDS in any way I could.

Like me, Carl was new to SDS, not a member of the "old guard" that had led the organization since the founding convention at Port Huron in 1962. I had not been at the SDS Convention held in Kewadin, Michigan, in June that had elected Carl president. SDS had doubled from forty-one chapters in December 1964 to eighty in June 1965. Many of the new recruits who came to the convention were from the Midwest and the Southwest. Often new to politics and the left, they brought a new sensibility to the organization, as well as work shirts, blue jeans and boots, and, for the men, Pancho Villa mustaches. Texan Jeff Shero, who was elected vice-president at the convention, dramatized later his view of some of the differences between the new recruits and the "old guard":

> "We were by instinct much more radical, much more willing to take risks, in a way because to become a part of something like SDS meant a tremendous number of breaks. If you were a New York student and became a member of SDS, it was essentially joining a political organization, which was a common experience. In Texas to join SDS meant breaking with your family, it meant being cut-off... Your mother didn't say, 'Oh, isn't that nice, you're involved. We supported the republicans in the Spanish Civil War, and now you're in SDS and I'm glad to see you are socially concerned.' In most of those places it meant, 'You Goddamn Communist'...." (Sale, p. 206)

My first SDS national meeting was the national council held in a park in Indiana in September 1965. Indiana is a long drive from Massachusetts. Like most people attending the meeting I arrived tired and left exhausted.

The meeting was held in a large room at a campground, with bunkhouses nearby to crash in. The first item of business at this and every other national meeting was to agree on the agenda. To my surprise, the agenda debate went on and on. Then it began to dawn on me that some of the experienced people in the organization had very clear ideas of what they wanted and did not want to happen at the meeting. They believed they could determine a meeting's outcome by determining the way the issues were posed and the order in which these issues were considered.

Unless you were an insider what was going on was rarely understandable. Many members simply got angry and frustrated. Often, after three hours or so of procedural discussion, a new member would stand up at the back of the room and denounce the proceeding, saying something like, "I didn't drive all the way from Oklahoma to listen to this kind of bullshit!" Realizing that the outsiders had had enough, the insiders would find a compromise order to the agenda so that the group could pull itself from the procedural swamp they had created to address the substance of what needed to be done.

The elitism of the "old guard" was very annoying. Despite this, I couldn't wait to become an insider myself.

The September 1965 national council was difficult, with many proposals and little agreement. I was concerned about the attacks on SDS coming from the League for Industrial Democracy (LID), which was still, in principle, our parent organization. After the Port Huron Statement, the relationship between parent and child had deteriorated considerably, and the LID had locked the SDS leaders out of the office space they rented. Things were patched up afterwards. Then, the day before the SDS March on Washington, LID leaders Norman Thomas and Harold Taylor joined a group of other peace notables and social democrats in issuing a very public statement, proclaiming that they, unlike SDS, were "not committed to any form of totalitarianism nor drawing inspiration or direction from the foreign policy of any government." (Gitlin, p.182) Maintaining a relationship with a parent organization whose leaders attacked us publicly as committed to a form of totalitarianism seemed like a bad idea.

At about 2 a.m., the last night of the conference, the issue of relations with LID came up on the agenda. Paul Booth, though barely awake, was chairing the meeting. Everyone was completely worn out. Dirty clothes and sleeping bags were everywhere. Delegates were sleeping on top of the tables or on the floor in of the meeting room. From time to time someone snored. I made a motion that we dissolve all relations with the LID. No one objected to the motion so it passed with the unanimous support of all those present and awake. Soon I was asleep myself. On October 4, 1965, the association between SDS and the League for Industrial Democracy was dissolved. (Sale, p. 239)

The September national council meeting did not provide a clear direction for SDS's anti-war work. This lack of direction did not prevent the pro-war establishment from portraying SDS as a well-organized enemy of society. On October 13, Senator Thomas Dodd's Senate Internal Security Committee characterized the national days of protest scheduled October 15-16 as marking the passage of the anti-war movement from the moderate elements "into the hands of communists and extremist elements who are openly sympathetic to the Viet Cong and openly hostile to the United States." (Sale, p. 228)

The next day the syndicated columnists Rowland Evans and Robert Novak weighed in with the accusation that SDS was about to embark on a major campaign to get American men to resist and evade the draft, as part of a "master plan" designed to "sabotage the war effort." (Quoted in Sale, p. 229)

All this attention by the pro-war forces was somewhat flattering. Actually, they seemed to think we were a lot more effective than we did. "Think of how well we might do if we had actually had that master plan" was a common view in SDS, particularly among the "old guard."

More successful efforts to isolate us and destroy our work came later. Despite, or because of these attacks at the national level, the local work surged forward in cities all over the country with the largest anti-war demonstrations yet. At the chapter level, a special SDS Bulletin noted, membership soared:

"Our Harvard organizer reports that he walked into Harvard Yard with 30 membership cards and had to go back for more 1/2 hour later.... He wasn't lying. We just got 50 new membership cards from him special delivery." (Quoted in Sale, p 230)

Getting Serious

In the fall, despite all the excitement, my life began to take on a more stable, adult form. I had become an official New England traveler for SDS, working out of the regional office in Cambridge. I also got a job as a teaching assistant at MIT. The MIT job paid little and the SDS job nothing. Frinde and I had also decided to get married.

Frinde and I had been living together since her return from England. I was in love and convinced that we would live together forever, raising many children. Frinde, I believe, felt the same way. However, marriage seemed to me a coercive, bourgeois institution, a potential trap to be approached with great caution. Having seen destructive marriages up close made me believe that the only principled way to look at relationships was as purely voluntary associations. Should the love leave, the relationship should be dissolved.

We decided to be together, but Frinde's family played a role in precipitating our marriage. One day when Frinde and I were visiting her parents, Mr. Aldrich summoned me to his paneled study for a private conversation. After I sat down, he turned to me and demanded to know my intentions towards his daughter: Was it fair to continue to live with her without the legal sanction that would make her an honest woman? I told Mr. Aldrich we would think about what he said. Frinde and I talked and decided, much to everyone's relief, that we would be married in a church in the fall.

One day, several weeks before the wedding, Frinde and I were invited to lunch with Mrs. William T. Aldrich, Frinde's grandmother. She was the daughter-in-law of Senator Nelson Aldrich from Rhode Island, the well-recompensed political ally of the Robber Barons, the powerful monopolists who ruled the American economy and dominated the government at the end of the nineteenth century. She was a great lady, powerful and opinionated, presiding over a large mansion for most of her adult life.

When we arrived, we were ushered into a large sun-lit dining room. I noticed that the two Irish servants waiting on our table were all aflutter, perhaps because I was the first person of Irish descent to sit down at the table with Mrs. Aldrich. After lunch had been eaten and the coffee served, the servants left the room. Sitting at the head of the table, Mrs. Aldrich prepared to lead the post-lunch conversation. She began by commenting in a loud and confident voice on those who had just left:

"The Irish are a wonderful people. They are so hardworking, loyal and kind, and so good with children, you know."

"Yes, m'am," I said, reddening slightly.

"But the problem is that they're not very smart," she said more softly, tapping her head to dramatize the disability.

"Oh?"

"Oh! Are you Irish?" she asked, a bit puzzled.

"Yes, m'am."

"Well, the Irish are such a wonderful people, loyal, kind, and so good with children."

Then she shifted the conversation to another controversial topic in inter-ethnic relations.

"Do you think my grandson Nelson [Frinde's half-brother] is going to marry that Jewish woman with four daughters?"

"Yes, m'am. He seems to like her a lot."

Another abrupt shift, this one in tone. "Fifty bucks says you're wrong," she said, relaxed and confident again.

"You're on," I said.

I'm happy to report that Nelson did marry the woman with the four daughters, with whom he had one more, and Mrs. William T. Aldrich did pay up promptly. Following our well-mannered confrontation over lunch, Mrs. William T. Aldrich joined the rest in welcoming me into the family.

Anti-Irish prejudice didn't usually bother me. I was proud of my Irish ancestors and their fight against the English. The Yankee gentry's views of the

Irish were very similar to those of the English establishment. I had found out long ago that the relationship between the Irish and the Yankee gentry was very similar to the relationship between Black people and rich white people in the South. Like Black people, we Irish were viewed as at best loyal, hardworking, and dumb, prone to drunkenness and violence on our days off. But unlike racism against African Americans, anti-Irish prejudice was fading dramatically, becoming much less intense even in Frinde's parents' generation.

Occasionally, I felt my in-laws-to-be were a little proud and preoccupied with their status as well-to-do members of the WASP gentry. At that point, I would comfort myself with the thought that while my ancestors on my mother's side were crossing the Appalachian Mountains and fighting their way to the Mexican border and beyond, the Aldrichs were standing behind a counter selling dry goods in Rhode Island.

The wedding, October 24, 1965, held a few small surprises. To please Frinde's mother the wedding was at Christ Church Episcopal in Cambridge. Frinde and I had met with the minister a few days before the ceremony and asked him to downplay the religious aspect of the service, since we were both non-believers. He seemed to agree. When the actual ceremony began, however, he reverted to the traditional service. There wasn't much we could do but go along. When he said "repeat after me," with us standing there in front of two hundred family and friends, we did what we were told. In the end the Father, Son, and Holy Ghost sanctioned all the promises we made to each other.

At the reception afterwards I was determined to be on my best behavior – no political disputes for me, whatever the provocation. It was a sign of the times that I was unable to keep this promise to myself to lay off the war for a day – Frinde, our friends, and I were not the only people at the wedding outraged by the war. About a half-hour into the reception, I saw David Rockefeller and his daughters coming our way as we stood in the receiving line. David Rockefeller was the president of the Chase Manhattan Bank. If the ruling class had a central committee, David Rockefeller was definitely on it. Later I found out he had come only as a gesture of sympathy and solidarity with his favorite cousin, Nelson Aldrich, whose oldest daughter was marrying a "notorious Communist," or so he'd heard. His attitude was not surprising, given the way SDS had been portrayed in the press.

As he and his daughters approached, I noticed his expression of intense discomfort. Suddenly his teen-aged daughter Abby was standing before me, looking me directly in the eye.

"You're an SDS organizer, aren't you?"

I glanced at David Rockefeller. Discomfort had moved on to pain. "Why, yes," I answered.

"So when are you guys going to get serious and start recruiting students to fight on the Viet Cong side, so they can drive the U.S. imperialists into the sea?"

Then I looked at her father again out of the corner of my eye. He looked truly mortified. Turning to Abby I said, "That's an interesting idea, perhaps you could discuss it further with my colleague Michael Ansara over there." I gave Abby a discreet nudge towards the punch bowl and turned around to greet her father.

In the early evening Frinde and I made our escape in a green VW. In the back window was a large heart over which someone had written "Withdraw Now." After a four-day honeymoon in a cheap hotel in New York City, we went back to work.

Noam

My paying job was as a teaching assistant at MIT in a course called "Intellectuals and Social Change," taught by Professors Noam Chomsky and Louis Kampf. Louis and Noam had been looking for a way to support the student movement, as well as for someone who could bring its perspective into their classroom. As the local SDS regional traveler, I fit the bill.

Louis and Noam were easy to work with. This helped a lot because there were a number of important differences we had to overcome to work together as a team. They were better read and more sophisticated, not to mention smarter, than I was. Also, coming from left-wing working-class backgrounds (Noam from Philadelphia and Louis New York), they had imbibed the class struggle with their mothers' milk while I had grown up on the other side of the class divide. At an early age I had reacted strongly to injustice, but I was just beginning to learn how ordinary people fight back. Motivated by loyalty to where they came from as well as a more general commitment to humanity, Louis and Noam had been fighting back for quite a while longer. I could never be as comfortable with my own class background as they were with theirs.

One of the books they assigned was George Orwell's *Homage to Catalonia*, in which Orwell describes his experience in a left-wing militia during the Spanish Civil War. Speaking about Barcelona after the Fascist uprising there in 1936 had been crushed, Orwell wrote:

> "... [T]he Spanish militias, while they lasted, were a sort of microcosm of a classless society. In that community where no one was on the make, where there was a shortage of everything but no privilege and bootlicking, one got, perhaps a crude forecast of what the opening stages of socialism might be like." (*The Orwell Reader*, p. 187)

Orwell's view of what socialism should mean became mine. It was far different from the Communism of the Soviet bloc, or the socialism of the U.S. social democratic establishment.

All three of us attended course meetings. When my turn came I gave lectures on topics like "The Radical Student: The Berkeley Rebellion" and "The Potential of Radical Politics in America" and later helped grade the papers. We have remained friends.

Shortly after the course was over, Noam summarized the themes of the course in a talk "The Responsibility of Intellectuals" he gave at the Harvard Hillel Foundation. In his talk, he attempted to define the responsibility of intellectuals as well as of peoples for atrocities committed by their governments.

> "For a privileged minority, western democracy provides the leisure, the facilities, and the training to seek the truth that lies behind the veil of distortion and misrepresentation, ideology and class interest through which the events of current history are presented to us. The responsibilities of intellectuals, then are much deeper than ... the 'responsibility of peoples,' given the unique privileges that they

enjoy." (Noam Chomsky, "The Responsibility of Intellectuals," text
of a talk given at the Harvard Hillel Foundation, March, 1966, p. 2)

Do American intellectuals live up to their responsibilities? Often not, he
says:

> "It is the responsibility of intellectuals to speak the truth and to ex-
> pose lies.... For the modern intellectual, it is not all obvious.... Thus
> when Arthur Schlesinger was asked ... to explain the fact that his
> published account of the Bay of Pigs incident contradicted the story
> he had given the press at the time of the attack, he simply remarked
> that he had lied." (Chomsky, text of speech, p. 3)

Another failure of American intellectual life is the willingness to exempt our
own government from the same skeptical analysis we direct toward others.

> "He [Henry Kissinger] observed, rather sadly, that what disturbs
> him most is that others question not our judgment, but our mo-
> tives ... it is an article of faith that American motives are pure and
> not subject to analysis. (Chomsky, pp. 5-6)

In conclusion, Noam gave a call to action still relevant today:

> "MacDonald quotes an interview with a death-camp paymaster who
> burst into tears when told that the Russians will hang him, asking,
> 'Why should they? What have I done?'... The question 'What have
> I done?' is one we may well ask ourselves, as we read, each day, of
> fresh atrocities in Vietnam – as we create, or mouth, or tolerate,
> whether with amusement or contempt, the deceptions that will be
> used to justify the next defense of freedom." (Chomsky, p. 24)

Eva and the FBI

Noam Chomsky and the SDS regional organizer teaching a course on politics
and political responsibility got both the FBI and the local anti-Communist
establishment pretty worked up.

One day in the early fall, Eva, a Hungarian immigrant who worked around MIT, approached us each separately with the same story. She told us that there was a group of young men in Pennsylvania who wanted to escape to Canada to evade the draft. They needed our help, she said.

Noam and I quickly compared notes. Then we went for a walk in a garden nearby, where we could continue our conversation unrecorded. Helping young men to escape the draft was abetting a crime and itself a crime. Why would this woman approach two people so much in the public eye to engage in illegal, clandestine acts? Why would people from Pennsylvania approach us to help them get to Canada when firmly anti-war Quakers based in Philadelphia had had generations of experience running the Underground Railroad? Eva's story just didn't add up. Eva, we concluded as we walked around the garden, was an *agent provocateur* trying to lure us into committing illegal acts so we could be arrested and put away. We decided to be the trappers rather than the prey.

I told Eva that we were interested in helping, but that all arrangements had to be made through a friend of ours whose phone number we gave her. When our "agent," actually a lawyer friend of mine, was called by a mysterious Pennsylvania contact, he taped the conversation. At the end, for the record, he made it clear that Noam and I were not interested. After the conversation was over, he called back the mysterious contact, identified himself as our lawyer, and played the tape. Then he warned that if they tried again to entrap his clients, he would take the tape to the *Boston Globe*.

After the call, Eva immediately disappeared. Six months later, I read in the papers that she had emptied her pistol, presumably Government Issue, into her boyfriend's stomach. *Agents provocateurs* had a reputation for instability and violence. We were lucky to get rid of Eva so easily.

Following the national press attacks on SDS, Gordon Hall also came after us. He was usually careful to avoid outright slander of his opponents, but in a radio exposé about the October demonstrations, he made a mistake. In one part of the broadcast, he said that Noam and I were the organizers of the demonstrations in Boston, and in another part that the organizers were Communists (just as Senator Dodd said). The clear implication was that Noam and I were Communists.

After our experience with Eva the *agent provocateur*, I had my Irish up. I asked my lawyer friend to call around to the radio stations to let them know that his clients were upset at this allegation that we were Communist Party members, which we most definitely were not. He told them that we were considering suing Gordon Hall for damages, and would love to include any radio station that helped him spread this untruth. Gordon Hall was off the air for quite a while after that.

One attack on us was successful, however. In 1967, Frinde had applied for a teaching job at Newton North High School, for which she was well qualified. Newton turned her down. Later we found out that a MIT professor on the school committee blackballed her application because she was the wife of a notorious subversive. Some professors' commitments to academic freedom turned out to be fragile. As for Frinde, she was able to get a job teaching at Wellesley High School.

Vlado

One weekend Marty Peretz called me up for a favor: "There are some Yugoslav visitors at Harvard, friends of mine, who want to buy a used car. Being from Texas, you should know about things like that. Meet us at Kirkland House in an hour to go out car shopping with them." Car mechanics was a total mystery to me. I knew little about new cars and less about used ones. I was reluctant but game.

When Frinde and I arrived, we met Vladimir Dedijer, his wife, Vera, and their children Marko, Bojanna, and Boro. Vlado was a huge bear of a man, descended from Slavic mountain people, a volcano that erupted passionate conversation. Vera was quiet, a tall, blonde Slovenian from the part of Yugoslavia closest to Western Europe in culture. Marko was the kid, the youngest. Bojanna was blonde like her mother; she was quiet and very attentive to the discussions that raged around her. Boro, the New Leftist, challenged his father at every turn.

While we drove around used-car lots, Vlado told us his story. He had been a member of the Communist underground in the pre-war kingdom of Yugoslavia, and had served as a Partisan commander in the war against the Germans from

1941-1945. His first wife, a doctor, had been killed, and he himself had been grievously wounded in the head, at the battle of Sutjeska in 1943. After the war, he had represented Communist Yugoslavia at the United Nations, and participated in the Yugoslav leadership at the time of their break with Stalin. After the break, Vlado had written a biography of Marshall Tito, which explained the evolution and development of the Yugoslav brand of independent Communism.

As Vlado told his story, his son Boro kept bringing the story back to the present, the corruption and high living of the Yugoslav leaders and the lack of democracy for everyone else.

By the end of the afternoon, the Dedijers drove away in a second-hand Chevy sedan, and we had made some new friends. I came to know Vlado well, and he was one tough character. In the face of first the Germans, then Stalin, and finally Tito, Vlado had refused to knuckle under. When he was brought before the party's Control Commission, Vlado made a statement to the *Times* (London) about why he had refused to boycott his friend Milovan Djilas, as the Party leadership had demanded of him:

> "I disagreed with him [Djilas] on theoretical matters, but I cannot stop seeing a friend who is so very much alone. In my view, a Communist should be first of all a human being, and every political movement which puts aside ethics and morals carries within it the seeds of its own destruction." ("Mr. Dedijer's Personal Statement," *The Times*, Wednesday, December 22, 1954)

Shortly after this interview, Vlado was ousted from the party. In 1959, most tragically, Branko Dedijer, Vlado and Vera's oldest son, harassed at school for the political stands his father had taken, came home and committed suicide by hanging himself in their back yard.

Vlado's commitments, which he lived as well as talked about, brought together values I admired but that were then thought to be contradictory – Communism and democracy, revolution and ethics. For many American social democrats at that time, socialism had nothing to do with actual workers. Democracy meant that U.S. leaders got to decide what happened in countries like Vietnam and the Dominican Republic, because, as we all know, the U.S. is a democratic country. When social democrats criticized President Johnson's Vietnam policy, it was to point out that they knew some better way to beat the Viet Cong, not that there was anything inherently wrong, or undemocratic with the United States intervening militarily to control another country. To me, Vlado's willingness to defy illegitimate authority in Yugoslavia gave real meaning to revolutionary ethics and democratic socialism, and it provided an example to follow in my own land.

More Problems with the Social Democrats

One day in the fall of 1965, Paul Booth, the new national secretary of SDS, called with a request I couldn't refuse. Norman Thomas had asked for a meeting to air his concerns regarding SDS's break with the League for Industrial Democracy (LID). Norman Thomas had led the Socialist Party more than four decades. To refuse to meet with him would be unforgivably rude and insulting. Since someone had to go, Paul said, it should be me. Since I had made the motion that led to the breakup, it was only fair I should take the heat that came from it.

The break with LID was forced upon us by their attacks, but what I wanted was a friendly divorce rather than perpetual war. Alas, the conversation I had hoped for did not take place. When I arrived at a rundown office where the meeting was supposed to be, there were four middle-aged men waiting for me – pale, heavyset fellows who looked to be party hacks rather than intellectuals or organizers. They put me at one end of a long table, with a vacant seat at the other end. Norman Thomas, when he entered, took this seat, opposite me. His aides surrounded him, two on one side, and two on the other.

One of his aides began the meeting by lambasting SDS. After about ten minutes, the next guy to him picked up where he had left off. Each of the four was eager to get some airtime in the presence of the chief. Each speaker looked up at the ceiling as he orated and waved his hands around, while the other three glared at me, softening me up for the knockout. But because they were so focused on themselves, and me, they missed certain vital signs. Norman Thomas's eyes began to close and his head slumped down slowly to the table. Poor man, I thought, he's probably heard this horseshit so many times before. Suddenly his head hit the table, with a loud bang. Norman Thomas was out for the count. I was led swiftly away, as if my bad behavior had provoked his sudden nap.

Now that I myself am an aged leftist, I am sometimes seized with the desire to lecture the young, to set them straight, to remind them whose shoulders they stand upon when they try to catch a glimpse of a better world. Then I think of Norman Thomas, who by the time I met him had apparently lost the capacity to listen to new ideas and welcome the contributions of the next generation. Sometimes I hold my peace.

A few weeks after the meeting with Norman Thomas, Marty Peretz asked Paul Booth and me to participate in a forum at Harvard with Irving Howe, the editor of the socialist journal *Dissent*. Irving Howe was a respected historian and an icon to the previous generation of social democrats. Naturally we accepted.

A few days before the forum, Marty broke the news. "Irving is going to kill you guys," he said, rubbing his hands with glee. "Gee, I didn't even know he had it in for us," I said to myself, "maybe I better find out why." I decided to prepare. I found that Howe had recently published in *Dissent* an article "New Styles in Leftism." This article was an attack on the "fringe" among the "newly blossoming young radicals" whom he identified as "new leftists": "sometimes it looks like kamikaze radicalism, sometimes like white Malcolmism, sometimes like black Maoism." ("New Styles in Leftism," *Dissent*, fall, 1965, p. 295) His caricatures were amusing, but caricatures. By focusing on "styles," Howe avoided discussing the issues that motivated these "New Leftists." Howe seemed to be promoting himself as the elder statesman of the movement, the gatekeeper who identifies what is acceptable on the left, and what is not.

The forum was in the common room of one of the Harvard houses. Irving Howe, Paul Booth, and I stood facing a crowd of about a hundred people sitting in folding chairs. Paul went first and talked about what SDS was doing. Then came Howe. After a few general remarks, he took out his recent article and began to read from it at length. I rearranged my note cards to correspond with the passages he was reading, while Howe read on, with an occasional dramatic flourish. Then he stopped and smiled.

I lit into him. Youth were revolting worldwide, but particularly in the Third World, over issues of foreign domination, declining standards of living, unresponsive local elites, a lack of democracy and civil liberties, I said. Youth were leading the revolution in Latin America because of the failure of urban-based "Old Left" parties, including the social democratic parties Howe had praised, to effectively address these issues. Howe's contribution was to attack the young people who were putting their lives on the line.

Afterwards members of the audience came forward to talk to the speakers. John Clayton, a young Boston University professor, came up and told me that the BU Socialist Club had come as a group to hear their leader Irving Howe. After the debate they had caucused, and decided to drop their affiliation with the Socialist Party. Could they join SDS as a group? With Howe standing nearby I gave John twenty membership applications and welcomed him into the organization. I never saw Howe again.

In retrospect, it's amazing that Howe and social democrats like him still could have been taken seriously as leaders of the left. The battle against Stalinism, which Howe had waged in his youth, in the United States, where it was safe to do so, was still twenty years later the defining moment of his political life. Of course, people who believed in democracy had to oppose Soviet dictatorship. But unlike Vlado, my Yugoslav friend, who had fought Stalin and Stalinism up close, anti-Communism had so distorted Howe's judgment that he denied for the Vietnamese the freedom he had so ardently wished for the Hungarians, Poles, and Yugoslavs. Howe wanted to be the gatekeeper for a movement whose goals he did not share.

Bringing 1965 to a Close

In the middle of November 1965, I debated a member of Congress at the Harvard Law School Forum. The next day the *Boston Globe* misquoted me as saying that in an election held in Vietnam in 1954, 80 percent had voted for Ho Chi Minh. What I had actually had said was that President Eisenhower wrote that 80 percent of the population would have voted for Ho Chi Minh *had* an election been held in 1954. (See Dwight Eisenhower, *Mandate for Change*, p. 449.) The next week the *Boston Globe* published a letter from Reverend

O'Connor, a Catholic priest from St. Columban's Foreign Mission Society, challenging the facts as I had supposedly presented them. My reply was published the next Sunday. The exchange between the two of us continued on alternate Sundays through February 1966. In Boston, at least, the debate over the war had become part of the mainstream.

On December 22, 1965, I wrote my brother Albert a letter in New Mexico, where he had turned up after he left Cambridge: "I am convinced we have Bubba Lyndon by the balls. More and more people are coming to the conclusion that this war is no damn good."

By the end of December, SDS had grown to an estimated 124 chapters in 38 states (Sale, p. 246), but we still had a distance to go, to say the least.

Discovering Sexism in the Movement

When I came to SDS, two and a half years after the founding Port Huron Statement, I was struck by how intellectual and thoughtful they all were. Men and women seemed to work together in harmony. However, there was a lot I didn't see or understand, about myself and many of the other male activists.

The "old guard" founders of SDS wanted to bridge the gap between the new recruits and themselves, so an SDS National "Rethinking" Conference was held at the Illinois University campus in Champaign-Urbana over the Christmas vacation in 1965. This conference was also the first national meeting where the issue of sexism in SDS was brought up in an organized way. The efforts of the old guard to renew its influence in the organization collided directly with the desire of some female veterans of SNCC and SDS for gender equality in the movement and a more inclusive, participatory style of leadership.

In their "kind of memo" sent out before the conference, Casey Hayden and Mary King talked about a caste system that "dictates the roles assigned to women in the movement, and certainly even more to women outside the movement."

> "Within the movement, questions arise in situations ranging from
> relationships of women organizers to men in the community, to who
> cleans the freedom house, to who holds leadership positions, to who

does secretarial work, and who acts as spokesman for the groups."
(Sara Evans, *Personal Politics*, p. 236)

At the conference, a workshop was called to discuss the problems of women in the movement. A women's statement that came out of the workshop called for greater "initiative and participation" by women and greater understanding of the "woman question" by men in the organization. "Many women feel that the problem of participation by women is a special problem – one that reflects not only inadequacies within SDS but one that also reflects greater societal problems, namely the role of women in American society today." (Quoted in Sale, p. 252)

For some of the male members of the old guard the effect of this workshop on "women in the movement" was traumatic. One of my "old guard" friends broke down in tears and kept saying, "It's all over, all over," meaning that something, a certain kind of trust perhaps, had been broken and could never be repaired. At the time, my friend's reaction seemed to me overwrought. Gender equality was certainly a reasonable demand. What we men had to do was simple, I thought: clean up our act so that women could be full partners in changing society. Perhaps he's in tears because he can't take criticism, I thought, somewhat smugly. Had I the imagination to see how intractable sexism would prove to be, I might have understood better my friend's tears. Men, myself included, resisted change.

In the beginning was the "old guard," the co-authors of the Port Huron Statement. But as Gitlin points out, "for the most part women were not the writers or speakers, the men were. The original circle of SDS male heavies was well read, well spoken, adept at circulating in a man's world." (Gitlin, p. 367) Men gave long speeches and dominated meetings. Women who were not confident enough to speak at great length were shunted aside, pushed towards the traditional role of scribe, logistics coordinator, comforter, and sustainer of the male leaders.

SDS men seemed to me more sensitive than the American average to women's feeling and women's concerns. But sensitivity stopped when it interfered with another man's right to run his personal life as he pleased. I was struck by the insensitivity of one of the "old guard" leaders, who sat there in the meeting circle smooching with his new girlfriend, while the wife he had left, a gifted organizer and talented leader of the organization, was also present. The spectacle was painful to watch.

Sexism was deeply rooted in the movement, as in the rest of American society. Some women in SDS were leaders, particularly in the community-organizing projects, but SDS in 1965 was a man's world, and, unfortunately, it remained so. Women's feelings were disregarded and women's voices often were not heard. Todd Gitlin relates a telling incident the night after the women's workshop:

> "The evening deepened as the argument proceeded about whether women were essentially passive. It grew chilly. Barbara [Haber] proposed that the group continue the discussion around the corner, away from the wind. No one noticed. She raised the point two or three times; talk ambled on. Her husband nudged her and said, 'Watch this.' He repeated the same proposal in the same tone of voice. Everyone moved." (Gitlin, p. 370)

As the war ground on, discrimination in SDS against women grew only worse. One reason was the draft and the way some activists in the anti-war movement viewed the fight against it. Men were drafted into military service; women were not. One wing of the draft resistance movement focused on encouraging and supporting individual young men who with exemplary courage said no to the draft. Of course, refusing the draft was a very courageous thing to do, but emphasizing the unique role of men in resisting the war mirrored the sexism of American society at large, which highlighted men's unique and courageous role in waging it. In this part of the anti-war movement, as in the war itself, women became exclusively auxiliaries and sex objects. "Girls say yes to guys who say no" became a popular slogan that captured this point of view.

There was, of course, nothing intrinsic to anti-war organizing that made it man's work as opposed to woman's. The Vietnamese recognized this even when Americans did not. Sara Evans recounts how Vivian Rothstein was chosen to go on a delegation to Hanoi only because the Vietnamese insisted that women be included.

> "In Vietnam the Vietnamese elevated the status of women delegates further by always requesting that they speak first, stressing their importance in view of the fact that there were many barriers to women becoming active, and pointing out the accomplishments of Vietnamese women in surmounting them." (Evans, p. 188)

Another way in which the war undermined the status of women in SDS was by overshadowing the earlier focus on community organizing. According to the original strategy formulated by Tom Hayden and others, young men were the key population and jobs the key issue. But the projects that succeeded were ones in which women in the community were seen as the key strategic population, with welfare and housing as the key issues. "Almost all the leadership-type women who were around the organization in sixty-three went into ERAP (the community organizing department of SDS)," according to Steve Max, a member of the original group which founded SDS at Port Huron. (Quoted in Evans, p.138) In the communities themselves the SDS women were often more successful organizers than the SDS men, partly because women are more likely to have the interpersonal skills necessary for good community organizing, the ability to listen and learn from people in the community, and above all the desire to develop the leadership abilities of the people they were organizing. When funding and support within the SDS for community organizing dried up, some women leaders had to leave the organization to continue their work. They were joined by other seasoned women leaders who departed simply because they couldn't stand the sexism of the organization.

As SDS became more a male-dominated organization, a style of leadership developed that was antithetical to the egalitarian aims articulated by the movement. Towards the end of the 1960s, "in the rush toward the phantasmagorical revolution, women became not simply a medium of exchange, consolidating the male bond, but rewards for male prowess and balm for male insecurity." (Gitlin, p. 372)

I knew that I was not the perfect person, but there were some forms of exploitation I wanted to avoid and did. Trustworthiness was essential for an organizer and leader of the movement. People, women as well as men, had to trust me. Sexual exploitation, and the lying, cheating, and self-deception that goes with it, makes real trust impossible. I was a married person. I wasn't going down that road.

But in retrospect, I was less of a fine fellow than I thought at the time. I didn't fight even the sexist practices I knew were wrong. Friends of mine in the leadership traveled around the country like superstars, sleeping with whoever was attractive and available. I thought what they were doing was destructive and wrong, but secretly I considered my conscience a liability and admired them. While I rarely hesitated to take someone on over some issue relating to political analysis, I never confronted my male peers, publicly or privately, about their sexual exploitation of women. I thought sexual exploitation was a serious problem, but not serious enough to fight about.

I also tended to recognize leadership only when it came packaged in the kind of articulate, abstract, academic reasoning at which some men of that era, including myself, were so adept. My commitment to equality was deeply undercut by this notion that leadership was not a broad set of skills and attributes that could be developed and learned. To me leadership remained a kind of genius that some people, mainly men, just had. This self-serving notion that to be a political leader at the highest levels required a narrow set of attributes that men were more likely to have, distorted my personal life as well as my political judgment throughout the sixties.

Frinde was the breadwinner for most of the 1960s, as well as a volunteer in many important movement projects and campaigns. In principle, I recognized that household chores were men's work as well as women's. In practice, I, the political genius whose insights were indispensable to the movement, claimed all sorts of special privileges and exemptions when it came to actually getting the housework done. To make matters worse I gave my supposed superior politics as a justification for demanding to be pampered. Of course Frinde found this line of specious reasoning infuriating. In retrospect, I look upon myself as lucky that she didn't put arsenic in my soup.

I spent a lot of time in the 1960s thinking about how to train people as speakers and organizers. But since I saw leadership as an innate quality that some few had and others didn't, I never thought systematically then about how people could learn to be leaders and strategists. That came later, when I learned to plan meetings and share responsibilities with younger organizers.

Rarely was I aware of how distorted and self-serving my view of leadership was. A flash of insight occurred once in a conversation with Clark Kissinger, at the time SDS national secretary. We were discussing some issue or another, and he referred to the "Councils of the Mighty" as the body in SDS that would have to rule on the topic. I smiled a smile of instant recognition. Socialists though we SDS leaders were, we functioned ultimately in a feudal way. SDS national council meetings and national conventions came and went. But to make something happen in SDS required the consent of the "mighty" leaders. Without necessarily having a formal position in the organization, they had or were thought to have great strategic insight, connections, and powers of persuasion.

Consent came through behind-the-scenes consultations. Some people lost their influence or quit the "Councils of the Mighty." Newcomers like me were sometimes able to push their way in. But this group maintained at least a minimum of cohesion and exercised enormous influence over the life of the organization. The "mighty," of course, were all men.

Clark and I were both participants in these councils without accountability. He at least had the insight to identify and articulate them as a problem. From that moment on, I also recognized that this was not a good way to make decisions, but once I became an insider myself, I never thought systematically about how to address this problem. Lack of leadership accountability eventually led to the destruction of the organization.

Jerry Rubin

Jerry Rubin and I had met for the first time at the December national meeting in Champaign-Urbana. Short, with dark hair and dark eyes, he radiated the intensity and charisma of an organizer at the top of his game. He had led extremely successful Vietnam Day demonstrations in Berkeley in the fall of 1965. We had lots to talk about when we came together over a quiet lunch in the student cafeteria at Champaign-Urbana. I wanted to learn about how he did this great work, the best in the country. However, I had a burning question, one that could only be discussed in private.

"Jerry, you give speeches about the role of marijuana in building a new consciousness. But when I smoke even a puff or two of the stuff, I can't think straight. How the hell do you smoke all that dope and get anything done?"

Jerry's answer really blew me away. "Marijuana is pure poison! I only say that shit about dope because that's what people expect and want. I'd never use the stuff myself."

Jerry Rubin gave me a lot to think about.

❦ ❦ ❦

What I Learned from SDS in the Early Days

- Nothing justifies an organization or an organizer putting aside ethics and morals.
- The previous generation can give advice, but not orders, to the current one.
- Never underestimate the power of the prejudices of the past, and the ability of old patterns of domination, men over women, insiders over new people, etc., to carry over into an organization or movement ostensibly fighting for democracy and against oppression of all kinds.
- Organizations trying to fight for democracy can only succeed if they are democratic themselves. Patterns of discrimination within an organization make real accountability and democracy impossible.

VII

Trying to Develop New Leaders, New Strategies, 1966

THE DIRECTOR OF THE SELECTIVE Service System announced in February 1966 that "lower level" students would be subject to the draft. Who was "lower level" would be determined by academic rank in each college class on the one hand and the results of a national intelligence and achievement test on the other.

The fat was in the fire. College students realized that enrollment in higher education no longer guaranteed deferment and their safety from the horrors of the Vietnam War. The national office saw this escalation in the draft, which flowed of course from the escalation of the war, as an opportunity for SDS to take united action and to regain its leadership of the anti-war movement. Lee Webb, an "old guard" leader who had been national secretary in 1963 suggested a national counter-draft exam, giving questions and answers on Vietnam and American foreign policy, to be handed out nationwide on the day of the exam at the Selective Service exam centers. (Sale, p, 254) Here is a typical question:

> Which of the following American military heroes has, in the past, warned against committing a large number of troops to a land war on the Asian mainland: (A) General Douglas MacArthur (B) Pres. Dwight D. Eisenhower (C) Gen. Matthew B. Ridgeway (D) Gen.

Maxwell Taylor (E) Gen. James Gavin (F) Gen. Omar Bradley?
(Answer: All have made such warnings.) (Sale, p. 255)

The exam itself was the result of consultations with Vietnam experts from over a dozen campuses around the country. The national office printed 500,000 copies of the exam and installed an unlimited long-distance line, a major expense at the time, to coordinate the campaign. On May 14, 1966, the exam was handed out at 850 of the 1200 Selective Service System examination centers. (Sale, p. 255)

The plan was a carefully designed educational program, tied to a national issue of direct interest to SDS's key constituency, and it was confrontational enough to make people think, without, however, demanding that students do something they might be afraid of doing. I thought it was a great idea. As an educational device, the counter-draft exam may have been well conceived. But as a means of unifying SDS around a high-impact national campaign, the counter-draft exam was a flop, failing to engender any significant protests or ongoing campus campaigns.

SDS older strategists including me had misjudged what would move the campuses. Successful campaigns around international and national issues need a local hook. Many chapters figured this out for themselves or learned it from others. They focused not on the national draft exam, but on their university's complicity with the Selective Service. Local committees formed at many campuses all over the country trying to block their university from sending information about academic ranking to the Selective Service System.

At Harvard, the local chapter gained significant faculty as well as student support. In response, the Harvard administration claimed that it was not supporting the war per se, but simply passing information along. "We're only licking the envelopes," they told the faculty. But like many other areas of collaboration, the first step led down a slippery slope. In a faculty meeting Professor Renato Poggioli spoke for many when he warned, with his heavy Italian accent, "First, you licka da envelope, then, you licka da ass!" (According to Marty Peretz, who told me the story just afterwards.)

In 1966, American colleges and universities began to see the first serious resistance to their complicity in the war effort. By June 1966, there were 174 SDS
chapters, compared with 124 at the beginning of the year. SDS as an organization was succeeding when its national campaigns were not. In retrospect, I
think that my desire to lead an organization with a coherent program on issues
like the war blinded me to the reality that for many student activists democracy
was the program and they wanted democracy now. SDS chapters drew people
who wanted a better future for the country, but they didn't want to wait twenty
years to exercise their leadership and make their voices heard. For a program
to work it had to be their program, not something imposed by faraway national
leaders.

Problems

For all its success in remaking the political landscape on campuses, SDS as a
student organization faced two tremendous problems. One was how to develop
leadership on the campuses when students' life on campus is short-lived.
Building a movement, student or otherwise, requires experience. But the most
experienced people in SDS, members of the "old guard," and people like me,
were too distant from campus life to provide good leadership for high school or
campus based organizing. But sending inexperienced young people who had
never done a campus campaign out on their own as regional travelers was a disastrous idea, both for the "travelers" and for the work.

The solution that appealed to Paul Potter, the former president of SDS, and
me was to look to the student leadership of the larger and more experienced
chapters, like Harvard, as a source of a new cadre who, with help and support
from us, could begin to assume regional responsibilities and help develop the
newer chapters. In the New England region in February 1966, we had twenty
high school and college chapters. Perceptive and committed students like Hal
Benenson and Sarah Eisenstein from Harvard SDS began to lead the regional
organization.

A second problem had to do with the fact that SDS's ambition to change
American society far exceeded the resources any student organization could
possibly have. Throughout the world, students have played an important role in

many struggles for greater democracy, but victory came only in alliance with other forces – workers, farmers, intellectuals, etc. In the United States in the mid-1960s, we found ourselves virtually alone.

With a few notable exceptions, labor unions had become undemocratic institutions led by men who were committed to the anti-Communist crusade that had brought the United States to Vietnam. Dissident rank and file labor organizations that might have allied with us were absent from the scene in the 1960s.

What about the left? It had been years since the social democrats had tried to organize anyone outside their ranks – they were more isolated than we were. Besides, to them we were ungrateful children who had betrayed our heritage. The Communist Party treated us and our work with respect, at least to our faces. But to many of us they seemed less a potential ally for the future than a relic of the past, tired, and hopelessly compromised.

❧ ❧ ❧

What I Learned in 1966 from Some of SDS's Weaknesses

- All struggles are local. National campaigns have to have a local hook.
- National organizations must be rooted in the local chapters that actually carry out these struggles.
- The most useful thing experienced leaders can do is help develop new ones.

Relations with the Communist Party

I spoke at a forum at Harvard with Gil Greene, one of the major leaders of the Communist Party, in the spring of 1966. He was slender, dressed like a worker in a nylon shirt and cotton pants, with a careworn face. Gil Greene's modest manner was in sharp contrast to the Harvard setting – the leather couches and carved wood – as well as to his reputation for commitment and courage. He had been a union organizer for most of his adult life. In the 1950s, during the worst of the anti-Communist purges, he had gone underground. Subsequently, he had done time in prison for his beliefs. In 1966, he was the Communist leader most respected outside the party.

In the forum, I laid out sharply but respectfully the issues I saw separating
the New Left from the Communist Party. One was the party's seemingly unconditional support for the Soviet Union – despite Stalin, despite the invasion of
Hungary (and even despite the invasion of Czechoslovakia, which occurred in
1968 two years after the forum). Fighting for human liberation, I said, meant
that all government actions and the actions of all governments had to be open
to criticism. No special exemptions for the Soviets.

The second issue was that the Communist Party had gravitated to the position that the left had no future in America outside the Democratic Party. To
make matters worse, obsessed with the fear that they might lose the little influence they had in the Democratic Party, Communist Party leaders refrained
from saying anything that wasn't being said already by at least some prominent
Democrats. We New Leftists saw no reason to let Bobby Kennedy set the bound-
aries of political discourse. While New Leftists campaigned for immediate and
unconditional withdrawal from Vietnam, Communist Party activists campaigned for negotiations, which was the position of the Kennedys at that time,
and sometimes hard to differentiate even from the position of the Johnson
administration.

Gil Greene was polite, listened, asked clarifying questions, and said he and
the party would think seriously about the points raised. The forum ended with
a common theme of continuing the dialogue and finding ways to work
together.

One criticism of the Communist Party that I did not bring up at the forum,
but developed in a paper for the SDS Convention at Clearlake, Iowa, August 27
– September 1, 1966, was the semi-clandestine way in which the CP worked in
SDS. (*NLN*, August 24, 1966, p. 14) Gil Greene spoke in public as a leader of the
CP, but party members active in SDS did not reveal their affiliation to those
with whom they worked. This struck me as a self-serving but self-defeating policy. After all, the government probably knew the identities of the party members in SDS, because the FBI had so heavily infiltrated the Communist Party.

The danger for both SDS and the CP was that at the moment of their choosing, the government or other opponents of SDS could unmask the party members, confirming the anti-Communist cliché about duplicitous leftist infiltrators,

thus discrediting the CP as well undermining the unity of SDS.

I had attempted to persuade a colleague who worked with me in the New England Regional Office to trust the SDS membership and go public with her party affiliation. Like most party members in SDS, she was a "red diaper baby"– her parents had been party members. Younger than me, she was truly a child of the 1950s, traumatized by the red-baiting. Nothing I could say helped her overcome her fear, almost phobia, to go public.

One skill I learned early on was to listen carefully to what people said, not only about politics, but also about their goals for themselves, their friends, and their families, and use this information to construct a picture of what kind of person they were and what they really believed. Party members had a somewhat distinct profile. They were committed pragmatists at a time when that was rare. They tended to gravitate towards administrative jobs. Getting the press release out or the money raised was more important than wasting time in general political discussions. When they did speak out, their politics were always sensible, conventional even. But sometimes, if they trusted you, they let you know they were more left than they appeared. They were discreet, but for support sat together in public meetings.

Police agents had a different profile. I learned to be wary of people who mouthed the left-wing clichés of the day. People who appeared from nowhere advocating violence against the cops and the system were almost certainly cops themselves. One guideline that kept me out of jail was never trust anyone completely until you got to know their friends and family.

The most serious consequence of the destruction and self-destruction of the Old Left social democrats and Communists was that we American New Leftists were orphans, cut off from our own history. I have learned many things since that forum with Gil Greene in the spring of 1966. But on reflection I realize that most of my discoveries are simply rediscoveries of strategies and tactics that were commonplace and well understood by U.S. organizers in the 1930s and 1940s – patience, focus, respecting the opinions of the people you're trying to reach, and understanding that people change only gradually. As it was, we New Leftists, for all our bravery and resourcefulness, often disregarded this and proceeded throughout the rest of the decade to make just about every mistake in the book. Some of the best among us burned out, and others turned to silly cult figures for guidance.

When I look back on that spring evening when I spoke with Gil Greene at Harvard, I have no regrets about the criticisms I made of the Communist Party. But despite their faults, there was much we could have learned from experienced organizers like him. Without mentors we continued for the rest of the 1960s to lack political realism and a disciplined approach to organizing,

Outside the campuses, there was a tremendous vacuum on the left. Given the small number of potential coalition partners, most of the work had to be done from the grassroots up. At the time, I was confident that we could succeed. One step towards building an off-campus left was to find some kind of organizational structure to consolidate the off-campus supporters and activists of SDS. At the time this seemed to me a sizeable group of people – a survey conducted in March 1966 found that 20 percent of the 5,500 national members of SDS were non-students. (Sale, p. 271) Chapter membership, most of whom were not members of national SDS, was of course much larger, close to 15,000, nearly all of them high school or college students.

Tom Adams Runs for Senate

Electoral politics was one way for SDS to expand off campus. I became involved in a campaign to win Tom Adams the Democratic nomination for U.S. Senate. Thomas Boylston Adams was a New England patrician, a Brutus defending the republic against Lyndon Johnson's Julius Caesar.

The first problem with the campaign was that the leadership was weak; from the very beginning I had a bad feeling about the campaign. The second problem with the campaign was the way I handled the first problem. I had chosen to run the campaign in a district that included Cambridge, Brookline, and Somerville, prime territory for SDS to begin to build a base in the community. After the election, we could have consolidated the volunteers we'd recruited from the neighborhoods into an organization, which among other things could have begun to pressure the Eighth Congressional District Representative Tip O'Neill, then Speaker of the U.S. House of Representatives. "Using" the campaign in this way would have been good for SDS and great for Tom Adams, who would have recruited more volunteers and gotten more votes overall if we had added a grassroots component to the campaign.

Instead of doing what needed to be done, I sat around the office, dithered, worried about the lack of direction of the campaign, and wrote memos. I knew, in principle at least, what needed to be done. As one of my memos to local coordinators pointed out, "Door-to-door canvassing is the most direct and personal form of vote getting.... Ultimately it is the only way to build a permanent broadly based political organization."

To make this happen would have required me to do some things I was reluctant to do. First, I would have had to model correct behavior. Campaign volunteers don't canvass door to door in response to memos, but when they see the leadership going door to door, they will go with them. Given my connections with the campus movement, if I had modeled correct behavior, I could have recruited dozens of activists to go with me.

I was also reluctant to learn new things. I knew how to talk to people on their doorstep and how to recruit volunteers. What I didn't know then was how to put together a systematic series of communications and events to get the campaign's sympathizers out to vote on Election Day. I didn't know how to do this, but I could have learned from dozens of political operatives in Massachusetts. Why? I don't know. But the shame of it all kept me from making the same mistake again.

On Primary Day Adams received 51,483 votes, or about 8 percent of the total. One conclusion many radicals of the 1970s, 80s, and 90s drew from the 1960s was that elections can never be used to advance the organizational agenda of the left – building strong independent political organizations accountable to the base in the neighborhoods. The sad story became a mantra: "The bad guys always screw us. They usually win. Good people, if elected, always turn bad. Our organizations fall apart after elections." Because of this attitude many radicals sat on the sidelines for thirty years as working-class, minority and low-income voters were driven out of the electoral process. The fault lay not with our opponents, but with ourselves.

Boro's Death: Accident? Murder? Suicide?

The New Left was an international movement. We felt very much a part of the struggles in other countries, those in France and Germany in particular. Because of my friendship with the Dedijers, I also followed events in Yugoslavia as carefully as I could. Boro Dedijer, Vlado's son, was my friend who had become a New Left activist when he returned to Yugoslavia from the United States. Students demonstrated and workers struck against the Communist government there. The repression did not seem as severe as it had been in the Soviet Union and elsewhere in Eastern Europe. But I worried about Boro – his older brother Branko had committed suicide in 1959, due to the pressure put upon him at school as the child of a critic of the regime.

I wrote to Boro suggesting he come and visit me in the United States, see how we were doing our work, and relax for a while. Unfortunately, my letter arrived two days after Boro was dead. He had died while climbing a mountain near Bohinj in Slovenia on July 13, 1966. Vlado and Vera were devastated. Had he fallen by accident? Had he thrown himself off? Or had he been pushed by the secret police, as Vlado thought possible? I have a picture of Vlado taken by Anne Peretz shortly before Boro's death. Vlado is leaning against a wooden gate, with a mountain rising gently behind him. Vlado looked so young then.

Later on in the 1960s Vlado became the chairman and president of the Russell Tribunal on Vietnam, founded by the British philosopher Bertrand Russell, which inquired into U.S. war crimes there. Taking on the U.S. government was a courageous step for an itinerant scholar often on the outs with his own government, living off the earnings of his books in the West as well as temporary academic appointments at American universities. Three Americans, Stokely Carmichael from the Black Panthers, the pacifist leader David Dellinger, and Carl Oglesby from SDS, also sat on the Russell Tribunal.

Vlado's moral and physical courage continued to inspire me. He also admired our work and had high hopes for the New Left. He expressed this admiration and his expectations for us in an open letter to Jean Paul Sartre, his colleague on the Russell Tribunal, published in the *New York Times* in 1971, expressing in public things he had said many times when we were together during the 1960s. Noting the American New Left's spontaneity and enthusiasm, as well as its lack of ideological commitment and organizational discipline, he went on:

> "Let us, as Europeans, pay special respect to the internationalism of the New Left. These Americans oppose the war of their establishment against Vietnam much more strongly than the French Communist Party or the working class of France opposed the Indo-China or the Algerian war or than the Russian working class opposed the invasion of Czechoslovakia....

> "The future of the world depends so much on the American New Left. Nowhere are the social contradictions deeper, and nowhere does a rebel have a greater opportunity to demonstrate the firmness of his convictions than here. Therefore it is the greatest country in the world." (*New York Times*, Thursday, February 4, 1971, p. 35)

About the same time this letter was published, Vlado returned to Yugoslavia leaving behind his war diaries and other documents, some of which had recently been smuggled out of Yugoslavia to the United States. He was afraid the government would seize them because the truth could tarnish some of the glitter attached to the party leadership and compromise the official view of the role of the Yugoslav partisans in World War II.

Vlado's health deteriorated throughout the 1970s, as he suffered from diabetes and pain from his old war wounds. He died in November 1991 of a heart attack while he and Vera were visiting Bojanna and her daughter in Tivoli, New York. When I heard the news, I thought to myself, "What a stubborn and brave man he was." The next morning I went to Tivoli to help the family. When his ashes were returned to Yugoslavia, Vlado was given a military funeral by the government, as befitting a partisan officer. Vera and Marko still live in Slovenia, now an independent country, in the apartment in the capital Ljubljana where Frinde and I had visited them three decades ago.

When Vlado returned to Yugoslavia in the early seventies, leaving behind his papers, he had named Noam Chomsky and me his literary executors to act on his behalf should he be arrested or killed. I hid his papers in a safe place in Houston where they stayed for the next decade. They are now part of a collection at the University of Michigan.

From Campus to Community Organizing

The fiasco of the Adams for Senate Campaign made me angry and determined. I had wasted three months. I wanted to wash away the taste of failure. Instead of just talking about building a base in the community, and wondering abstractly whether working-class people could be reached and moved to oppose the war, I decided to go door to door in my own neighborhood to try to build a neighborhood-based anti-war organization. Clark Kissinger and James Weinstein had been doing local New Left political organizing in Chicago and New York respectively, working to build Citizens for Independent Political Action (CIPA) groups in their neighborhoods. They planned to recruit a core group of fellow radicals already living in the neighborhood and build a larger group around them which would be active in elections around a comprehensive program of New Left concerns, including housing and employment as well as the war.

I was inspired and encouraged by their examples, but I had another goal in mind. I decided to focus on the war, at least in the beginning, because I thought it was the most important issue around which radicals needed to work at that time. Once consolidated, the organization could take on other issues, I thought, in coalition with other groups, or on its own. Secondly, I wanted to test a model of organizing, knocking on doors in neighborhoods to talk about the war. If this campaign were successful, campus anti-war activists around the country could replicate it in some form.

In the fall of 1966 before I began the work, I gave a speech at a student conference that laid out the rationale for SDS initiating community organizing around Vietnam: "Students feel intuitively that when the question is peace or war the power to say no lies in the community, where live the voters, workers, and for the time being at least the draft-age youth."

Frinde and I lived in an apartment building on Beacon Street in Somerville. The neighborhood I chose to canvass was in Cambridge on both sides of Oxford

Street, down to the Harvard campus. At that time, before Harvard expansion began to drive rents up higher than working-class people could afford, it was a mixed neighborhood of graduate students, young professionals, and workers.

I wanted this organizing project to be unencumbered by endless discussions with other radicals. Some people want a guarantee that something will work before they try it out. I wanted to try it out on my own to see what happened. If it succeeded, then we would have a lot to talk about. As to how to make it work, I figured the best teacher would be feedback from the people on whose doors I knocked.

I wrote a leaflet for this project, but my real aim at the beginning was to talk to people about the war, and find out what they were thinking and why. When someone answered the door I usually introduced myself as a neighbor concerned about the war. What did they think? I went out in the early evening and met all kinds of people with all kinds of opinions about the war and the other issues of the day. I sat in their kitchens and talked it through, and then I went on and knocked on the next door.

I got lots of feedback, but no hostility. Very early on, some significant patterns emerged. Many people told me they supported the war. Some working-class people thought we should blow the place up, and then get the hell out. Their support of the war was shallow. Often it was easy to convince them of an even better idea – just get the hell out. Some graduate students had big theories about how we had to stop Communism, and Vietnam was the place we had to do this. But it wasn't difficult to show that the Vietnamese Resistance was deeply rooted in that country and not some invention of the Communist bloc, itself in deep disarray over disputes between Moscow and Peking.

I went back to see people who were interested. One young woman wanted me to talk to her officer boyfriend. The thought of a possible confrontation with an army officer made me nervous, but she was so concerned about her lover and so insistent I couldn't say no. One evening Frinde and I had them over for dinner. Trying to be hip, I had just bought an authentic Japanese hibachi. Unfortunately, I didn't understand how much charcoal even a small hibachi required. Fortunately, I was as generous with the wine as I had been cheap with the charcoal. We sat around, ate raw lamb chops, and drank red wine until early morning. I don't know whether he survived the war or not, but I think I convinced him that in a war with so many questions he should be very careful about committing himself and his men to combat.

In the late fall I called the first meeting of interested people I had talked with going door to door. We met at Phillips Brooks House in the northern corner of Harvard Yard, close to the neighborhood where I had been working. I don't remember exactly what the agenda was, but based on my plan we probably discussed how to get an explanation and some accountability out of our Democratic congressman, Tip O'Neill, Cambridge resident and Speaker of the House. The turnout – housewives, workers, young professionals, and graduate students – was sufficient to start the campaign. Barbara Ackerman, a rising politician, soon to be mayor of Cambridge, also turned up, uninvited and unannounced. I was somewhat annoyed to be upstaged by a real politician, but I knew that her presence there was a good sign that I was on to something.

The war had dragged on and on. During 1966 alone, the United States staged seven thousand air raids against roads, five thousand against vehicles, and more than a thousand against railway lines and yards in North Vietnam, hitting many of the same targets several times. (Karnow, p. 468) Like me, most Americans did not know that Secretary of Defense Robert McNamara was already beginning to privately despair of winning the war, short of annihilating North Vietnam and its people. (Karnow, p.469) What I did know was that some of the leaders of the anti-war movement were beginning to privately despair of our ability to stop the war.

One day in the late fall I heard that SNCC organizer Cleve Sellars was looking for me. Cleve had been with Bob Moses at the Institute for Policy Studies conference after the SDS March on Washington in April 1965. His message, I was told, was that Bob and Staughton Lynd thought that the leadership of the anti-war movement should go down to Washington to sit in, go to jail, get out, and continue civil disobedience until we had brought an end to the war.

I admired Bob Moses and Staughton Lynd. Bob Moses in particular seemed to model what movement leadership should be about. But it seemed to me that such desperate proposals were testimony to the tremendous crisis and demoralization in the leadership of the anti-war movement. Civil disobedience in the capital could mean serious jail time. I felt we had other cards to play before it came to that. I must admit I waited a day or two before trying to find Cleve, and by the time I got around to it, he was gone.

There had to be a better way. There were hundreds of thousands of college students who really did get it about the war. Middle-class parents already were being affected by the views of their children. Now, with the changes in the draft, students' lives were potentially on the line. Similarly, millions of working-class people with sons whose lives were already on the line had many questions about the war. If we could find a way to bring the students into dialogue with their parents and working-class people, we could turn this war around. Soldiers in our army, just like any other, I thought, will cease to be reliable instruments when the civilian population stops supporting the war.

This was the vision of where we needed to go. But there were many rivers to cross, and some doubt as to whether the bridges would hold. For one thing, "student power" was sweeping many campuses, and was very influential with the new leadership of SDS elected in August 1966. Paul Potter, Hal Benenson, and Sarah Eisenstein had pointed out in *New Left Notes* May 29, 1967, some of the strengths and some of the dangers in relying on confrontations to build the student movement.

> "The accusation by many people, some of them sympathetic, that SDS people are arrogant is a serious charge. It speaks to a real problem that we see: that somehow in our effort to disentangle ourselves from the brainwashing and moral corruption in this society, we do not lose the capacity to reach out to other people whose doubts are still tentative."

They concluded this section with a warning, prophetic as it turns out: "An apocalyptic brand of politics can only be diversionary."

Arrogant students, or students who couldn't deal with other people whose doubts were more tentative than theirs, could destroy the nationwide dialogue about the war I was envisaging. But based on my discussions with hundreds of anti-war students over the last year and a half, I felt confident that they would be motivated enough to try community organizing around the war. Arrogance, I thought, would be a problem for only some students.

One evening I had a few drinks with Gar Alperovitz, who had left his job running Senator Gaylord Nelson's office for an academic appointment at Harvard. We talked about the sorry state of the world, the absence of fresh and creative ideas, and the demoralized leadership of the anti-war movement. It turned out that we had both been dreaming of a nationwide dialogue between disaffected students and the rest of the community. Then and there we decided to make it happen, and to call it Vietnam Summer. Vietnam Summer 1967 became the largest mobilization of anti-war volunteers to date, and it played a key role in turning the country against the war.

VIII

Vietnam Summer, 1967

THE ANTI-WAR MOVEMENT WAS READY to bring its message to the country at large. By the end of the summer of 1967 more than 25,000 Vietnam Summer volunteers would be working in 700 local projects.

We choose the name Vietnam Summer as a tribute to Mississippi Summer 1964. Then, students from the North had gone down to join SNCC organizers from local communities in a door-to-door voter registration campaign to build the Mississippi Freedom Democratic Party, the first integrated Mississippi political organization since the end of Reconstruction. Mississippi Summer had transformed the way the country viewed the civil rights struggle. Now Gar Alperovitz and I hoped that students from all over the country would join with local peace activists going door to door to build community-based anti-war organizations and transform the way the country viewed the war. Inspired by Bob Moses, the SNCC organizer who coordinated Mississippi Summer, we too hoped we could strengthen grassroots power by helping to build organizations controlled by local people.

Tom Hayden and Staughton Lynd had proposed a Vietnam Summer project when they returned from visiting North Vietnam in early spring 1966 to turn America into a town meeting against the war. (Paul Booth, "National Secretary's report, *New Left Notes*, April 1, 1966, p. 1) In 1966, I had also proposed a

Freedom Summer: USA – a time of intense political activity for those who hope
to build a new America. Nothing had come of these proposals.

Based on several months of door knocking in my Cambridge neighborhood
and my feel for the mood on campuses across the country, I was confident we
could make this Vietnam Summer happen. All Gar and I had to do was work
like hell, use our complementary skills and contacts well, and encourage other
like-minded people to come into the project and become stakeholders.

Gar felt that we had to involve the religious community in Vietnam Summer
from the very beginning if it were to succeed. I on the other hand wanted to focus on recruiting radical organizers and student volunteers. We agreed on the
direction we needed to go, but he worked the right side of the street, and I the
left. In a memo to national organizations, we laid out where we wanted to go in
a way we hoped would be acceptable to both sides.

Our objectives were stated in "A Proposal for Vietnam Summer."

I.   To begin to create a new and independent political force, initially
     organized with the minimal demand that the United States with-
     draw from Vietnam, but subsequently and increasingly organized
     around multi-issue concerns.

II. To allow, through the creation of such a force, the anti-war move-
     ment to exercise such political power as may be brought together to
     end the war.

III. To prevent the peace movement from falling behind the band-
     wagons of politicians promising vague doveishness, but no real
     program against the war.

IV. To develop trained organizers who can move from the initial war
     issue into other community problems.

The heart of our argument was that while numerous organizations were currently working effectively in a variety of areas, each organization, working
alone, had yet to make a serious impact on the war. It was time to move beyond
frustration to a dedicated and coordinated national summer effort, a pooling of
resources, and a massive and dramatic assault on common problems.

We pulled together a steering committee from the Boston area to help shoulder the burden. Then we moved to gain the support of national organizations, enlist prominent individual sponsors, as well as find money, office space, national staff, local project sites, paid local staff, volunteers for the local projects, training sites, and curriculum, in that order more or less.

All my energy went into Vietnam Summer, which meant that I stopped organizing my Cambridge neighborhood. In the long run, it was worth it. By early summer there were not one but two Vietnam Summer projects with hundreds of student and faculty volunteers in Cambridge canvassing the city.

Organizational turf wars were just as common, just as intense, and just as destructive then as always. But Vietnam Summer had a number of things going for it that helped it succeed as a coalition effort. Donors and potential volunteers were ready for a new approach. Because they were ready to move, no organization wanted to be left behind. Secondly, Vietnam Summer was a summer project scheduled to close at the end of August. People and organizations with profound disagreements could work under the same rubric for the summer knowing that at summer's end each project and the individuals in it would decide what direction to take.

What we wanted from organizations was participation, not endorsement, to be part of the process one way or another, if only by sending out our materials to their constituency. In private, leaders could complain that Vietnam Summer was a tool of the Communists, the Kennedy family, or whoever, to try to take over the anti-war movement. But with the prospect of thousands of new volunteers and donors joining up, no one wanted to stay out. When the train left the station, everyone wanted to be on board.

Dr. King Sends Out the Call

We wanted Dr. Martin Luther King Jr. to support Vietnam Summer. To get Dr. King's sponsorship, Gar worked his side of the street, the National Council of Churches and Clergy and Laity Concerned about Vietnam, while I worked my side, the movement. I didn't have much of a relationship with Dr. King's organization, the Southern Christian Leadership Conference (SCLC), but I did have friends in SNCC, which had a relationship, often a tempestuous one, with Dr. King and the SCLC. One early spring day Ivanhoe Donaldson, a SNCC organizer, had called me up. He told me to get down to New York for a rally in April where Dr. King was perhaps going to announce his support for Vietnam Summer, or perhaps not.

The day of the rally, in a dingy passageway beneath the podium, Ivanhoe and I shared a package of Lucky Strikes as we listened carefully to Dr. Martin Luther King Jr.'s voice booming over the loudspeaker system at a New York City stadium. When we were told to be there, we weren't sure what Dr. King had in mind, but at the end of his speech came a brief statement calling upon people of good will to support Vietnam Summer. I was overjoyed. A few minutes later Dr. King hurried by. "Martin, here's the guy from Vietnam Summer," Ivanhoe said.

Dr. King turned his head quickly and said, "Well then, you go get 'em." Then he was gone. Only later did I fully appreciate how angry J. Edgar Hoover and Lyndon Johnson were at him and how much courage his support had required.

Famous sponsors were essential to recruit volunteers and donors. Dr. King's support gave us access to many people we needed. He was, of course, very busy with many demands thrust upon him. Since some establishment supporters of the Civil Rights Movement also supported the war, the issue was complicated for him. Add to this the pressure from the FBI and the right who saw as dangerous subversion any effort to bring together the two issues of the war in Vietnam and civil rights.

On April 23, 1967, a week or so after the rally, Vietnam Summer held a formal press conference in Cambridge. There Dr. King said, "It is time now to meet the escalation of the war in Vietnam with an escalation of opposition to that war. I think the time has come for all people of good will to engage in a massive program of organization, of mobilization." Carl Oglesby, the president of SDS, and Robert Scheer, the editor of *Ramparts Magazine*, as well as Dr. Benjamin Spock, the famous pediatrician, joined him in the call, backed up by religious leaders, scientists, and academics from around the country.

What Are You Doing During Vietnam Summer, 1967?

The basic recruiting brochure, yellow with a bright summer sun, had gone out to campuses all over the country just before the press conference, with a Guide for Recruiting Volunteers. After the press conference, recruitment of volunteers and staff went into high gear. Student recruitment had to be a major priority because students would be leaving the campus soon. We urged students who had already joined the project to put ads in the local and campus papers, put up posters, organize campus meetings, and go door to door in dorms to recruit more volunteers. We urged local peace activists to organize a community project, and to provide room and board to Vietnam Summer workers.

On May 1, I published an article about the project in the SDS newspaper *New Left Notes*. On May 8, a mailing signed by leaders of student organizations was sent to activists around the country. The letter laid out the kinds of activities Vietnam Summer would support by providing training, educational materials, and funds. "The Vietnam Summer embraces a variety of people who are interested in several different projects." These included Community Teach-Outs, an educational program designed for middle-class areas, projects designed to involve people in poor and working-class areas, university projects designed to get the Department of Defense off the campus, and draft resistance.

Occasionally, there would be a little dust-up over the participation of activists from the Communist Party or some other left-wing organization. At a steering committee meeting on May 28 the Midwest field staff coordinator working out of the national office reported indignantly that a newspaper in Milwaukee had identified someone both as a member of the Communist Party and a worker for Vietnam Summer. She decried our "lack of political definition." Gar put the issue to rest, "Everything is happening as it should." One of the secrets of our success was that we kept the organization politically balanced by bringing people in rather than throwing people out.

I spent a lot of time on the road, as did other members of the steering committee. Activists and thousands of potential activists were ready to hear and act on the vision we laid out. At Columbia University, for example, William Vickery, chair of the Economics Department, and other professors passed out Vietnam Summer recruiting leaflets on Commencement Day. With thousands of volunteer applications pouring into the office, I felt that at last we'd really connected with the mood of the country.

Not everything, of course, went as I would have hoped. One evening I made a presentation about Vietnam Summer in Chicago. I had agreed to meet afterwards with a group of ministers connected with Dr. King. After the others had gone, I left the podium and sat on the back of a chair while Dr. King's people, about twelve to fifteen Black men, continued to sit and stand at the back of the hall. I started by saying what was on my mind: Black people were bearing a disproportionate share of the fighting and dying in Vietnam. So I thought, Black people needed to play a major role in building and directing the anti-war movement, based on solid, well-funded organizing in the Black Belt in the South and in inner cities of the North. One of our four regional directors was Black, and I hoped that we would be able to recruit staff and volunteers from the Black community for a vigorous campaign in the Chicago area.

From the beginning, there was an angry undertone to the meeting. To be more accessible I had come down from the podium. They kept their distance. I was smiling, while they were glaring at me angrily. One man in particular, standing in the very back of the room began to interrupt me with questions I didn't quite understand, but the general thrust seemed to be "what's in it for me?" Then slowly what was going on began to dawn on me. "God damn," I said to myself, "these guys are trying to Mau Mau me like I was some big shot business or foundation executive. Little old me from a campaign that's barely off the ground."

(Mau Mauing was when angry Black activists tried to instill both guilt and fear in people they saw as representatives of the white power structure. Because the Mau Mau, a secret society dedicated to driving the British from Kenya, attacked and killed British farmers in remote areas they became associated in the public mind with Black terrorism against whites. In fact, the British army and police did much more killing in Kenya than the Mau Mau did.)

The ministers wanted to talk about jobs all right, but they didn't want any accountability to Vietnam Summer about what they did while on our payroll.

They were saying that they were the holders of the Martin Luther King Jr. franchise in Chicago. Now that Vietnam Summer was also raising money off Dr. King's name, we were taking money from the franchise too. We owed them, and jobs were a way of returning to them what was theirs.

Now I understood their position. But there was no way I was going to give them a penny of Vietnam Summer money for "no show" jobs. To pay them off would have meant betraying the people they allegedly represented, who needed for this anti-war work to get done. But saying that directly would have provoked an ugly scene, which I wanted to avoid. So, I kept coming back to our desire to hire Black staff committed to the goals of the project, while avoiding commitments to hire anyone there. I had to keep my cool while they raised the pressure.

Their message, not quite stated, was clear: Who was I, a snot-nosed white boy, to tell them what they had to do to get money that was theirs? Finally, they began to leave in disgust. Then I got out of there as fast as I could. That night was, however, just a brief storm in weeks of sunshine.

At some point in the spring Gar decided to step back from active day-to-day leadership of Vietnam Summer, although he continued to play a key role on the steering committee. Chester Hartman, a friend of mine who taught urban planning and helped recruit some of the major organizations supporting us, became acting director of Vietnam Summer. Then the steering committee hired Lee Webb, who in addition to serving as national secretary of SDS in 1963, had experience organizing and administering community groups. To balance possible public perception of radical tilt to the project from Lee's SDS background, Reverend Richard Fernandez, executive secretary of Clergy and Laity Concerned about Vietnam, was also hired. He and Lee became co-directors, but Reverend Fernandez did not play a significant role in day-to-day operations. Greg Finger, then working for the National Conference for New Politics, came on as director of development. I was in charge of the training institutes.

Five Days' Training

The organization was beginning to take shape, but for those trying to guide the effort the tension was terrific. None of us had ever attempted a project on this scale before. The staff field coordinators were flat-out recruiting workers and identifying possible projects. Every day hundreds of pieces of mail arrived at the doors. Thousands of student volunteers needed to be matched with projects, some of which didn't even exist yet. Money was coming in, but we needed a lot more of it.

Orientation and training for hundreds of local staff and volunteers was crucial to the success of the summer. Now I was sitting in the office in the middle of May without a clue as to how I could make this training happen. I was so overwhelmed I couldn't even begin to break the job down into manageable pieces.

In walked a young man of medium height, close-cropped dark hair, and an eager go-getter look in his eye. Fred Stout was graduating from Harvard in a few weeks. He wanted to volunteer. "Great," I thought, "one more volunteer, when already we have hundreds more than we know what to do with." I tried to explain to Fred my problem: training was essential for the volunteers but the obstacles to setting up the training institutes, including for starters where they would be held, seemed overwhelming. He started to take notes. Realizing that we were on to something, I laid out all the problems, and then we brainstormed possible solutions. Fred disappeared for an hour or two, and then came back with the draft of a plan. We were on our way.

We checked in every day. Fred was in charge of the logistics, how to get 350 staff and key volunteers to places where they could be trained. Finding a place to train hundreds of anti-war activists was not easy, particularly given the prejudices of the time against anti-war radicals. But Fred worked the phones and pulled it off, finding a location for the institute in his home state of Ohio. Shortly afterwards we recruited Bob Greenstein to our education and training department. Then we had a real team.

I believed that the courage and enthusiasm of the movement could overcome all obstacles. But I also believed that these young men and women who were going out to do the crucial work deserved the best possible preparation. My vision for the institute was that we would try to provide these Vietnam Summer organizers, some new and some experienced, with every skill and every insight the movement had learned since 1960. I saw my job as recruiting the best possible speakers and workshop leaders to communicate specific information and skills. I saw my job also as bringing together the best teachers in the movement, like Paul Potter and John Clayton, to ask the questions activists needed to think about to become self-conscious organizers, sensitive to the needs of the people with whom they would be working. Radical organizers, we believed, needed to learn how to question authority, including the government and business elites, but also ourselves. Only by constant evaluation and response to criticism could we succeed in building the democratic movement necessary to build a democratic society.

The Vietnam Summer Training Institute was held at Case Western Reserve University in Cleveland, Ohio, starting Sunday, June 18, 1967. A separate training institute was held the week following in San Francisco, California, for the West Coast, organized by Fred Stout and Norm Potter, Paul's brother. The Saturday night before the institute began I met with most of the twenty-five workshop leaders and resource people, including Les, my brother's friend who had returned to Cambridge and the movement. Participants would meet in regional groups to discuss coordination and coalition building, in constituency groups to discuss what tactics and strategies would work best where they were going to organize – in African American, or middle-class, or white working-class communities, or with young people and students. Five different skills were taught in small group sessions, including draft counseling, how to organize a public meeting, press work, legal support, and how to set up an office and raise money.

The next day close to two hundred organizers registered and the work began. The group was diverse in terms of race, age, experience, and ideology. Bearded middle-aged pacifists rubbed shoulders with young Black and white movement types. We had actually pulled it off!

As always there were a few surprises. Sunday afternoon a staff person came running up to me:

"I just registered a guy with a 45-caliber automatic in his brief case," he said. "What do I do now?"

"Nothing," I said. "Just give me his room number. I'll go talk to him and see what's up."

Participants were living in the dorms. Fortunately, the man with the pistol had a single. I walked up the stairs to his room and knocked. The door opened revealing a tall, muscular Black man in an elegant suit and tie. As we shook hands, I introduced myself as the director and welcomed him to the institute. He invited me in and when I sat down, I cut to the chase.

"I'm a little concerned about the pistol you got there," I said pointing to his briefcase on the table.

"You know damn well a Black man isn't safe in the country. I need it for protection," he said. (There had been riots in African American communities around the country. In 1967 alone, there had been riots in Newark, Boston, New York, and other cities. In Detroit the toll was 43 dead, 7,000 arrested, 1,300 buildings burned, and 2,700 stores and businesses destroyed, according to Ann Charters in *The Portable Sixties Reader*.)

"I know it's dangerous. But with the riots and all, if the cops find out the pistol's here, they could bust you and bust us. They'd like nothing better," I said.

We went back and forth in a friendly sort of way, finally agreeing that he could keep his pistol, in the briefcase, in his room. When he left about a day later, I was disappointed – I didn't think weapons were the way, but to win I felt we had to include just about everybody, and he seemed like a nice guy.

Also, on that Sunday a group of young African American activists from Cleveland itself turned up to register. Their leader put me on the spot right away. He wanted answers to questions like, "Where did the money for all this training and materials come from?" and "What kind of a movement are you guys trying to build?" I said that I didn't know where all the money is coming from, and I didn't care, as long as the money came to us without conditions. I also told him we wanted to fund organizing in Black neighborhoods. I told them that there would be a full discussion of all these issues when the whole group came together to discuss "Vietnam Summer and the Anti-War Movement" on the last day of the institute.

The Cleveland group was not going to be put off to the end of the institute. That night they turned their suspicions about where the relative wealth of Vietnam Summer came from into a song, based on the carol "The Twelve Days of Christmas." They taught the song to the whole group of 225 the next day at lunch in a large cafeteria. While I stood there trying not to look embarrassed, the group sang:

> On the first day of summer
> Bobby gave to me
> A middle-class constituency

> On the second day of summer
> Bobby gave to me
> Foundation money and a middle-class constituency

> Third Day: Three co-directors...
> Fourth Day: Four SDSers...
> Fifth Day: Five days training...
> Sixth Day: Six infiltrators...
> Seventh Day: Seven PR men...
> Eighth Day: Eight fundraisers...
> Ninth Day: Nine community organizers...

And for the finale:

> On the tenth day of summer
> Bobby gave to me
> The Kennedy Dynasty!

(As recorded in Alan Jehlen's Vietnam Summer Worklist Mailing #8, "The Ten Days of Summer.")

At first, I was annoyed. They had jumped the gun. A public discussion of these issues was scheduled for later on in the week, when the institute had picked up more momentum. Then I realized that what I had hoped would happen was happening right here. They were questioning authority – me.

"Bobby gave to me" in the first verse and "The Kennedy Dynasty!" in the tenth raised the central issue. Robert Kennedy, recently elected senator from New York, was heir to his brother John, the martyred president. Bobby was young, good-looking, vigorous, and intelligent, and many people believed he was the person who could defeat Lyndon Johnson. Many of us also believed that the movement for civil rights and against the war was a political asset that could help elect the next president. To win the movement's support by embracing key elements of the program was one thing, co-opting the movement by putting its organizers on the payroll was quite another. Was Vietnam Summer simply a way to put the movement on Bobby Kennedy's payroll?

"A middle-class constituency" raised another important question. Did Vietnam Summer really aim to organize a diverse anti-war movement that would reflect the issues and aspirations of Black people as well as white? My friends from Cleveland were certainly not against organizing middle-class people, especially if it were done in a way that made them allies of poor people and minorities. But did Vietnam Summer intend to put serious resources into organizing in African American communities, or were we going to take the easy out and focus on building white anti-war organizations, "a middle-class constituency," with a few Black faces around to reassure everyone that we weren't really so racist after all?

My answer to anyone who asked was that Vietnam Summer was a big gamble. We were ready to fund organizing in the Black community. We didn't know if these projects would succeed. We didn't know if donors would continue to fund them after the summer was over. We didn't know if we would succeed in building a diverse anti-war movement. Certainly not, if we don't try. "With the outcome uncertain," I told them, "the only answer is to figure out what will make a difference and organize your ass off to make it happen."

When the national office in Cambridge heard about the grassroots revolution at the institute, they were not nearly as happy as I was. Co-director Lee Webb flew out to Cleveland on the second day of the institute. I urged him to go to the workshops and let the participants get to know him as a fellow organizer. But he insisted I call a special meeting so he could "reassure" the group that no special interests controlled Vietnam Summer. Andrew Young, Dr. King's main assistant then, later to be mayor of Atlanta and U.S. Ambassador to the United Nations under President Jimmy Carter, came out to bless the proceedings. Neither Lee Webb nor Andrew Young could actually reassure the people who were raising the questions. Reassurance was beside the point. Vietnam Summer offered people an opportunity for action, and this diverse group of two hundred was going to take us up on that. Questioning now meant that they would be better prepared for the real challenges they would soon face in the field. As Gar had said, "Everything is happening as it should."

By the third day, participants were still engaged with each other, talking in small groups sitting under the trees and taking trips together off campus. But they were less engaged with the formal workshops of the institute. I was as tired as I had ever been. I ran around all day checking out the small group workshops. At the end of every evening session Ivanhoe Donaldson, Les, and I had retired to a rundown bar near the campus to analyze the day's events and prepare for the next day's challenges. Boilermakers, cheap Bourbon whiskey with cold beer as a chaser, were the refreshment of choice.

So, I was a bit hung over when the Black minister who had led the charge for "no show" jobs at the meeting in Chicago in May pulled up one morning in a red Cadillac. He rolled down the window and spoke to me as I stood on the sidewalk. "Andy Young talked to your group yesterday, so I want you to get everybody together so I can address them this afternoon," he said. For a few seconds I was so amazed I couldn't say anything. Here's a man who wants to chisel "no show" jobs out of the project, and now he wants me to assemble the institute to hear his sermon. "Yeah, sure. So why don't you turn that red Cadillac around and go fuck yourself all the way back to Chicago," I finally replied. He left fast. I wasn't about to let him spoil the day for me.

The song "The Ten Days of Summer" was sung many times over the course of the institute. The line that got the biggest laugh was "Five days training." Participants were truly grateful to have been brought together, but five days training was just too damn much. In less than five days, they wanted to be out there doing the work.

The Cleveland group offered to organize the send-off party. I was nervous about the party, which was taking place in a vacant lot close to the Hough neighborhood, where there had been riots and police repression earlier in the year. Would the police attack our party too? The fear was compounded by my sense of responsibility towards the movement and the participants who had just been trained. Was I putting the future organizers of the anti-war movement at risk? Or did I simply lack the confidence I should have that the Cleveland group knew what they were doing?

A truck delivered kegs of beer and food to the large vacant lot in the late afternoon. As the sun began to set there were about 250 people standing around drinking beer and talking, some from the institute and some from the neighborhood. When the sound system came on, people started singing and dancing. The party was going strong when the cops arrived, in a squad car that jumped the curb into the vacant lot where the party was and turned its spotlight on the crowd. People gathered in front of the squad car and started hollering for the cops to leave. It was "Black and white together we shall not be moved," as the old movement song said. I was so scared I practically peed in my pants. But after a very long minute, the squad car turned around and drove back to the street. It did not come back for the rest of the evening. "It doesn't get any better than this!" I thought.

Other things happened in Cleveland that were not on the printed agenda of the institute. One day, when as usual I was dashing from one meeting to another, a man who introduced himself as Ken Keniston caught up with me. The name was familiar to me because he had written a very well regarded book on alienated youth. As we hurried along he told me that now he wanted to study the process of "politicization" that had led young people like me to become committed to the "New Left." In essence, he wanted to find out why we had made the choices we had made. As part of his research, he wanted to do in-depth interviews of willing people on the staff of the national office of Vietnam Summer. What did I think?

Well, I thought, this could be a very good thing, or a very bad one. If it confirmed the right-wing stereotype that we were crazy people betraying our country to get back at our parents that would be very bad. A serious study that dispelled for the public the misinformation about our motives would be very good. Plus, if we learned more about how we got here, it might provide useful insights about how we could recruit others.

I slowed down for a second and looked him over. He seemed like a regular middle-class guy: khaki pants, colored shirt, short-cropped hair, and a summer tan. He wasn't all full of himself, or he wouldn't have spent the last fifteen minutes chasing after me. He wasn't a pompous academic, or he wouldn't have laid out what he wanted so clearly. He wasn't some con man pretending to be one of us. The thing about Keniston was that he radiated unpretentious honesty. I told him he had my vote to go ahead.

As I wrote him later, "You were received as you were because you were seen immediately as an honest man with good questions. If you had come on as 'Dr. Keniston, the mind expert,' our tense and fractured group would have affirmed its essential solidarity by running you out before the first day." He quoted my statement in his book *Young Radicals: Notes on Committed Youth*, published less than a year later.

The book fulfilled all my hopes for a serious effort to explain young radicals to the college-educated public. As Keniston wrote:

> "Working with, and writing about, the leaders of Vietnam Summer was in some respect a 'radicalizing' experience for me: I find myself more ready to understand, sympathize, and support many of their actions than I was before the summer.... [T]he hope that a better understanding of these young men and women – of who they are, what they object to in our society, and what they propose for it – might contribute to understanding our common desperate predicament led me to seek early publication of the book, despite my awareness of its many limitations." (Keniston, p. 296)

Over the course of the institute a series of informal meetings was held in quiet corners, outside, to avoid surveillance. Leaders of the anti-war movement gathered to consider how we could begin to reach out to GIs and how to support the growing anti-war resistance in the army. In the next few months coffee houses were set up near army bases in this country to provide support to soldiers who questioned the war but were trapped in the army.

How Vietnam Summer Worked

The national office of Vietnam Summer was set up to support the local work. Four field staff coordinators including one for African American communities outside the South (SNCC received a grant from Vietnam Summer to develop the work in African American communities in the South) were on the phone every day encouraging and troubleshooting with the local projects and regional offices. Vietnam Summer regional offices were in New England (Cambridge), the Midwest (Chicago), the South (Nashville), Pacific and Rocky Mountains Region (San Francisco), New York City, and Los Angeles.

After the training institutes were over, Fred Stout, Bob Greenstein, and I worked as a team to help the local organizations sort out what worked and what didn't and share successes around the country. Fred helped develop the Cambridge organization. Bob ran a publications program that produced and distributed what we learned in the form of an organizers manual, with a U.S. Navy survival kit on the cover, providing a general orientation to community anti-war organizing, an orientation to specific constituencies, how to do neighborhood work, and how to set up an office. We also published guides on how to set up a draft counseling center, fundraising, local referendum campaigns, and publicity.

By summer's end, there were at least ten local and state anti-war referenda. The Vietnam Summer Teacher Student Project worked with twenty teacher groups around the country, including one in the Boston area that my wife, Frinde, coordinated. She and a group of radical teachers had developed a high-school curriculum on Vietnam that was published and distributed by the *New York Review of Books* in 1966. Special efforts to reach out to low-income and Black communities were consolidated over the course of the summer, and much more serious efforts were begun to reach out to unions and local union leaders. Draft resistance moved from students signing petitions to setting up draft counseling centers as a part of local community based anti-war organizing, including outreach to working-class young men who were actually being drafted.

The Revolt of the Secretaries

When Lee Webb came in as co-director, he divided the staff along rigid lines. The "political staff" was concerned with program, public relations, fundraising, and the overall direction of the project. The "administrative staff" did the typing, addressed the envelopes, answered the phone, and printed or made copies of the vast quantities of material that went out the door every day. The two groups worked in the same office but had vastly different access to information and decision-making.

As so often happens, this effort to become more "businesslike" created its own inefficiencies. Even in the 1960s, many businesses were moving away from the factory model of worker discipline, with workers performing discrete tasks under the watchful eyes of supervisors. Managers were learning that workers produce more when they know what's going on and are encouraged to participate. In Vietnam Summer, where the energy, commitment, and enthusiasm of all the staff were one of our greatest potential assets, it was particularly wasteful not to draw them in. But the "administrative staff" was clearly left out of the loop in the new order of things.

Another reason for not dividing the staff along the lines of who made the decisions and who did the "shit work" was that the "administrative staff," largely female, wasn't going to put up with it. One day in the middle of the summer, the Vietnam Summer Revolutionary Workers Committee put out a manifesto that captures the spirit of the time:

> "To be human is to exercise and develop the capacity to think, struggle, and love. Submitting to the dehumanization of being placed in arbitrary slots and jobs without responsibility is a crime against those in the field who depend on the intelligence, creativity and responsibility of the office."

What followed were six reasonable demands relating to their desire for input in the campaign and for cooperation from the rest of the staff when big and especially burdensome mailings were being put together. Lee capitulated, and the distinction between political and office workers was abolished.

I had my own particular reasons for supporting this change. In fact, I had started a discussion group for the administrative staff so that they could learn how to be speakers and organizers. For me, one of the basic premises of Vietnam Summer was that people new to the movement could, through training and practice, become speakers and organizers. If the national office didn't demonstrate some attention to developing our staff, why should we expect the local projects to do better?

Also, the input of relatively inexperienced people is often a very useful reality check. Under the intense pressure of a fast-paced campaign, experienced leaders can sometimes become trapped in their own hopes and assumptions, losing touch with the reality of what ordinary people out there in the real world are actually thinking.

Another reason for supporting the office revolution was that I needed allies in the office. Fred, Bob, and I worked in a classroom at the end of a long corridor in the Cambridge Friends School. At the other end of this corridor was the co-director's office and the offices of the people he considered his management team. From time to time Lee had put out a memo in which the political staff was listed top to bottom in terms of "responsibility." My name started close to the bottom and went lower with each new edition. The door to my "office" was almost always open, his often closed. Lee Webb kept his own counsel, but the signs were there that he wanted to make Vietnam Summer permanent. I thought this was a bad idea, as did most of the staff, because over the long term an unaccountable national apparatus would try to dominate the local work. It was not in my interest to have my potential allies excluded from the decision-making process.

Not all the political staff supported this effort to develop our human resources. One angry, burned-out manager told Keniston what he wouldn't have dared to say in public:

> "After the revolt, overworked political staff people sometimes could not find a typist for material which needed excellent typing on the mimeo machine.... What the revolt meant was that these girls... were now spending much of their time in the "glamour" roles of calling on the WATS line and arranging public concerts (none of which ever came off)." (Keniston, p. 161)

For the leaders of an enterprise like Vietnam Summer learning how to plan and communicate with the rest of the staff was a good thing, not a bad one. Actually, the office continued to run as smoothly as before, but sometimes you had to schedule your clerical work, rather than just dump it on a secretary's desk.

What We Accomplished

Approval for President Johnson's handling of the war had been declining steadily since the summer of 1965. In October 1967, one month after Vietnam Summer closed its doors, public opinion crossed a significant barrier when polls showed that 46 percent of the public regarded the commitment to Vietnam as a "mistake," as against the 44 percent who continued to back it. A poll comparing potential presidential candidates conducted in July 1967 showed Bobby Kennedy trailing Johnson by 39 percent to 45 percent. By October, a survey showed Kennedy ahead by a margin of 20 percent. These polls seemed to confirm our belief that systematic door-to-door outreach could have an effect on a public that was beginning to question the war. The polls also disclosed the continued support for the war among the college-educated, upper-middle-class people whose sons were least likely to be drafted. (For polling data, see Karnow, p. 502 and p. 524.)

The polls and our experience confirmed that the largest growth in the anti-war sentiment would come through organizing in working-class and minority communities. Because they were the ones being drafted and sent to war, the attitudes of working-class and minority young men, and their families, were critical to getting the U.S. out of Vietnam. On November 30, 1967, Eugene McCarthy announced he would run against Lyndon Johnson in the Democratic presidential primaries.

The impact of the anti-war movement on this change in public opinion is hard to measure. We don't know how much of this change would have happened without a national grassroots campaign, but there are a number of reasons to believe that Vietnam Summer made a difference. By the end of August 1967, the national staff estimated that there were 26,000 volunteers working in 700 local projects in 42 states and the District of Columbia. Of the full-time paid staff of 500, 125 were hired by the national office, 60 by regional offices, 65 by projects with seed grants, and 250 on the initiative of local projects. Vietnam Summer raised $500,000: $180,000 by the national office and the rest by regional and local groups. (Lee D. Webb, "Vietnam Summer shows what can be done," *Vietnam Summer News*, August 25, 1967, p.7)

Foreign policy is a national issue. The fact that Vietnam Summer was truly national and involved work in forty-two states and the District of Columbia affirmed that we were building a movement that was up to the task. It also refuted the notion that anti-war sentiment was a bi-coastal phenomenon. The fact that much of the national campaign involved grassroots outreach similar to an electoral campaign and that some of the groups were building referendum campaigns set the stage for the electoral efforts of Eugene McCarthy and Robert Kennedy the following year.

Without a national campaign, it is hard to imagine how local groups by themselves could have recruited so many student volunteers. Without the national training institutes and the follow-up work on the phone by the field staff coordinators, it is difficult to imagine how so many inexperienced people could have been given a basic orientation to grassroots organizing, the confidence to give it a try, and then the support to stick with it long enough to begin to learn on their own. A national campaign could get national press and help the local groups get local coverage. Without a national organization many local efforts, particularly those in remote locations, might have been overlooked. Press coverage helped the morale of the staff and volunteers and spread the message beyond those they had actually talked to.

One of the factors contributing to Vietnam Summer's success as a national campaign was that the programs had been field-tested at the local level first. Vietnam Summer's programs were built to a certain extent on the work I had begun in Cambridge. But they also drew on the experience of Hank Werner of the Milwaukee Organizing Committee, the first complete community-organizing peace project in the country. Hank served as the national field staff coordinator for Vietnam Summer. Another factor contributing to the success of Vietnam Summer was that the objective and time frame of the project was clear, at least initially. Vietnam Summer was a summer project to stimulate local grassroots organizing against the war in Vietnam. Another strength of Vietnam Summer was that it was inclusive and non-exclusionary. People who supported the program were welcome to join, be they pacifists, Communists, Republicans, Democrats, third-party and no-party people, and they did.

There were problems with the work in the field. At the beginning, some of our materials focused on neighborhood study groups as a way to build the local organization. However, attendance at study groups and discussions quickly dropped off unless they were tied to actions that people felt could make a difference in ending the war. In "We All Hate to Study," a piece by Alan Jehlen sent out as a mid-course correction, he laid out an essential truth about the relation between study and organizing:

> "... [A]t meetings people want to prepare for new activities, or evaluate old ones they participated in. They will also want to discuss questions about the war which came up in the course of canvassing.... [A]ction breeds discussion. It rarely works the other way around."

Like the rest of the national staff, I worked hard, but almost entirely in the national office. I thought I was at the top of my game, but actually I was out of touch. As an experienced organizer, I should have been on the road, problem solving and working side by side with the local organizers helping make Vietnam Summer real in local projects around the country. Fred Stout and Bob Greenstein could have run the program office while gaining valuable experience and insight by working in local projects in the Cambridge area as well as the national office.

At the end of the summer, Lee Webb proposed extending Vietnam Summer for a year, with "a two-million dollar budget, six thousand local projects, a newspaper with one million circulation, a vastly expanded program." Many people figured that only the Kennedys could come up with that kind of money. "Will Vietnam Summer become a clever trick to put the movement on the Kennedy payroll?" my friends from Cleveland had asked at the institute earlier that summer. "No," I had answered then. I planned to keep that promise.

A national meeting was scheduled in Washington to consider Lee's proposal. Before the meeting I was invited to a get-together with some other movement leaders, some of whom wanted Vietnam Summer to continue. One of those was Jerry Rubin, who turned up with what he described as some "really good stuff from Latin America"– apparently, marijuana was no longer poison for him. He rolled a joint, and I took a couple of hits to calm my pre-meeting jit-ters. Big mistake. The meeting started a few minutes later. When my turn to speak came, I pressed the "on" button but no words came out. "That bastard set me up," I thought. After what seemed an eternity, but was probably ten seconds or less, the words began to flow. Ivanhoe stood there in the back waving his fist to urge me on. Finally, I began to make sense.

That was the last time I ever smoked dope when there was work to be done. Vietnam Summer closed as scheduled.

In the end the sense of humor of the New Left at that time prevailed. In the last national mailing in September, Lee received the "New Left Executive of the Year" award: "As of one week before the closing of the office, Brother Webb had still not learned how to use the Xerox machine, because he had always gotten someone else to do it." I received the "Most Words Written by a Staff Member Whose Job Does Not Directly Involve Writing" award: "Brother Maher's 289,473 words far exceeded the efforts turned in by any staff members in his class." (Jehlen, Worklist #8.)

My last piece was an article in the newspaper urging local Vietnam Summer groups to go beyond the war as the single issue and to build power in coalition with working-class people and minorities who have other issues perhaps even more pressing than the war:

> "If we cannot bring ourselves to care deeply about what happens to us and our own people there is nothing we can do for the Vietnamese. Political necessity (an electoral majority, for example) if nothing else dictates that the anti-war movement must go beyond itself. What holds us back is the fear that conflicts far away can be solved more easily than conflicts close at home. History will un-doubtedly prove that fear justified." (*Vietnam Summer News*, August 25, 1967, p. 8)

❦ ❦ ❦

What I Learned During Vietnam Summer

- Campaigns need to be field-tested at the local level before they are rolled out at the national one.

- While all organizing is in a sense local, organizers should focus on strategies that if replicated can have a national impact.
- Keep your coalitions balanced by bringing people in rather than by throwing people out.
- Reading and workshops are important, but people learn organizing primarily on the job.
- Action demands study and discussion. Study and discussion are no substitute for action.
- A noble cause does not excuse top-down leadership and oppressive conditions where the people who do the work are not listened to.
- Political campaigns and organizations require timely decision-making. Democratic and effective organizations require broad input into the decisions. Leaders must learn how to balance the two.
- The most experienced organizers in a campaign need to get out into the field to help develop new ones, not move papers around the national office.
- Self-pity and taking yourself too seriously are symptoms of burnout. Organizers and leaders experiencing burnout need to take a break. Those who consider themselves indispensable are reluctant to take a break, which is all the more reason for them to do it.

Predictions

While Vietnam Summer was going on, Gar Alperovitz had convened a group to plan a "Seminar on Fundamental Social Change in America" to take place at Harvard in the fall of 1967. Besides Gar, the planning group included Michael Walzer, Stephen Thernstrom, Christopher Jencks, Paul Potter, and me.

At the very outset, we asked every member of the seminar including ourselves to write an outline of a case, an argument, a "brief" of his own prediction of whether fundamental social change is possible in the United States. My own brief, "Imperialism and Fundamental Social Change," came down on the side of certainty: "Fundamental social change, the destruction of private ownership capitalism by revolution or by war, is not only possible but inevitable."

U.S. corporations' need for profit threatens the interest of the people of the underdeveloped world, I argued, by seizing their natural resources and exploiting their labor power in ways that make it impossible for them to develop. Their resistance to U.S. corporate dominance leads to perpetual war, which destroys the American way of life at home. Two outcomes are possible, victory by the opposition in the United States, or destruction of the world by those who will not accept change.

Looking back on what I thought then, I still believe now that our drive to empire is the greatest danger our country faces. But now I have more questions and fewer answers. I think I was mistaken to ignore the unique features of U.S. behavior, and not look for its unique causes. I don't think now that the need of U.S. corporations to maintain their profits can by itself explain why the United States intervened in Vietnam, or the Dominican Republic, or Guatemala, Iran, Chile, Afghanistan, and Iraq.

Most developed countries have economies dominated by large corporations. Few if any developed countries, capitalist or not, have clean hands when it comes to using their economic power to exploit the underdeveloped world. But with the exception of the U.S., no developed country since the decolonization process ended in the mid-1960s has risked a major war to assure their political and economic domination of a faraway nation. The United States is unique in that respect. Why?

New Politics, Old Prejudice

There was one more ordeal to endure between leaving the national office of Vietnam Summer and resuming my life as an organizer. A group called the National Conference for New Politics (NCNP) had called a national convention of the opposition to Lyndon Johnson's policies. I was amazed at their presumption. Did they have any appreciation of how fragmented the opposition actually was – the lack of shared history, political perspective, or personal relationships between white and Black, poor, working class and middle class, Black Power, Old Left, New Left and the just plain new to politics? I thought that people could overcome these barriers by working together as we did in Vietnam Summer, but in America for the most part people of different races and classes lived separately. Just because Reverend King and Dr. Spock could have a courteous conversation did not mean that different perceptions based on hundreds of years of racism would vanish when white people from Summit and Black people from Newark came together for a New Politics Convention at the Palmer House in Chicago. I felt a disaster in the making. But when the time came, I got in a car and went to Chicago.

The convention took place August 29 to September 4, 1967. The purpose of the convention was to choose among three possible strategies for the opposition to pursue: support the third-party candidacy of Martin Luther King Jr. and Dr. Benjamin Spock for president and vice president; support campaigns to send anti-Johnson delegates to the Democratic Party Convention; and support local organizing campaigns. (*New Politics News*, August 28, 1967, p.1) In the several weeks leading up to the convention, special, if belated, efforts had been made to recruit African American delegates.

No one had a plan for how the political needs of hundreds of African Americans attending the convention were to be synchronized with the agenda of thousands of whites who had come there to debate which of the three programs would be better for the anti-war movement. The first day almost all of the several hundred African American delegates withdrew to a Black Caucus that met behind closed doors throughout most of the five-day convention. The forming of a Black Caucus should not have surprised anyone who had thought about the last three years of Black life in America, not to mention the last three hundred.

Stokely Carmichael from SNCC was one of the leaders of the Black Caucus. The year before, Stokely had been among the first to call for "Black Power" and articulate within the Civil Rights Movement the idea that Blacks had to organize separately. The Lowndes County Freedom Movement in Lowndes County, Alabama, that Stokely had helped organize adopted the Black Panther as its symbol for the local elections in the summer of 1966. The struggle in Lowndes County inspired the Black Panther Party that was organized in Oakland, California, in the months following.

At some point in 1967 Ivanhoe Donaldson had taken me to hear Stokely speak at a Black Power rally in Roxbury, then the center of the Black community in Boston. I stood at the back of the crowd and listened very carefully as Stokely described the U.S. policies towards Black people as genocide. Stokely's message offended many, but as far as I was concerned the people in the movement were still my brothers and sisters, whether we organized separately or together.

Stokely and I talked once briefly during the convention. Ivanhoe and I met almost once a day to try to figure out how to overcome this crisis of mistrust and get the movement, if not working together, at least moving towards some common goals. A Black Caucus walkout, publicly confirming our lack of unity, loomed as a disastrous possibility.

The Palmer House Hotel felt like a special circle of hell. I never left the hotel, except to sleep for a few hours. The red carpets and the gilt furnishings radiated the negative energy of the proceedings. What a contrast with the Vietnam Summer Institute only months before! There people of all classes and races sat together in small workshops, ate together, drank together, danced, and stood up to the police together.

Engulfed in a hot, stale atmosphere, we were 2,500 people trapped in our separate groups, large and small, desperate for fresh air, with no countryside to walk in to restore our stamina and perspective. At times, my only consolation was the thought that since no one had yet died, or been killed, things were not as bad as they could be.

The Black Caucus demanded that their several hundred members be given votes equal to the two thousand whites also present – otherwise Black delegates would walk out. A minority in the convention as well as in the country and accustomed to being patronized, passed over, and ignored, African Americans had decided to take a stand.

In the Radical Alternatives Caucus to which I belonged, I argued that the demand for equal representation reflected a certain rough justice. "Eighty-five percent of the delegates at this convention may be white. But if you look out into the streets about one-half the people in motion against the government are Black. But many African Americans who might have come here as delegates aren't here, either because the groups they come from can't afford to pay for the trip, or because they had never heard about the convention in the first place." One reporter construed my argument to mean that Black people deserved more votes because they were so poor. Actually what I called for was justice, not pity.

The debate over the Black Caucus demand almost sent the whole gathering over the cliff:

> "Arthur Waskow summed up the views of many who opposed the demand. 'There are 1000 good liberals in this room who think the way to become good radicals is to castrate themselves,' he said. 'But after you castrate someone, you don't sleep with him.'" (Alan Jehlen, "William Pepper's Lonely Hearts Club Band," p. 6. William Pepper was the executive director of the NCNP.)

Whatever Waskow intended, the debate got stupid fast. Self-styled members of a White Organizer Caucus walked out because the Black Caucus demand was "an attack on our masculinity." Others asserted that the Black Caucus demand was really a test for white radicals. If they "gave in," Black radicals would "lose respect" for them because they had shown themselves to be not true radicals after all. This view was like the 1950s take on relations between the sexes – real men "lost respect" for women who "gave in" before marriage. These themes of castration and "giving in" were widely echoed in the press coverage of the convention. But despite all the rants, the white delegates passed the resolution giving equal voice to the Black Caucus by a vote of three to one. On the whole, the liberal peaceniks showed more political maturity than many of the radicals.

The Black Caucus resolution on Israel, submitted less than three months after the Six Day War in which Israel had conquered the West Bank from Jordan, Gaza and the Sinai Peninsula from Egypt, and the Golan Heights from Syria, also provoked a lot of anger and dismay among some whites. The resolution read, "Condemn the imperialistic Israeli Government; this condemnation does not imply anti-Semitism." Later a number of the resolutions were reexamined. In its final version the Middle East resolution included a plea: "We implore the Arab people and nations to try to live with the reality of Israel and not try to uproot its people." (Jehlen, p. 6)

The Black Caucus proposed that to ensure future racial parity, twelve directors were to be chosen by the Black Caucus, six by the Radical Alternatives Caucus, and six by the Third Party Caucus. This proposal was adopted by the convention. I was elected to the NCNP Executive Board from the Radical Alternatives Caucus. I went to at least one meeting, but my heart wasn't in it.

At the end there were a few victories, but at what cost? To prevent a terrible public split in the movement along racial lines, elements of the New Left, white and Black, had taken over a weak national organization that had far over-reached its capacities and soon would die. Worse, some of the angers and preju-dices nurtured in the hothouse atmosphere of the Palmer House would last a long time. Some thought that when it came to foreign affairs Black people should mind their own business. That's what the right wing said when Dr. King or Mohammed Ali talked about Vietnam. With the Black Caucus resolution on the Middle East, some on the left joined the right in angrily questioning wheth-er Black people had a right to an opinion on such weighty matters.

Marty Peretz's attitude towards the Black movement was never the same after that, and he moved quickly to the right. Ironically, whereas Black opinion on foreign affairs often is seen as out of step in the U.S., it is in fact much more in harmony with the rest of the world than the mainstream U.S. version.

Never underestimate the power of racism in American society. To para-phrase William Faulkner, the past isn't over yet – it's not even past.

Another disturbing trend that surfaced at the convention was the political immaturity of some radicals. Working on elections was seen as a "sellout." This radical rhetoric about elections weakened our appeal to middle-class people at the convention, who tended to respond well to a more comprehensive view of local, grassroots work, including elections, when it was presented. Later raised by some radicals to the status of religious principle, the prohibition against electoral work was to hamstring their efforts for decades.

Alan Jehlen's judgment was that "the local organizing forces were strong... but they lacked clarity and effective organization. White radicals had an oppor-tunity at the convention to lead a broad movement for local, radical organizing and they muffed it." (Jehlen, p. 7)

Despite the disaster in Chicago, I was optimistic. After nine months as a movement entrepreneur, I joined up as an organizer at the Boston Draft Resistance Group. I came home to what I saw then as the real work – building the local base at the grassroots level that could one day sustain a truly national campaign to change the country. I felt that Vietnam Summer, for all its faults, had turned around a situation that at the end of 1966 appeared to many, including leaders of the anti-war movement, as almost hopeless. Now in September 1967, we knew that the majority of the American public was open to an anti-war message, and that thousands of students were prepared to go door to door to end the war. The soil was fertile, the first seeds had been sown, and the only question left seemed to be who would reap the harvest.

IX

Resistance, 1967-68

RAMPARTS MAGAZINE PUBLISHED IN OCTOBER 1967 a dozen or so brief takes on the National Conference for New Politics Convention in Chicago. Mine concluded with this prediction: "People who jostled each other in the hallways of the Palmer House Hotel will learn to work together because survival demands it. Out of local work come national networks and will come, someday, a national movement. There is no other way." With somewhat desperate optimism, I threw myself into the work of the Boston Draft Resistance Group (BDRG).

Based on the success of Vietnam Summer, I knew that public opinion was turning in our direction. But by then I was convinced that the success of the anti-war movement depended on its support in working-class and minority communities, where the war hit hardest in terms of its economic consequences, lives disrupted, and lives lost. In twelve months spanning 1965-66, 85 percent of all men drafted had a high-school education or less. (See Barrie Thorne, "Resisting the Draft: An Ethnography of the Draft Resistance Movement," PhD Dissertation, Brandeis University, 1971, p. 5.)

The New England Resistance focused on encouraging students to engage in public and often dramatic acts of non-cooperation with the Selective Service System, such as burning draft cards, which could be punished by a term in prison. In contrast, the BDRG emphasized anti-war education and draft counseling in working-class communities. The young men involved in the New England Resistance were mainly college students. The BDRG was a disciplined and creative effort to build the anti-war movement in working-class and minority communities, and help young men from these vulnerable communities stay out of the army and out of jail.

The BDRG filled a one-story, one-room dilapidated building at 102 Columbia Street in Cambridge, in a low-income neighborhood just off Main Street. The office was often filled with draft counselors and young men seeking help, up to thirty a day. When I first arrived, I had to go through a rigorous training program so I could become a draft counselor as well.

By the time I starting working there, the BDRG was already a serious organization with a coherent program. Vernon Grizzard and Nick Egleson, both former national officers of SDS, had been working there for some time. Their influence had helped to foster a thoughtful, low-key, participatory atmosphere. They themselves spoke softly and encouraged everyone to participate in the meetings. Unlike most anti-draft groups women were leaders in the BDRG, and there were organizers and activists of color.

Ads in alternative papers, leafleting, canvassing in working-class and minority neighborhoods, and word of mouth helped bring in young men, sometimes with their family and girlfriends. But the most effective means we had of reaching working-class young men about to be drafted was the "early morning show."

The Early Morning Show

Every month each draft board in the Greater Boston area sent potential draftees to the Boston army base for a pre-induction physical. There their fitness for military service was ascertained by medical exams and various pencil-and-paper tests. They also might be interviewed by a psychiatrist or by military intelligence. If they were determined fit for military service they would probably be drafted soon. We wanted to have a dialogue with young men about the war and the draft at a time when those subjects were uppermost in their minds.

At the beginning of every month, a BDRG volunteer called each local draft board claiming to be living in that town but registered with a draft board far away. "My draft board asked me to call you up. When are you sending men from your town to their pre-induction physical? I want to go with them, instead of going back to my hometown halfway across the country."

From these phone calls, we made a schedule of when each board was sending pre-inductees to the base. Staff and volunteers would get up very early in the morning and drive out to talk with the potential draftees. When the thirty or so potential draftees showed up at their local draft board to be checked in and board the bus for the Boston army base, a carload or two of men and women from the BDRG would be there handing out leaflets with information about the war and legal options to avoid military service.

During the winter, the Boston area was still dark and cold when we piled out of our cars, leaflets in hand. The potential draftees were standing outside the building where the draft board was located, usually on the second floor of a run-down office building. People aren't that expressive early on a freezing morning, but usually they were surprised to see us and curious about why we had come. We talked to them one by one or in small groups before they went up the stairs. Then we talked to them again when they came down the stairs and were waiting outside for the bus to take them to the Boston army base.

We asked questions in a friendly and low-key way: What do you think about the war in Vietnam? Do you think it's right that you have to go fight there? Do you know there are alternatives to the draft? We listened to what they had to say. If we got a good discussion going, we would urge them to call us up and come by our office. If someone didn't want to talk, we respected that and moved on to the next person.

Our presence made the staff of the draft boards uptight and sometimes belligerent. Occasionally, they called the cops. I was arrested once, at the draft board in Roslindale, at that time one of Boston's all-white working-class neighborhoods. I was talking to the potential draftees when along came two cops called by the draft board. They arrested me and put me in a paddy wagon, with the usual kick in the ass while I climbed in. At the preliminary hearing at municipal court later on that day, two Boston police officers gave a great demonstration of "testilying." On the witness stand they testified that they had seen me forcibly blocking the main door of the small office building where the draft board was located, to prevent the thirty or so young men from going outside to get on the bus. Just imagine that! At the trial itself, my lawyer produced in court two pre-inductees who had been there that morning. They gave up a day's pay to come set the record straight. The judge threw out the case, and I was freed. The cops also walked free, of course, with big sheepish smirks on their faces.

Our draft counseling leveled the playing field and reduced the gap in risk between upper- and middle-class guys, who were almost never drafted, and low-income and working-class guys, who often were. When well-to-do kids wanted to avoid military service, they brought in letters from doctors, psychiatrists, or social workers documenting their disabilities or the hardships military service would bring to their families. Our counselors and panels of experts provided the same support to low-income registrants. If the counselee appeared to be a pacifist, we could help him write the personal statement he needed to attain conscientious objector status. We felt committed to support whatever position a counselee wanted to take. In general, we encouraged counselees to stick with the truth in their dealings with the Selective Service System, because most people hate to lie about themselves, and because facts can be more easily documented than fictions.

In the end, however, not everyone could qualify for a legal deferment. For those who didn't qualify for legal deferments but were strongly opposed to the war, I was the counselor of last resort. The program I helped run was known as the "horror show."

The Horror Show

My brother Albert's experience had first suggested to me how a "horror show" might work. Because he had gone to Cuba in violation of the state department's travel ban, he was targeted by the Selective Service System for immediate induction. When he reported for his pre-induction physical in Puerto Rico, they asked him if he was going to refuse induction into the army, certain to mean jail time in federal prison. "Hell no," he replied. "I *want* to serve in the army, to learn how to shoot a gun and blow up bridges so I can fight the bad people who are trying to take over the country."

When he wouldn't leave, they threw him out. Several months later, he received notice of his "1-Y" deferment, and never heard from the Selective Service System again.

The army was prepared to make some hard choices. Individual nonconformists or "fuck-ups" could be isolated and broken in basic training. But a man who appeared to be an organizer, a person who could build a group on the inside to challenge the legitimacy of the army and the war, was dangerous to them and had to be kept out.

Students or ex-students connected with the New England Resistance had disrupted their pre-induction physicals at the Boston army base by passing out leaflets and making speeches. My job was to design a program that would work for people who were new to the anti-war movement – to help them become part of a group that could support their efforts to stay out of the army and out of jail.

I chose carefully the candidates for the horror show. I met Herb when he came by the office. He was tall and good-looking with black hair – one of the black Irish. He had a notice for a pre-induction physical coming up in a couple of weeks. I talked with him for a while. There was no way he could qualify for conscientious objector status – he wasn't a pacifist and understandably didn't want to lie about his beliefs. After a couple of years of community college, he had started a training program to become a lineman for the phone company, which had given him a physical and found no problems. He didn't want to see a shrink. Not 4-F (physically or mentally unfit for military service) material, for sure. I had him read a short article from the Progressive Labor Party (PL) newspaper *Challenge* that described a "horror show" by one of their sympathizers who had come close to starting a riot at his pre-induction physical. I asked Herb whether he would be up for something like that. He said he would think about it.

Later on I dropped by his house – partly as a security precaution. I always wanted to know the people I was working with, who their friends were, and what they did in their daily lives. I met some of his friends and we talked more, particularly about how the army brainwashed draftees. He definitely got it. He told me how the phone company was trying to brainwash as much as train the newly hired linemen. The phone company and the army used the same methods, developing group solidarity against a common enemy, the "fuck-up."

Herb told me this story: "One day the trainer asked us to talk about what really annoys us in a co-worker. So one guy in the back says, 'you know what really freezes my shit is when the guy you're working with doesn't do his own job so you have to always cover for him.' The trainer picks up on that right away and says, 'Let's call the guy who freezes your shit a frostie. Now what can we do to keep frosties from fucking up our jobs at the phone company.' He used the term 'frostie' for weeks afterwards."

I felt Herb could pull off a horror show. When he decided to do it, we sat down and wrote a flyer that expressed in his words his reasons for opposing the war. We also outlined and practiced the speech he would use at the army base. Besides helping him prepare beforehand, my role was to go with him to the draft board, pass out his flyer, line up support on the bus, work up the crowd at the army base when he started his speech, and then use the chaos and confusion as cover to get the hell out before they arrested me.

The day of the pre-induction physical there was no problem getting inside the local draft board office. I wore a watch cap to cover my thinning hair, to help me pass for a pre-inductee. Getting on the bus, however, was always something of a challenge. The day's catch of potential draftees sat on benches in the office as the clerk called the roll. I knew that there would always be "no shows." The trick for me was to wait just long enough after a name was called to make sure he wasn't there, then take his name and place on the bus. When I said yes to "O'Leary," for example, there would be some snickers of surprise from the other registrants – they had gone to high school with "O'Leary" and knew that I wasn't he.

Once on the bus, the real work began – talking to the other registrants about the war and lining up their support for the coming action. Sometimes a person unknown to us before wanted a piece of the action, volunteering to play a role in disrupting the process, gambling that he too might be forbidden to join the army because of his bad attitude.

Horror shows developed more or less like this. When we arrived at the Boston army base, we would file quietly off the bus so as not to give the game away. The army viewed the first roll call and orientation at the pre-induction physical as crucial to socializing the draftees:

> "The attitudes of the pre-inductees toward military life will be influenced by the manner in which they are treated during pre-induction processing. All phases of pre-induction processing will be conducted in a dignified and professional manner." (U.S. Army Regulations 601-270, ch.2, p. 2, cited in Thorne, p. 241)

I hadn't yet read the regulations but I knew that during the roll call we had to hit them hard and disrupt their "process." I would start the leafleting, while the person I had come with talked to the other pre-inductees who had come on different buses. When the sergeant began his roll call and orientation, the potential draftee I had worked with would step forward and say something like the following:

"Before I go in the Army I want to know why we are in Vietnam. If we're there to protect freedom why—"

"You can't do that! Be quiet while the roll is called," the sergeant would interrupt.

"Let him speak! Let him speak!" several other inductees would holler.

"And after he finishes speaking I have some things to say," says the backup we had met on the bus.

"You can be court-martialed for this," the sergeant threatened.

"The hell we can. We're not in the army yet," says my guy, letting the sergeant have it.

"Then shut up before I break your goddamn neck!" the sergeant might scream, blowing his cool.

"Try it, you fat-assed motherfucker!" says the backup, seeing the sergeant had lost control.

Once the "horror show" was going good, I snuck out through the huge, empty warehouse next door. Herb got the letter he was looking for, barring him from the army, and I think the backup did too.

After a while, I began to hear that the army was looking for a "Mr. Big from PL" who was orchestrating disruptions at the base. College students with whom I had had no connection, arriving for their physical doped up or filled with lust for their fellow males, were being interrogated about their relationship to "Mr. Big from PL." "Who can this 'Mr. Big' be?" I wondered. Suddenly one day it occurred to me that I was "Mr. Big from PL," the person who gave pre-inductees *Challenge*, the Progressive Labor newspaper to read before their trip to the Boston army base.

I turned my mythological status to my own advantage. Once I was leaving a "horror show" through a large deserted warehouse on the base when a security guard caught up to me. He was an "old" guy, mid-forties maybe, short and stocky, with a very long billy club. "I've got you," he said, "come along."

"If you wave that club at me," I said, "I'll take it away from you and stick it right up your ass." Not a serious threat, of course. But he, suddenly aware of the danger of trying to bring in Mr. Big by himself, took off like the wind while I sauntered out through the back way.

Guerrilla tactics rely on popular support. The "horror show" depended for its success on the others on the bus headed for the Boston army base. Their attitude ranged from sympathetic neutrality to enthusiastic participation. They knew I was an infiltrator, but no one ever reported me to the officials of the draft board. No one ever sided with the officers during the "horror show" at the base. By late 1967 the working-class draftees from the Greater Boston area, though for the most part not yet ready for public protest, no longer supported the war.

The Boston Draft Resistance Group was a remarkable organization. Staff and volunteers became professionals committed to laying out the options and supporting as best we could the decisions of each potential draftee we met. The BDRG was also a remarkable community. The work could be heartbreaking. Sometimes guys lost their nerve and let themselves be drafted when they needn't have been. We mourned with the communities where we were working the predictable casualties of the war. We took risks all the time at the early morning and horror shows. The young men we were reaching out to had to trust us, and we had to trust each other.

We relied on the group. The clear moral vision that brought us together in this work was the foundation for a great sense of common purpose and love for each other. Like the "beloved community" of the early civil rights movement, our "beloved community" was held together by trust, a feeling that each person in the group was prepared to do the moral thing regardless of the personal consequences.

Then after the work came the parties, wild with drinking, singing, and stories. I remember that spring lying on the grass with thirty others while a half-gallon of Scotch was passed from mouth to mouth until it was drained to the bottom. Without the love and joy we could not have sustained the effort for as long as we did.

❦ ❦ ❦

What I Learned at the Boston Draft Resistance Group

- What the soldiers, their families, and the communities from which they come think about the war is crucial to the success of an anti-war movement.
- To succeed, the anti-war movement must figure out ways to challenge the process by which the military seeks to mold the minds of new recruits, soldiers, and reserves.
- The anti-war movement must find creative ways to reach out to and engage soldiers and potential soldiers.

Vietnam GI

Vietnam GI, published in Chicago by Jeff Sharlet and David Komatsu, reached out to the most important constituency of any anti-war movement, the troops. *Vietnam GI* covered everything from combat in Vietnam, strikes by enlisted men at army bases, lying politicians, brutality in military prisons, and the day-to-day struggle between ordinary soldiers who wanted to stay alive and officers who wanted them to risk their lives in a dirty war. The paper had headlines like "... he threw his rifle at the commanding officer ..." (January 1969) or "We had 11 of us left now out of 237 people" (June 1969). One of my favorite stories was

"Phucatruc" (August 1968), about how the soldiers in a transportation company manipulated army regulations to keep two-thirds of its trucks out of service until the officers met their demands.

Jeff himself was a Vietnam Vet, giving him great insight and credibility in carrying out the work. Jeff had learned Vietnamese at the Army Language School in Monterey, California. In 1963, he was sent to Vietnam. There he spent a lot of time talking with South Vietnamese officers, soldiers, students, Viet Cong agents, and former French soldiers in the colonial army. By the end of his tour of duty, "he'd put a lot of the pieces together" (*Vietnam GI* special edition in his memory). Coming back to the States, he went to college and became the chair of his local SDS chapter. But he became disillusioned with the student movement's "snotty attitude" towards working people.

Jeff had started *Vietnam GI* in 1967, and he worked like crazy from that moment on to build the paper and the movement it served, always on the road looking for correspondents and distributors, people inside and outside the military who would pass the paper on to GIs. I helped raise money for the paper and distribute it around the Boston area. When the work was done, Jeff and I loved to sit around and drink beer and talk politics. We became close friends.

Organizers at the BDRG distributed *Vietnam GI* every chance they got. One day a man in civilian clothes came by the office and told me he was a soldier at Fort Devens. He said he could help me sneak into the base and show me some great places to distribute the paper. I violated my own rule and went off on a mission with someone I had just met and didn't know. He took me down a country road beside the base where we crawled through a fence. No sooner were we on the base than the military police drove up. They took me to an office for interrogation and ordered me to sit down at a large old-fashioned wooden desk to await the arrival of the military intelligence officer in charge. On the desk, I noticed a metal box labeled "Forbidden to come on the base" and filled with three-by-five cards. "Boy, are these guys stupid!" I thought. Whenever the guard wasn't looking, I would take a bunch of cards out of the box and drop them in the wastebasket or hide them around the desk.

Then the officer in charge came in and caught me doing my dirty work. He screamed at me. On the wall, I had noticed a plaque commemorating his service in Korea. To impress the soldier who had been arrested with me, who was being held in the next room I thought, I asked the officer how many babies he'd raped while serving in Korea. He raised his fist and lunged at me. We squared off. Before the fists started flying the MPs stepped between us. I was taken to the gate and thrown off the base.

When I got home and cooled off, I went over the incident carefully in my mind. Was my arrest the moment I slipped on the base a coincidence? Or was I set up by the soldier who had come to the BDRG and brought me onto the base, and whom I had tried so hard to impress by insulting the officer? Was my guide actually a military intelligence officer? Had they thought that if they lured me on the base and arrested me that that would be intimidating? If so, it hadn't worked. But, I had been stupid to get busted – I hadn't taken the time to get to know the "soldier" and his friends. I was lucky to get away with as little damage done to me as I did. Of course, I never saw the "soldier" again.

The Tet Offensive Breaks U.S. Morale and the Viet Cong

In 1968, Tet, the lunar New Year, was celebrated by the Vietnamese on January 31. That evening the Viet Cong, violating a truce they had pledged to observe, attacked over one hundred cities and towns, including Saigon, shifting the war from the countryside to the supposedly impregnable urban areas. (Karnow, p. 536) Nineteen Viet Cong commandoes attacked the U.S. Embassy in downtown Saigon. The war exploded on U.S. television screens right in front of all of us.

> "... [D]ead bodies lay amid the rubble and the rattle of automatic gunfire as dazed American soldiers and civilians ran back and forth trying to flush out the assailants. One man raced past the camera to a villa behind the chancery building to toss a pistol up to Colonel George Jacobson on the second floor. The senior embassy official shot the last of the enemy commandos as he crept up the stairs." (Karnow, p. 539)

No one watching the television news in 1968 as I was can forget the summary execution of a Viet Cong captive by General Loan, head of the South Vietnamese national police.

"He wore black shorts and a checkered sports shirt, and his hands were bound behind him. The soldiers marched him up to Loan, who drew his revolver and waved the bystanders away. Without hesitation, Loan stretched out his right arm, placed the short snout of the weapon against the prisoner's head, and squeezed the trigger. The man grimaced – then, in almost slow motion, his legs crumpled beneath him as he seemed to sit down backward, blood gushing from his head as it hit the pavement." (Karnow, p.542)

The Viet Cong captured for a time Saigon's main radio station and tried to capture the national palace. (Karnow, p. 540) The Viet Cong and North Vietnamese troops captured the imperial city of Hue in central Vietnam and held out there until the old citadel was finally recaptured by U.S. troops on February 24.

In November 1967, General Westmoreland, the commander of the U.S. Forces in Vietnam, had been brought home by President Johnson to shore up support for the war.

"... [H]e promised a National Press Club audience that 'we have reached an important point where the end comes into view.' And he defied the Communists to stage a massive attack. 'I hope they try something,' he told a *Time* interviewer, 'because we are looking for a fight.'" (Karnow, p. 527)

With the Tet Offensive, the truth of the war, brutal and unwinnable, was revealed to a broader spectrum of the American public than ever before. When the enemy was able to attack from one end of the country to another, the administration's lies about success made the setback all the more apparent.

For me, however, there was a dimension to the Tet Offensive beyond what it revealed about the administration's lies and the terrible suffering of our soldiers. As I saw the story unfold on television and in the newspapers, it seemed obvious to me that the Viet Cong had made a terrible miscalculation. The popular, anti-U.S. uprising in the southern cities that the Viet Cong seemed to have anticipated was simply not happening. Without popular uprisings, local revolutionaries, developed over decades of clandestine organizing and guerilla warfare, stood their ground alone in the cities; instead of falling back into the jungles, they fought in the streets, and were slaughtered. It will take a generation to replace such people, I thought.

The decimation of the Viet Cong was terrible. I didn't "support" the Viet Cong – who ruled southern Vietnam was for the people there to determine. But I identified with the Viet Cong in a way I did not with the Communists of the North. The Viet Cong were revolutionaries rooted in their communities, fighting to build a more egalitarian society free from foreign domination. The Viet Cong government, the National Liberation Front, although committed to unity with the North, was also committed to representing the enormous diversity of southern political and religious forces opposed to U.S. intervention. The Viet Cong had only turned to violence as a last resort, when the U.S.-backed Diem government began tracking them down like animals. If I had been a Vietnamese living in the South, I would have supported the Viet Cong and the National Liberation Front. The destruction of the Viet Cong brought home the utter futility of the war.

Interviews after the war's end confirmed my suspicions then. In an interview with Stanley Karnow, General Tran Do, one of North Vietnam's most distinguished soldiers, made this concession: "In all honesty, we didn't achieve our main objective, which was to spur uprisings throughout the south. Still, we inflicted heavy casualties on the Americans and their puppets, and that was a big gain for us. As for making an impact in the United States, it had not been our intention – but it turned out to be a fortunate result." (Karnow, p. 558)

Another Communist figure was more blunt: "'We lost our best people,' she said mournfully, recalling that Vietcong military units composed mostly of indigenous southerners had borne the brunt of the fighting, and suffered the heaviest casualties." (Karnow, p. 547)

The decimation of the Viet Cong brought no consolation to the Johnson administration. Viet Cong units destroyed in the Tet Offensive were replaced within weeks by soldiers from the North. By destroying the Viet Cong as an effective force, the U.S. had simply brought about what it said it had intervened to prevent, a South Vietnam ruled by the North. (See Karnow, p. 256 for a similar view.) As Truong Nhu Tang, the Viet Cong Minister of Justice put it:

> "When the time came... we assumed power in South Vietnam, not as a government constituted and guaranteed by international agreements, drawing on various sources of domestic and foreign support – but riding on the back of the North Vietnamese Army's tiger; precarious and tentative guests in our own house." (Truong Nhu Tang, *A Vietcong Memoir*, p. 218)

Backed by the Soviet Union and China, the North Vietnamese were prepared, to use the rhetoric of President Kennedy, to "bear any burden and pay any price" to expel the foreigners from their country. Tet may have broken my heart, but U.S. morale was also broken, irretrievably. In Washington, there were high officials smart enough to realize that the game was up. Clark Clifford, the secretary of defense who replaced Robert McNamara, presented the issue to a cabinet meeting on March 4 as follows:

> "Do you continue down the same road of more troops, more guns, more planes, more ships? Do you go on killing more Vietcong and more North Vietnamese? As we build up our forces, they build up theirs. The result is that we are now fighting at a higher level of intensity.... We seem to have a sinkhole. We put in more, they match it." (Quoted in Karnow, p. 569)

Obviously, I was not privy at the time to the disarray in the Johnson administration, nor was the American public. But the public grasped the fact that we were losing the war, and President Johnson paid the price with his political future.

> "During the six weeks following the initial Communist attacks, public approval of his overall performance dropped from 48 percent to 36 percent – and, more dramatically, endorsement for his handling of the war fell from 40 percent to 26 percent." (Karnow, p. 559)

In early March, Senator Eugene McCarthy, running against a sitting president of his own party, received only 300 fewer votes in the New Hampshire

Democratic Primary than Lyndon Johnson did. A few days later Bobby Kennedy announced his candidacy, and by the end of March Lyndon Johnson had announced, "I shall not seek, and I will not accept, the nomination of my party."

After the war, General Westmoreland claimed that the distorted press and TV coverage of the Tet Offensive turned the Communist military defeat into "psychological victory" for the enemy. Holding the press responsible for the defeat in Vietnam was a variation of the familiar right-wing scapegoating: "we'd have won if the press or the anti-war movement hadn't stabbed us in the back." But in fact, Vietnamese victory wasn't based on psychology but on reality. After the decimation of the Viet Cong, the North Vietnamese quickly showed they could make good the loss. The Vietnamese had the resources and the will to drive us out, regardless of the cost, and they did. To cover their rear ends, generals could, and did, ask for hundreds of thousand more men, and even nuclear weapons, so that later they could say "We would have won, if only...," as if "stopping the Communists in Vietnam" was worth risking a world war.

The reality was the war was lost. Unfortunately, the American political figures that could deal with reality were murdered in the coming months.

The Vietnamese had defeated the U.S forces, but it took the anti-war opposition five years to get us out of Vietnam. More American soldiers in Vietnam were killed in the five years after the Tet Offensive than before. With no way to win and no will to get out, keeping our soldiers in Vietnam to kill and be killed seemed to politicians like the path of least resistance.

Prolonged strategic bankruptcy, however, carries with it a certain price. Ordered to risk death in a pointless war, and moreover a lost one, our soldiers were in a most difficult situation. Abandoned by the country's leaders, they had to make hard decisions about the circumstances under which they would, or would not, risk their lives.

Trying to force soldiers to do something they don't want to do can be a very risky business. After all, they too have guns. According to Chris Hedges, author of *What Every Person Should Know About War*, more than six hundred U.S. officers were killed by enlisted men before the war was over. When the army started to fall apart, the leaders finally found a way to bring them home.

X

Storms Are on the Ocean, 1968

I WAS SITTING IN A beat-up old car in front of the SDS national office, on the second floor of a rundown building at 1608 West Madison Street, on Chicago's Near West Side on April 4, 1968, in the late afternoon. Mike James, an organiz-er with JOIN (Jobs or Income Now) in Chicago, and I were in the front seat smoking cigarettes and disagreeing about Dr. Martin Luther King Jr.

Mike worshipped Dr. King. I respected Dr. King and was extremely grateful to him for his support in launching Vietnam Summer. But like my friends in SNCC, I had a number of reservations about King. He seemed too close to the Kennedys. He supported the use of force by the state police and National Guard in putting down "riots" in African American neighborhoods. His organizing through the Black ministerial alliances was top down rather than bottom up, and some of his people, like the minister in the red Cadillac who had tried to get "no show" jobs out of Vietnam Summer, were dishonest. Mike knew the crooked minister well, but nothing I said could shake his faith in Dr. King.

Then news came over the car radio that Dr. King had been shot and killed. We were both stunned. We assumed, along with millions of others, that his kill-er was white and that the assassination was part of a racist conspiracy. I sat there for a moment, realizing that everything critical of Dr. King I had just said was irrelevant to what needed to be done now. While many African Americans disagreed with Dr. King around one issue or another, he was their national leader. His murder was an assault on the whole Black community – African Americans were not about to take this assassination lying down.

An apocalyptic vision unfolded in my mind's eye. It would be another Tet Offensive, but hopeless from the very beginning. Black communities would rebel, even though they lacked sufficient power and support to resist the repression that would inevitably follow. The "riots" would provide the government with the excuse to send in the National Guard, and perhaps even the army, to put down the rebellions and crush the movement by killing as many Black activists as they could get their hands on.

The response of SDS had to be to mobilize white opinion and to organize demonstrations that interposed sympathetic whites and the media between the National Guard and the ghettoes. This is the only way, I thought, to make a real difference in this unfolding tragedy. But the SDS national office, in the Near West Side of Chicago, was a dangerous place to be. If the police or the National Guard attacked this neighborhood, largely African American, we would be easy to spot because we were white. Killing us could be a bonus outcome on top of whatever damage they could do to the Black movement.

I put all that aside. There was a job to do, a job that had to be done here in the national office, the communications center where the lists were. I bought a quart bottle of Scotch, and bounded up the stairs to the office.

There were four or five beat-up old desks in a large room. The national secretary sat at his desk, rubbing his cowboy moustache, saying nothing, staring off into space, too preoccupied perhaps with his own mortality to say anything. "Too much acid'll get you eventually," I thought.

Cathy Archibald was also there. Fortunately, she was disciplined and tough minded. We had worked together setting up Vietnam Summer. Now she was the office manager. After a brief discussion, we agreed on what needed to be done. Cathy mobilized the rest of the staff to help us call every chapter leader and contact around the country. The national secretary disappeared and did not return. Each one of us sat down at a desk with a phone. I passed the Scotch around and we got to work.

People were grateful we called. Isolation at such a traumatic time was a terrible burden. SDS people needed to be in touch with someone who could help them put what was going on into a context they could understand. Better yet, we were proposing a course of action that made sense and gave them a reason to pull their own people together to organize public demonstrations that might make a difference.

Most SDS people were ready to try to do what needed to be done. But one Progressive Labor member leading a Boston-area SDS chapter assured me in her soft Southern accent that the rebellions I saw coming wouldn't happen, because Black people had already seen through Dr. King. Since no one supported him now, there would be no riots. She's living on another planet, I thought, and moved on to the next call.

At about one o'clock in the morning, the calling started to wind down. We had accomplished a great deal, and we felt close for having worked so hard together. But an apocalyptic mood still reigned in the office. We knew the riots would start tomorrow and that everyone in or near Black communities was in danger. Including ourselves. I had drunk most of the Scotch during the calling, with, remarkably, no effect on the intense alertness I felt. It was a relief to relax after all that effort, but relaxing did not make the fear go away.

The next morning Cathy sent me out for supplies – soft drinks, potato chips, and the other junk food that the workers at the national office lived on. I went to a small grocery store nearby. There were a lot of people in the store when I arrived, but few came in afterwards. When I got up to the register I saw why. A group of about a dozen men had gathered outside, and three of them were rehearsing the moves they would make to shatter the large front window. I was the last person in line at the register. I paid for the groceries and headed for the door. As I walked outside, the men who had been getting ready shattered the glass, and the people with them prepared to go in. One African American man about my age, obviously in charge, turned to me with a friendly smile. Reaching a hand across the racial divide, he asked me, the only white person on the street, "Why the fuck did you pay for all that stuff, when we would have given it to you for free?"

I went back to the office with the supplies. By the early afternoon, I was restless and wanted to move on. The protests were unfolding more slowly than I had imagined. Cathy had the national office under control, and she had enough ties to the neighborhood to assure the safety of the staff, if they needed to leave the office to escape the police. Perhaps I could do more in Boston.

When I heard that leaders of the Chicago movement were gathering in an office downtown, I decided that was where I should be. I had come to Chicago to raise money for trainings to share what we had learned in the BRDG with other draft resistance groups. I put the clothes I had been wearing in a briefcase, and put on the suit and tie I had brought for my meetings with donors. When I hit the street, I realized that I had made a big mistake. Older people had stocked up on supplies and gone home. The streets were filled with young African American men, angry and hostile. With my suit and tie and briefcase, I wasn't just an ordinary white person, I was "the (hated) man." Sticking out the way I did, I was a prime candidate to get my ass kicked.

But I was already a block or so from the office, and it seemed more dangerous to turn back than to go forward. Every time I passed a group of young men, threats and abuse rained down on me. No eye contact – I kept my head down and my feet moving. Getting out of there in one piece was the priority. This was no time to stop and try to explain what a good fellow I really am.

Fortunately, a city bus came by. When I got on board, I saw to my relief that the passengers looked largely middle-aged and headed for work. No one took any notice of me. I was the only white person on the bus, and I had become invisible: people were talking quietly about the situation, as if I were not there. An African American woman said, somewhat absently, to no one in particular, but loud enough for me to hear, "He was their best friend, and they killed him. I wonder why?"

When the bus arrived in downtown Chicago, I got off and walked to the tall office building where the meeting was being held. Many movement "heavies" were there: Clark Kissinger, Rennie Davis, a founder of JOIN, and a number of others I recognized but didn't know very well. With all of us there, it seemed like we should come up with a grand plan to respond to the terrible crisis. We talked for a while at cross purposes, and paced around the room, looking out the window as plumes of smoke began to rise above Chicago. Heroic visions of death on the barricades were replaced by the cold reality of being in a room with a bunch of isolated white guys wasting each other's time.

Then Clark Kissinger, always fast on his feet, got up and said, somewhat proudly, that he had an organization in his neighborhood to go mobilize and he was going. Then he walked straight out the door and was gone. It occurred to me that that was my cue to leave also, go home, and do something useful. I left for the airport and arrived in Boston in the late evening. The next morning I found out that SDS had responded to the call, and much was happening. This allowed me to be a participant rather than a leader, which suited me just fine, because I was totally exhausted.

African Americans responded with outrage at Dr. King's murder:

> "As many 'civil disorders' took place in the twenty-five days after King's death as in all the previous year, with more arrests and injuries. 'Violence in varying degrees, ranging from minor disturbances to major riots, erupted in more than 100 cities,' according to the ever-watchful J. Edgar Hoover. 'The April outbreaks and the subsequent disorders resulted in more than 60 deaths, injuries to thousands of persons, and millions of dollars in property damage.'"
> (Sale, p. 424)

I was certainly overly apocalyptic about how the government would use "civil disturbances" as a pretext to destroy the movement. But sixty people were killed, and thousands injured. "Federal troops were called into Wilmington, Delaware, Baltimore, Chicago, and the nation's capital.... Jerome Skolnick, in his report to the National Violence Commission, determined: 'Never before in this country has such a massive military response been mounted against racial disorder.'" (Sale, p. 424)

I was most proud, of course, of the response from SDS, protesting the assassination of Dr. King and demanding that the police and National Guard stay out of Black communities.

> "Some two dozen black colleges and more than a hundred white institutions mounted protests led by SDS chapters in many places. SDS mounted or participated in demonstrations in several major cities: Rennie Davis, Clark Kissinger and Noel Ignatin, and others

organized marches in Chicago; SDS chapters and Resistance workers led a massive rally in Boston; regional SDS people picketed the
White House.... Detroit radicals, many from Wayne State SDS held
a memorial demonstration; and in New York a conglomerate of militants turned up in Times Square...." (Sale, p. 424)

This same spring of 1968 in France "civil disturbances" broke out, involving
millions of workers and students. Many French observers at the time thought
these disturbances threatened the constitutional order of the Fifth Republic.
However, in contrast to both the U.S. experience and their own bloody history,
no protestors were killed by the "forces of order" in the entire Paris region
in 1968. Changes in police training and procedure had made this dramatic
improvement possible. (See Jean-Paul Brunet, *Charonne*, pp. 299-301)

Bobby Kennedy Murdered

The night he won the crucial California presidential primary, June 5, 1968,
a deranged Palestinian murdered Bobby Kennedy. I did not fully grasp what
a catastrophe this was for the country. Maybe my lack of awareness was due
to overload. Our soldiers dying, brutal police and National Guard incursions
into Black neighborhoods, the destruction of the Viet Cong, and the assassination of Dr. King were all weighing heavily on my mind. I just shrugged my
shoulders and kept going, doing what I could do at the Boston Draft Resistance
Group.

Was Bobby Kennedy's murder a turning point in U.S. history? With his
money, connections, and charisma, no doubt he could have beaten Richard
Nixon. Would Bobby then have dealt directly with the Vietnamese Communists
and found a formula to get us out of Vietnam, or would he have fallen back on
the unreflective anti-Communism of his brother's day? Would he have kept the
promises of his high-energy campaigning in African American and Latino
neighborhoods and carried through the civil rights revolution, or would he have
reverted to the Bobby Kennedy of 1962, the cautious little rich boy who didn't
want to rock the boat? At the time, I didn't trust him. Now I think that in 1967

and 1968 he may have burned all the bridges leading back to the old Bobby. The transformation of his brother Teddy from a careless young man to one of the few truth tellers in the U.S. Senate makes me think it's possible.

Bobby Kennedy's murder was a turning point, for the worse. The African American community was able to replace Martin Luther King with new leaders. But the Bobby Kennedy some on the left hoped for has not been replaced.

Ellwood Comes to Visit

One day "Ellwood" turned up at my house. He wanted to speak to me in private. He had run a field office for Vietnam Summer, and I had seen him once or twice when he came to Cambridge for meetings. I remembered him with great fondness. But he was not the same cheerful confident person I had known before. He looked tired and nervous, desperate in a word.

Quickly he came to the point. "What do you know about organizing armed resistance?" he asked. "Black people can't take any more of the police attacks without shooting back."

"Nothing really," I said. "I know how to shoot a gun, but that's about it. There are some Black leaders around here who know a lot more than I do about what you're asking about. I can set up a meeting if you want." Then I said to myself, "Yeah, that is the best you can do. And you, John, are a chicken-shit coward. God, let him be careful." Then I set up the meeting.

Ellwood had always struck me as the most careful, sensible person on earth. That it had come to this, for him, was a measure of how little hope there was among Black activists that a peaceful resolution to the race war they saw on the streets of their communities was possible.

I never carried a gun, much less intended to use one, except to defend my home. But once I did spend an afternoon with some Black and white activists wandering through the park where the National Guard had gathered for its last assault on Roxbury in Boston's Black community several months before. We were looking for positions from which the community could be defended from assaults by the National Guard in the park. I knew I would fight to defend my own home. Would I fight to defend theirs? I hoped not to be put to that test.

Tom Hayden's Trip

Various plans for demonstrating at the Democratic Convention had been circulating since the beginning of the year. After the murder of Bobby Kennedy in June 1968, most people in the movement saw little good coming out of the convention. Vice President Hubert Humphrey, committed to the war policies of President Lyndon Johnson, was almost certain to win the Democratic nomination for president over Eugene McCarthy, the remaining peace candidate. Mayor Richard Daley ran the city and had been an ally of the Kennedy family. Now he was with Johnson and Humphrey. Laying down very restrictive conditions on demonstrations around the convention, he threatened that the police would deal harshly with anyone who crossed the line. With Chicago's reputation for police violence, Mayor Daley's threats had to be taken seriously.

Tom Hayden, one of the New Left's most influential thinkers, writers, and leaders, took a trip around the country in the early summer to build support for his plan to demonstrate at the Democratic National Convention in late August. A number of leaders of the movement in Boston gathered in a house off Rindge Avenue in Cambridge to hear what he had to say. Tom stood at the front of a sun-drenched room and laid out his proposal to about twenty men and women sitting on sofas and chairs in front of him. "Whatever happens we must be in Chicago to stand up for peace and justice," he said. "If Mayor Daley won't let us demonstrate at the convention site, then we must find ways to disrupt the Democratic Convention and shut down the city." The people I talked with afterwards didn't like the proposal, left the meeting in a hurry, and as far as I know had nothing further to do with the demonstrations at the convention.

Tom was playing a complicated game. He showed his disparate allies only the cards he wanted each to see, while the hand as a whole was held very close to his chest. Before Bobby's assassination he had played the role of key intermediary between the Kennedys and the movement, planning a much more respectable event. With Kennedy's death, the plan had changed. Now to get the anarchist "kids" to come to Chicago he embraced Jerry Rubin and Abby Hoffmann, founders of the Yippies, the "Youth International Party," who threatened to "fuck on the beaches" and "burn Chicago to the ground." (See James Miller, *Democracy in the Streets: From Port Huron to the Siege of Chicago*, p. 286.) To get the pacifists and the traditional peace movement to come, he promised to try to obtain permits for large and legal demonstrations, knowing that there was little chance Daley would agree. To the militants like Bill Ayers, he promised a first step towards the guerilla war of their fantasies, forgetting to mention that no guerilla war could succeed without support from the people. To us in Boston, he suggested that the demonstrations could help elect Gene McCarthy.

This is the way Bill Ayers, later to become a leader of the Weathermen, heard Hayden in a pitch to him and his affinity group in a private meeting after a public rally in Ann Arbor, Michigan. Here he quotes Hayden:

> "This demonstration has the potential like nothing we've done be-
> fore to expose the face of the enemy, to strip him naked, to force
> him to reveal himself as violent, brutal, totalitarian, and evil. It will
> be difficult – and dangerous, taunting the monster, stabbing him in
> his most exposed and vulnerable places, but it's got to be done."
> (Bill Ayers, *Fugitive Days*, p.122)

The "guerillas" would come for the opportunities to test their mettle in the streets of Chicago. Rubin and Hoffmann, shameless self-promoters, were in because they would thrive in the chaos and media attention. The pacifist leaders would go along, however reluctantly, because national mobilizations were essential to their strategy. Rank and file protestors would come with no idea of what was in store for them.

My negative feelings about Hayden's plan divided the Boston Draft Resistance Group. No one defended Hayden's plans. But I upset his friends when I attacked his plans as irresponsible to the other staff and volunteers. Did they think that if we kept a discreet silence this mess would go away? Movement leaders had to live up to our responsibilities. Silence was, I thought, a form of complicity in the execution of an irresponsible plan.

One Selfless Act

I drove to Chicago with several other people. On the outskirts of the city, the police pulled over our car and ordered us to follow them to the station. At the station several officers explained in a calm, straightforward way that if we broke the rules, they would beat the living shit out of us. Then, they let us go. I couldn't help noticing that each police officer carried two pistols: a large caliber automatic and a smaller caliber revolver. "These fuckers are serious," I thought. "One to pistol-whip you with and one to shoot you if you fight back."

The word had gotten out that this was a good demonstration to stay away from, and only about ten thousand people participated. As a leader of the movement, I felt responsibility towards the naïve who might have been sucked in. If I could persuade some of the demonstrators who were already there to stay away from dangerous and stupid events, the trip to Chicago would be worth it. I knew it was a bad plan, but in the end, I went to Chicago.

As soon as I arrived I went to one of the "movement centers" that had been set up to orient people coming in from out of town. I found myself in a church basement in a middle-class neighborhood. I hoped that the meeting there would be a good place to begin to put forward my point of view: we should demonstrate as a way to communicate with Chicago residents and the American people, to broaden, not narrow, the appeal of the anti-war movement. We should carry signs that had something comprehensible to say and stick to large daytime demonstrations, when the media could see us. Large groups marching during the day, like the upcoming march of thousands of striking Chicago transit workers, were less likely to be attacked. But if we were attacked in daylight, at least the media would be there to make our pain a public issue.

A hundred or so white people of all ages gathered at this "movement center," sitting down on the floor. Some were teenagers out for adventure, but some were middle-aged people, pacifists perhaps. A few looked like movement people who might be connected with Hayden's operation.

Just as the meeting was about to begin, two young men came running in and shouted, "They're beating our people. They're beating our people. Everyone out in the streets."

"This could be a setup by the leaders, to get people out into the streets," I thought. "If people are not being beaten yet, they will be soon." I immediately got up and spoke urging caution and common sense. Night marches were illegal. We were a small group in a neighborhood far from the center of things. What could we accomplish now that couldn't be better done tomorrow?

There was also a New Left film crew there. They had been doing some film biographies of movement leaders, myself included, and had shot some footage of me in Cambridge and on the North Shore where Frinde's family lived. When I stood up to speak, the lights went on, and the film crew pointed the camera in my direction. But when they realized what I had to say, the lights and camera went off. I never saw or heard from them again. I had a short run that year as a movement hero. By criticizing the movement leaders to "outsiders," at the event itself, I had crossed the line.

In any event, excitement and curiosity overcame my words of caution, and young and old alike filed quickly out the door and into the streets. I was one of the last to leave the movement center, and thus I found myself at the back of the march. Then three young men wearing football helmets and carrying clubs appeared, as if by magic, at the front of the line, now about a block and a half long. "There's nothing spontaneous about this march," I thought; "the whole thing was set up in advance, with 'they're beating our people' as a bit of theater to get people out into the streets." Off we went, with me tagging along at the tail end.

The cops appeared soon enough, about a dozen or so of them. The three "street fighters" were immediately knocked to the ground and hauled away. The marchers panicked and ran, as well they should. I jogged up to the front of the line to buy a little time for the old and slow to get away.

I knew that if directly challenged by a weaker opponent, like the three young men in football helmets, the police would attack. But cops don't like to get hurt either. Over the years, I had learned that a serious, calm, and alert demeanor, strong but not directly threatening, causes cops to hesitate. When I got to the front of the line, directly facing the police, about six or seven yards away, I began to walk backwards, slowly. As I anticipated, the police slowed to my pace. As I backed down the street, I noticed a young African American man alongside me, but on the other side of the street, playing the police the same way I was.

"What the hell's he doing here," I thought, "risking his neck for a bunch of white people from out of town?" Together we walked slowly backwards for another half block, keeping a sharp eye on the police.

Suddenly a cop rushed forward. Bam! The young man hit the cop on the helmet with a metal bar he had concealed under his sleeve. The cop staggered back. The game was over. The remaining police charged, and the young man and I ran for our lives. Fortunately, by then, the rest of the marchers had gotten away. I got away too, but I never saw the young man again. I prayed he made it. His was the most selfless act I saw all week.

Later that week I did march with the striking Chicago transit workers. It was great – Black and white, men and women. Some of their marshals had real heft – the police were not going to mess with us here. The march got some attention in the media, but not as much as the Yippies did.

The Whole World Was Watching

In the late afternoon of Wednesday, August 28, 1968, a few hours before the Democratic Party nominated Hubert Humphrey for president, I was standing on the sidewalk by the Hilton Hotel, where most of the delegates were staying, talking to a journalist I knew. A prominent pacifist leader began to gather a rally there in the street, alongside the hotel. I'd had enough of the whole mess, and I didn't want to join the rally. Down the street, at the end of the block, were about a hundred or so police.

The police began to advance, first a walk, then a jog. On the streets for a few days, I knew what step three was – a wild, club-swinging charge. At the very instant that the police began to jog, the pacifist leader asked the demonstrators to sit down. Incredibly, they did.

I was horrified. Should I deck the pacifist leader, grab his microphone, and yell for the demonstrators to run for their lives? I hesitated for several seconds, paralyzed by fear. The police line hit the demonstrators like a tidal wave, knocking them right and left. Because they were sitting down, it was simple for the police to club them on the head before dragging them away by the hair. It was a revolting display of raw brutality. I continued to stand there on the sidewalk.

Those demonstrators who were able to get away retreated into the park nearby. At least there were trees to hide behind, and rocks and garbage to throw. As the sun began to set and a cloud of tear gas floated over the scene, war whoops came from the park and an eerie chant I had never heard before, "The whole world is watching, the whole world is watching."

I had witnessed this horrible event and done nothing. Ashamed of myself and not wanting to remain powerless, I decided to go into the hotel and talk to the McCarthy campaign volunteers about what I had just seen, and recruit them to work with SDS when their schools reopened shortly.

Because I was fairly well dressed, I had no trouble getting past security and into the hotel. I walked up to the mezzanine and looked out over the crowd, trying to figure out where I should go next. Down below me I saw a police captain, a big beefy man with golden epaulettes, holding a photo and talking to another officer. The captain looked up, photo in hand, and pointed me out to the other officer. Suddenly I found I could read lips, and those lips I was reading were saying, "Get that motherfucker!" I took off running.

Several months earlier a left-wing newspaper had obtained and published the FBI's list of key New Left activists, about forty or so of us, Black and white. I was pleased with myself to have made the list, even more so because, unlike most others on the list, there was no photograph of me to distribute. Organizers were supposed to work through others, I believed, and keep themselves and their pictures out of the newspapers, out of the public eye.

If you were a New Left organizer, the Hilton Hotel in Chicago on the night of August 28 was a bad place to have your cover blown. I knew I had to find a place to hide, and fast.

I dashed into an elevator. There I found an acquaintance from long-ago SDS national meetings. We had disagreed in a friendly way about many things, including his commitment to the Democratic Party. Now I was really glad to see him here in the Hilton, an official delegate to the Democratic National Convention, with a room in the hotel. His shoulders slumped when he saw me, and he looked grimly ahead, facing the elevator door. He knew I wasn't a delegate and that my presence here with him meant trouble. Quickly, I confided in him my situation, holding on tightly to his jacket to let him know I wasn't leaving him until he found me a place to hide – his safety and well-being now depended on mine, he had to understand that. After a little hesitation, he gave me his room key. I went to his room, lay down on the thick rug, and fell fast asleep.

Shortly after midnight I woke up, figured that the coast was clear, and went downstairs again to find the McCarthy volunteers. I found several dozen of them in a large room watching television, in shock at the events of the day, including the mayhem I had witnessed just outside the hotel, which was being broadcast again and again. There I found out about another incident, when the police had leapt through the broken windows of the Haymarket Lounge on the ground floor of the hotel and beaten all the customers they could get their hands on.

I was too intimidated to stay in the Hilton. After a few tentative tries at conversation, I left the hotel and departed for Cambridge the next day.

The whole world may not have been watching, but a big part of the American public learned about the brutality of the Chicago police by watching the repression on television. The Walker Report to the National Commission on the Causes and Prevention of Violence concluded that it was a "police riot." (See Gitlin, p. 326.) What I saw and experienced was not primarily a riot, but police carrying out orders, albeit with considerable ferocity. To this day, I am amazed that only one person was killed.

I was grateful that the casualties had been fewer than I had feared. But I returned angrier than before I left. The police had controlled the demonstrations. *Agents provocateurs* were everywhere. Time and time again, I saw guys with big arms and tattoos, pretending to be demonstrators, yelling "kill the pigs" at their fellow police officers on the other side of the line. A later estimate by CBS, based on army sources, put the number of undercover agents among the demonstrators as one in six. Jerry Rubin's "bodyguard" was a government agent who distinguished himself by pulling down the American flag in an incident that discredited the demonstrators and provided an excuse for yet another attack by the police. (See Miller, p. 297.)

Police agents are always a problem. Organizations like SDS rely on volunteers. One of these may be a police agent who could steal a copy of the membership list, for example. That is a risk, but manageable. When police agents shape the message, the movement is in real trouble.

I blamed Hayden for this mess. Only the naïve were ignorant of the government's effort to infiltrate the movement. Hayden, clever and suspicious, was anything but naïve. Once, Hayden and I had been at a meeting with a political hustler who worked his charm on a group of older, peace movement leaders. As I walked out, sickened by the performance, Hayden said softly to me, "You know that guy is a fucking cop." Why did Hayden let the cops play such an important role in his operation? I knew he knew better. Why hadn't he publicly exposed the police provocateurs that got so much media coverage? Was he too desperate to think straight, or simply out of control?

Even though he won the nomination, Hubert Humphrey obviously lost big in Chicago. But what killed his chances for being elected president was not the demonstrations, but the fact that he refused, even at the convention, to separate himself from Lyndon Johnson's war policies. To many Americans in the middle, Richard Nixon, elected president by a narrow majority in November 1968, had become the candidate who could get us out of Vietnam.

I also lost big in Chicago. At the beginning, the national movement had been "beloved community" sustained by love and ruled by trust. Tom Hayden had close personal relations with many other leaders, including some of the founders of the Boston Draft Resistance Group. But when I criticized Hayden publicly, to some of Hayden's old friends, I became the one no longer to be trusted.

Most of all, our movement lost big in Chicago. Others had taken control of the message and made us look like simple-minded martyrs or self-serving fools thrilled by violence. Nixon cleverly used these themes to feed the backlash to the movement. Some people regard the demonstrations at the Democratic National Convention as a signature event of the 1960s and wish they had been there, but for the most part what happened in Chicago was a gigantic fuck-up.

❦ ❦ ❦

What I Learned from the Demonstrations
at the Democratic Convention

- A movement is in big trouble if its leaders are not accountable.
- In situations of conflict, the government may try to discredit a movement by

attacking and/or infiltrating its demonstrations to provoke violence. Leaders have to be prepared to deal with these problems.

- A demonstration needs a clear political purpose, a clear message, and a clear discipline.
- Disaster comes when *agents provocateurs* are allowed to shape the message.

The Decline of Draft Resistance

The summer of 1968 was the high point of the draft resistance movement. After that, doubts grew stronger about both non-cooperation and draft counseling as effective strategies to build the anti-war movement. (See Thorne, p. 66.) I and others became discouraged as it became clear that draft resistance was not going to be the breakthrough strategy we had imagined. I felt that without a base of support among working people our movement could not succeed. I adored the BDRG, but the work did not appear to be getting us any closer to where we needed to be.

The staff and volunteers of the Boston Draft Resistance Group came together in the late fall of 1968 to honestly evaluate what we had learned in the last year and a half. The early BDRG members who had come from SDS, like Nick Egleson and Vernon Grizzard, had hoped to organize community-based draft unions, a vision they had shared with other SDS leaders and the originators of the "We Won't Go" statements. (Thorne, p. 107) But their expectations about organizing community-based draft unions had not been fulfilled.

Vernon Grizzard, who had brought his community-organizing experience in Chester, Pennsylvania, to the Boston Draft Resistance Group, summed up our experience this way:

> "No community–based draft resistance union, or anything resembling it, emerged from our work.... The inevitable result of all our talking with potential draftees was not collective action, but individual draft counseling, which often required months of study and legalistic criteria for one deferment or another.... If the draft affected

enough men at the same time within a given community, then perhaps the problem of individual counseling could be overcome. But the number of men threatened at any one time is small and the threat exists only for a limited time (no matter which way it is resolved)." (Quoted in Thorne, p. 108)

The BDRG as a social service agency had always conflicted with the BDRG as a political organization. The "horror show" was the most political program of the BDRG – a dramatic way to show opposition to the military and involve other pre-inductees in resistance to the war. But the "horror show" was the program of last resort. Few were actually driven to take the step of disrupting their pre-induction physical. This was because draft counselors were so adept at developing other, less demanding, options, like a letter from a doctor or psychiatrist attesting that the registrant was not fit to serve in the military.

The BDRG was caught in a vicious circle. The young men who would naturally drop by for draft counseling were college students and those from middle-class backgrounds. To get working-class and minority registrants into the office we had to do outreach. But outreach programs like the "early morning show" took a lot of effort. The effort was worthwhile if it built a base for the anti-war movement in working-class communities. But if it didn't, organizers had to find other strategies that did work and leave the draft counseling to others. Thus the BDRG became more a social service agency with a largely middle-class clientele, and less a political organization reaching out to working-class young people. Organizers like me began to pull away, and to urge other, politically motivated staff and volunteers to do the same. In the fall of 1969, BDRG closed its doors.

The breakup of the Boston Draft Resistance Group was painful for everyone involved. It was a wonderful group and I had so wished that we could have succeeded. Its failure underlined the need for a broader approach to organizing working-class communities around economic needs as well as the war.

At the end of 1968 Jeff Sharlet, the editor of *Vietnam GI*, came to visit us in Somerville. He was tired, lonely, and burned out. He was hurting, and I wanted to help. I introduced him to someone, and within days they were in love.

I believed that love cured all. But instead of growing stronger, Jeff got weaker and began to suffer terrible abdominal pains. After a few weeks, Jeff flew home to Florida for medical tests, which revealed that cancer had already destroyed his left kidney. Surgery and radiation did not seem to be able to stop its spread. I realized that soon my friend might be dead.

Mrs. Brown Comes to Visit

A few months after the demonstrations at the Democratic National Convention, Frinde was getting ready for a job interview with the director of the elementary school library program in the Boston Public Schools. Frinde had just graduated from library school and really wanted the job.

Since the director lived in Cambridge, she had asked if the interview could be conducted at our home, on the top floor of a three-decker. Her request increased my paranoid sense that we were being watched.

Frinde and I scoured the apartment and put away all the incriminating literature. We both dressed respectably. When Mrs. Brown arrived, I shook hands and was on my best behavior. After the interview began, I retired to the bathroom. No sooner had I sat down than I heard an urgent knocking. Frinde whispered softly, "The FBI are at the front door and want to interview you about the demonstrations in Chicago!"

My heart sank. They had caught me with my pants down. If Mrs. Brown found out the FBI was after me, we could kiss that job good-bye. Once again, Frinde would lose out because of me, in this case not for something I organized, but for something I opposed. But I wasn't going to share my disagreements with the FBI.

By the time I got to the front door, I was furious. "I'm not talking to you guys," I hissed through the door. "Get the fuck out of here." I was greatly relieved when I heard their footsteps going back down the stairs.

Mrs. Brown seemed very friendly when she left. Our apartment was quite small, and the living room was just off the front hall. What, if anything, had Mrs. Brown heard of the ruckus at the front door? After a nervous week or two, we heard that Frinde got the job. Later on, we found out that Mrs. Brown, Margaret Brown, had been a left-wing activist all her life. She and her husband had been put through the mill during the McCarthy period. Now she was creating the elementary school library program because she thought that working-class kids in Boston needed libraries just like the kids in the suburbs. The sincerity of her commitment must have impressed even the right-wingers in the school department. I never did ask Margaret about what she heard at the front door that evening. If she heard me cussing the FBI, it probably helped Frinde get her job.

XI

Off Course, 1969

IN NOVEMBER 1968, RICHARD NIXON was elected president, but that was not my only worry. The New Left had failed to develop organizations involving working people. A left movement without the support of those who have the most to gain from change is not going very far, I thought.

A movement that working people participated in and controlled seemed to me the essence of the "participatory democracy" SDS had talked about for years. But all of the short cuts the New Left had taken had turned into dead ends. Although we had influenced working-class opinion about the war, our specific efforts to bring working people into our movement, from SDS's early efforts to organize an "interracial movement of the poor" to our recent efforts to build community-based anti-draft unions, had all failed. The New Left had not fulfilled its mission, and it was beginning to come apart.

My friend Carl Oglesby, former president of SDS, had asked me to join him and Staughton Lynd in an effort to try to head off the coming war between Progressive Labor (PL) and anti-PL forces in SDS. The two sides seemed determined to slug it out, and unaccountable elder statesmen like us were part of the problem, not part of the solution.

For a long time I hadn't taken Progressive Labor seriously. I remembered the pot-smoking ne'er-do-wells who had delivered too few pamphlets too late to the SDS March on Washington in 1965. Then there were the "true believers" in New York who combined a lack of intelligent curiosity about the world with faith that all major problems could be solved by referring to the works of Marx, Engels, and Lenin. The New York group put out the newspaper *Challenge*, which tried to imitate a tabloid's common touch. Many of the articles had the same story line – the bosses are screwing the workers, the workers are rebelling, the union misleaders are trying to persuade the workers to give in, but their clever plots are being unveiled here on the pages of *Challenge*. In the end, the bosses and misleaders will be thrown out, and the workers will triumph. *Challenge* was not only unconvincing but also boring.

Also, I didn't trust "Jeremiah," the Boston area Progressive Labor leader. He was one of these people who needed to win every argument. In meetings, he was usually on the attack, talking faster and faster, as if the flood of words washed away any other point of view. Since some arguments are more important to win than others, trying to win every single one seemed to reflect a major lack of judgment. But I knew two national PL leaders well, Levi Laub, my brother-in-law, who was on the national committee, and Milt Rosen, the national chair. Levi was bright, sophisticated, and well read – a person who could discuss political topics in an open, undogmatic fashion. Milt seemed balanced, experienced, and trustworthy in an avuncular sort of way. Between them, they could keep Jeremiah in line, I thought.

I decided to give the Progressive Labor Party a second look. What was required, I thought, was a democratic, disciplined, and results-based approach to the essential issue of reconstituting the left in America. I felt that there were people in PL who shared my conception of how to build this movement. Progressive Labor members in New England were an impressive bunch. Many of them were bright, hardworking, open, and fun to be around. I decided to throw my lot in with PL, and disregard my previous reservations about the organization.

The Cambridge Rent Control Referendum Campaign

After I joined the Progressive Labor Party, I went to work with the Cambridge Rent Control Referendum Campaign. After years of being the outside organizer, always the person from somewhere else, I loved my role as an organizer and activist in my own community. Frinde and I lived on Prospect Street in Cambridge and became close friends with our next-door neighbors. On February 15, 1969, our daughter Sarah was born. Four days later we took her to a fundraising party featuring Dr. Spock who pronounced her strong and fit. Now we were a real family.

The need for rent control in Cambridge was very real. Harvard and MIT expansion into working-class neighborhoods was creating a housing shortage, and rents increased dramatically. A July 1968 survey of elders by the local anti-poverty agency found that 57 percent of the elderly living alone in Cambridge spent more than half their income for rent, and that many of them were forced to deprive themselves of adequate food, clothing, and medical care to meet the cost of shelter. (*Cambridge Chronicle*, 8/1/68, p. 5)

By the time I began volunteering there in the early spring of 1969, the Cambridge Rent Control Referendum Campaign was already a thriving operation with 80 or so volunteers on its way to collecting 8,000 signatures of registered voters in Cambridge. I loved collecting signatures and speaking about rent control at small neighborhood meetings in my own town, where I could follow up with the people I met and get to know them better. At one meeting in East Cambridge, I tangled with City Councilor Al Velucci, who at that time opposed rent control. Velucci was a populist and a bit of a demagogue, suggesting once that to solve Cambridge's parking problems the city should turn historic Harvard Yard into a parking lot.

I challenged Velucci to support the tenants in the room, myself included, rather than the landlords who were exploiting us. I talked about how mean our landlord was, about how I had to change my baby daughter's diapers on the stove because our apartment was so cold. Though true, this was also a bit of an exaggeration. Changing Sarah on the stove was an inconvenience I hardly noticed.

Velucci heard with his own ears that most of his constituents in the room supported rent control. After the meeting, he asked me if I would like to take a walk around his neighborhood, East Cambridge, home to Italian immigrants for several generations. As we walked along I talked about rent control, and he gave me an education about the anarchist traditions of the Italian working class. He made me feel that I was no longer his antagonist, but a pupil and potential ally. Looking down the dark streets, I could imagine the torch-lit marches through the neighborhood in support of Sacco and Vanzetti, Italian anarchist revolutionaries framed and executed by the state of Massachusetts in 1927.

At the end of our walk through East Cambridge, I was totally charmed. In the decades that followed, I always included Al in my list of who to vote for. A few weeks later, he came out in support of rent control.

Despite Velucci's switch, the city council defeated rent control in July 1969, thus allying with the landlords and the real estate developers. An enraged crowd forced the councilors to leave by the rear exit, an event described in Bill Cunningham's book *Which People's Republic*. Cunningham's book provides an insightful analysis of the class and race issues underlying the conflicts in Cambridge over rent control, urban renewal, and governance.

Since lobbying the city council had failed to get rent control, the Cambridge Rent Control Referendum Campaign seemed like the best way to win. The struggle continued in September. The city solicitor instructed the election commission not to put our referendum question on the ballot because impartial experts had not confirmed the housing emergency. In response, we planned a protest sit-in at the next meeting of the election commission. When the police tried to bar us from the building, several of us broke through their lines and charged up the stairs to the meeting. I was arrested along with forty others, tried, convicted, and fined. We blockaded several houses during the next few weeks to prevent the sheriff from evicting the families living there. But when the court upheld the city's right to keep rent control off the ballot, we didn't have the popular support to continue the struggle on our own terms.

The fight for rent control in Cambridge had begun long before Progressive Labor came on the political scene, and would continue long after we had moved on to other issues. Collecting 8,000 signatures, and the discussions that went with them, was real work and did a lot to build support for rent control in Cambridge. That grassroots effort was crucial to the eventual passage of the rent control law. But we in PL focused too much on the accomplishment of the campaign and too little on the other work being done on the issue by potential allies.

The Cambridge Civic Association won a city council majority in the 1971 elections and passed a strong rent control ordinance in 1972. Rent control did much to preserve a strong working-class presence in Cambridge, until a state-wide referendum supported by landlords and real estate interests narrowly won in 1994. It took away the local option for rent control. Now, other than in the housing projects, few working-class tenants remain in the city.

The Harvard Strike, 1969

In April 1969 I was asked to set up an off-campus print shop for the Worker Student Alliance in a third-floor apartment on Massachusetts Avenue across from Harvard Yard. Harvard-Radcliffe SDS was headed for a confrontation with the university administration. While I ran various copy machines, Sarah, a little less than two months old, lay on her back in a crib and smiled and gurgled, as happy as she could be. Occasionally, I went out for a while. When I returned she was kicking her little feet in the air as happy with the people I had left her with as she had been with me. From time to time Frinde would take a break from organizing, come in and nurse her, and then go back out again. When I look back, it is sometimes hard to remember that all this bliss took place in a country torn by war, and that a major battle was looming just across the street in Harvard Yard.

SDS had been booming, with roughly 350 chapters by the end of the school year 1968. Over 3,000 campus protests took place during that year, from coast to coast, North to South, small Catholic colleges to major state universities. (Sale, pp. 444-446) Many different organizations were involved in these protests, but the student strike at Columbia University in New York City led by SDS had been the one most widely covered in the media. As Che Guevara had called for "two, three, many Vietnams," SDS then called for "two, three, many Columbias."

The Harvard-Radcliffe SDS chapter, the largest in New England, had been for a long while a world unto itself. Now this world was splitting apart. Two factions, the Worker Student Alliance Caucus, organized by Progressive Labor, and the New Left Caucus, opposed to PL, were increasingly at odds over each and every issue. I thought there were good people on both sides, and I tried to maintain good relations with everyone, hoping that at some point the animosity would decrease as the need to work together to win became clearer.

The issue of the Reserve Officer Training Corps (ROTC) on campus dominated the Harvard political scene for the academic year 1968-69. As of the fall of 1968, ROTC nationwide provided 85 percent of the junior officers required by the army. (Lawrence Eichel et al., *The Harvard Strike*, p.61, cited in Amy Perry, "Harvard/Radcliffe Students for a Democratic Society 1960-1972: The Origin, Growth and Demise of a Movement for Social Change," Harvard University undergraduate thesis, March 20, 1986, p. 54) By the winter of 1968/69, there was substantial agreement between students and faculty that something had to be done about ROTC. The question was what. SDS wanted ROTC abolished at Harvard. (Perry, p. 55) Most faculty and students were prepared to settle for ending ROTC's academic credit, professorial appointments, and free use of facilities. (Perry, p. 57) But the Harvard Corporation provoked a crisis when it rejected the faculty's proposals on ROTC and other related issues, such as how protestors from a previous sit-in should be punished.

The Harvard-Radcliffe SDS chapter called a meeting on April 8, 1969, "to decide further strategy in the anti-ROTC campaign, including the possibility of militant action." (*The Harvard Crimson*, April 8, 1969, p.1, cited in Perry, p. 62) I went to the meeting for about an hour and then went home, dismayed by the divisive atmosphere in the middle of such a crucial campaign. That night the Worker Student Alliance Caucus had advocated for an immediate building seizure, while the New Left Caucus argued that more time was needed to win students over. At the end of four hours of debate, 400 SDS members voted not to seize a building at that time, but authorized the taking of a building at some unspecified time in the future. The meeting also produced six demands: the immediate abolition of ROTC, the replacement of ROTC scholarships with university ones, restoration of scholarships for students being punished for an earlier sit-in, a roll-back in rents on Harvard-owned buildings, and no destruction of workers' homes for the proposed expansions at the medical school and in the area of the Kennedy School. (Perry, pp. 62-63)

On April 9 I was told to sell *Challenge* at a Worker Student Alliance Caucus (WSA) rally at noon in Harvard Yard near University Hall, a historic eighteenth-century white building with a bronze statue of John Harvard mounted on a large marble pedestal in front. The deans had their offices there. After a few short speeches, the WSA students, forty or so, walked up the steps to the offices in University Hall. A few minutes later, the WSA students escorted the deans down the steps to the Yard. SDS had occupied University Hall, to the total bewilderment of the small audience of SDSers and others gathered outside under the trees.

Since those gathered by University Hall had as little interest in reading *Challenge* as I had in selling it, I started talking with the students milling about. They were not pleased with what had been done by the Worker Student Alliance group in SDS's name. The New Left Caucus students were furious that the compromise made at the meeting the night before when 400 SDS members voted not to seize a building at that time, but authorized the taking of a building at some unspecified time in the future, had been tossed aside. WSA members tried to split hairs, arguing that what they were doing was within the guidelines. Clearly it wasn't. More moderate student opinion ranged from puzzled to pissed off. Something had had to be done, everyone agreed, but occupying this building now was not it. The only people who agreed with the action seemed to be already in the building, and they were a small minority. SDS seemed to be too far ahead of student opinion, setting it up for isolation and defeat. It was an unpromising beginning to a big campaign.

But what happened in the next sixteen hours validated the SDS action. After the takeover, a search of the files at University Hall revealed a secret relationship between Harvard and the CIA. I had suspected that the administration had been dealing with the students and faculty in bad faith, but I didn't realize that University Hall was where they stored their dirty linen.

One professor came in to persuade the students to leave. As he was puffing on his pipe and offering avuncular criticism in an Australian accent, his file detailing a secret paid relationship with the CIA was brought into the room and passed around. He left quickly. So much for the otherworldly academy dedicated to the pursuit of truth.

A second gift to SDS was the way the administration decided to clear University Hall of protestors, now numbering several hundred. Campus moderates, including some deans and faculty, had urged that any police action be taken in the daytime with ample notice. Instead, the administration agreed to an early morning attack with only two minutes' warning.

The Bust

I was working in the print shop that night, preparing the materials for canvassing dormitories the next day. The night was very still, and I could imagine for a while that I was the only person awake. But as I bent over the printing press, WHRB, the Harvard student-run radio station, began describing a major police build-up several blocks from Harvard Yard – many hundreds of officers, including state troopers and police from Cambridge, Boston, and other outlying communities. At about 3:00 a.m., as they began to march to Harvard Yard, it became clear the attack was about to begin. "Go pull all the fire alarms in the dormitories in the yard, where the freshmen live, and then go down to the river and do the same in the houses where the upperclassmen are," I told a colleague in the print shop. Stopping the attack was impossible, but we could make sure the bloody job wasn't done in secret.

The student occupation of University Hall had happened without violence. But the police, undisciplined and under the cover of night, went berserk when they came to clear the building. Hundreds of students in the yard watched their fellow students, women and men, dragged bleeding down the steps and taken away. Moderate opinion was outraged. Later that morning, 2,000 students met in Memorial Church and called a strike.

Throughout the complicated political struggles that followed, SDS properly stuck to their demands dealing with the impact of the university's actions on the Vietnamese, whom our country was attacking, and working-class people in Cambridge and Boston, who were being displaced by university expansion. But moderate students wanted the university administration to pay more attention to student and faculty opinion around ROTC and other issues, and not use outside police to deal with internal university matters. For most students, Harvard's expansion into the community was a new issue, one they were prepared to say should be studied now and acted upon later. When large numbers of students decided to move, it was around their demands, and not those of SDS.

At a meeting of 800 students on April 11, SDS set up a strike steering committee around the six demands. But SDS decided to boycott the mass meeting of 10,000 students at the football stadium on Monday, April 14, because a vote would be taken on whether or not to continue the strike. SDS had decided to continue its strike, regardless. On April 17, the faculty approved, and the Harvard Corporation agreed to, a proposal relegating ROTC to the status of an extracurricular organization without special privileges or facilities. (Perry, p. 68) On April 18 a second mass meeting at the stadium, this one with 5,000 people, voted to suspend the strike. (Perry, p. 69) After the vote to suspend the strike, the two factions within SDS were unable to agree on a common course of action. Each faction tried to continue the struggle, with little effect. The strike was over.

During the early days of the strike, Harvard was a place to behold. When I walked through the yard, strike posters with big red fists were on display in and outside the university buildings. Few went to class. Meetings were held everywhere, in classrooms and under the trees. Everyday, SDS would publish documents revealing what had actually been going on behind closed doors all these years. But after the early days of glory, support for the strike began to decline, and "normal life" returned to the campus.

While complete victory for SDS's original demands was not in the cards, I have always believed that SDS made a mistake in not participating in the two mass meetings. That the majority did not agree with us was a reason to attend rather than a reason to stay away. Also a moralizing tone hurt SDS in its dealing with the majority and made common ground more difficult to find in the increasingly intense faction fight that tore apart the chapter in mid-April and the national organization in June. These tactics and tone isolated SDS from the majority of students, and made it harder for SDS to carry on the struggle after the strike had ended.

In the end, the Pentagon withdrew ROTC from Harvard after it was denied academic status. The proposed medical school expansion was moved to another location. Three faculty student committees were established. (Perry, p. 103) Nathan Pusey, unresponsive to student and faculty demands and responsible for the decision to bring in the police in the dead of night, resigned as president of Harvard. Derek Bok, who brought a more democratic style to the governance of the university, replaced him.

Had the administration been more solicitous of student and faculty opinion, these changes might have happened without the occupation of University Hall and the ensuing mayhem. Would there have been any substantive reforms without the occupation of University Hall? Probably not.

Twenty-five years after the event I attended a reunion of those who participated in the Harvard Strike. No one there regretted the stand they had taken. The Harvard they had entered was one where students could talk about whatever they wanted to, as long as they did nothing to interfere with the university's support for the army and the war. The Harvard they left had changed, because the students had learned that they could act to force the university to recognize the humanity and rights of those outside the ivy-covered walls.

The Strange Story of Cambridge Iron and Steel

A prominent Massachusetts businessman gave $25,000, and pledged an additional $75,000 in the fall of 1968 to a Massachusetts corporation called Cambridge Iron and Steel. A regional traveler and fundraiser for New England SDS set up this corporation in secret to receive and disburse the funds. Then he placed his wife and a number of his friends and close political associates on the board of directors. Cambridge Iron and Steel had nothing to do with metals and manufacturing, and everything to do with influencing the internal politics of SDS.

Although no report of this gift was ever made to SDS, word began to get around. As an elected member of the Regional Interim Committee of New England SDS, the body that supervised the office between regional meetings, I felt some responsibility to investigate this strange occurrence.

We had some clues about the donor's business and philanthropic interests, but the man himself remained a mystery. However, one day Frinde and I were sitting in her parents' living room talking to a student from England. He was writing a book about the New Left in America and his adventures at Harvard. He spoke fondly of the wisdom and understanding of his rich American patron. As his story unfolded, I realized that his patron was the mystery donor to Cambridge Iron and Steel. Seizing the opportunity, I politely said I was interested in meeting his wise friend. The English student invited us to brunch at his patron's house in Newton the following Sunday.

That morning I sat at the foot of the table, a humble and attentive guest at brunch. Other guests were there, but I remember only my conversation with our host. The mysterious donor explained to me how extraordinarily influential he had become in SDS through his investment in the Cambridge Iron and Steel Corporation. He referred to the SDS regional fundraiser to whom he had given the money to set up Cambridge Iron and Steel as "my man in the white community" parallel to "his men in the Black community" whom he had acquired through similar contributions to a fund he had set up in Roxbury. My questions were general and appreciative. My warm response encouraged him to expand on his accomplishments.

At a certain point, I felt I had learned as much about Cambridge Iron and Steel as he was going to volunteer at the brunch table. Then I asked him, "Why did you do all this in secret?"

"Who was told about this transaction and who wasn't is a matter of the internal processes of SDS and no concern of mine," he said.

"But I'm on the regional committee of SDS, so it is a big concern of mine," I told him, revealing that I had known much of the story before he had begun the telling of it. The atmosphere suddenly became very cold.

Then he turned to me, and said menacingly, "You know I could have you killed." The interview was over. Frinde and I promptly left.

As movements become more powerful, inevitably there are efforts to buy the leaders off. About a year before this confrontation, I had been offered a job at a think tank connected to MIT studying dissident groups in Latin America. My main qualification, I was told, was my experience as a SDS leader, which would help me empathize with the rebels and understand what they really wanted. What I would be doing would not be spying on these groups, I was assured, but helping American decision-makers understand them and their motivations, so that our country could design more appropriate policies regarding the region. The job paid $25,000, which was good money at a time when a nice apartment in Cambridge could be rented for $135 a month. ($25,000 in 1968 is equivalent to $162,500 in 2011.)

One evening the people recruiting me for this job invited Frinde and me to a party at a townhouse in New York City. The partygoers had been assigned to teams representing nation states to play a game of "Atomic Diplomacy." On the top floor was a large general assembly room. Nations caucused on the lower floors. Beautiful people combined political science and decadence as they drunkenly wandered up and down the stairs commenting on the coming end of the world.

The party and the job were an effort to lure me to the other side. Clearly if these people really cared what dissident groups in Latin America "really wanted," they didn't need to hire me; they could get on an airplane and go talk to them. Even if I told them nothing, every day I spent on such a bogus job was one less day spent organizing. But the allure was there, a nice comfortable office, money, access to decision-makers, no more hard, and dangerous work organizing. Nonetheless, I was insulted. Did they really think that whatever I knew or could learn I would share with the CIA, responsible for so much suffering in Latin America, which had to be behind this whole thing? I turned them down.

Cambridge Iron and Steel struck me as a similar effort to subvert the movement we had and to distract us from building the movement we needed. Some capitalists, a minority, alas, have funded the progressive movement ever since the birth of capitalism. But the fact that this donor had pulled a wide network of important movement activists into a secret deal indicated a desire to subvert SDS and our institutions. Some of the activities he was funding were also questionable, I thought, like opening new coffee shops in Cambridge, Massachusetts, and New Haven, Connecticut. What better way to divert activists from building a movement than to persuade them that running cafés in college towns was the "left" thing to do. I never saw the donor again.

As far as I know the donor still lives in the Boston area and has been involved in a number of business and entertainment ventures since. More likely, he was a rich egomaniac than a dangerous government agent, although for several months I slept with a pistol under my pillow. But apparently he did not have the authority to order my execution.

XII

Things Fall Apart, 1969-1970

SINCE BAD THINGS HAD HAPPENED in Chicago, I approached the SDS National Convention, held at a coliseum in Chicago starting Wednesday, June 18, 1969, with great foreboding. I had come to Chicago with Frinde and our little daughter, Sarah, but we would not get a chance to spend much time together. Over the next few days I was totally absorbed in the struggle fought out in this huge, ugly, dirty, half-empty hall over whether the national office faction of SDS, now called the Revolutionary Youth Movement (RYM), could get the votes to expel the Progressive Labor Party (PL) and its allies from SDS. To do this the RYM forces would have to persuade a substantial bloc of delegates not allied with either side that SDS should abandon a policy of non-exclusion, an article of faith since the organization was founded in 1962.

Relations between the two factions were so bad, and paranoid posturing so great, that each side had its own "security," supposedly to protect it from the other. I was part of the security team of the Worker Student Alliance Caucus, allied with Progressive Labor. I quickly reached an understanding with my counterparts in "security" on the other side. Let the big talkers do their thing. Our job was to keep cool and make sure that no one on either side got into a real fight. I liked being on "security." I could stand unobtrusively on the sidelines, looking tough and vigilant, and leave the chants and catcalls to those who thought that got us anywhere.

SDS had appeared to play a leading role in the U.S. student movement for many years. In Latin America, China, and Europe similar organizations of young people were shaking the regimes to the very core. SDS was the most visible New Left organization in the United States and was part of an international movement that seemed to be sweeping the world. Leading SDS seemed like a prize worth fighting for.

In 1968, even in the U.S., hundreds of thousands of students considered themselves revolutionaries. The Daniel Yankelovitch poll, fall 1968, for *Fortune* magazine found 5 percent of U.S. students, or 368,000, "strongly agreeing" with the need for a "mass revolutionary party" and 14 percent "partially agreeing." (Cited in Sale, p. 713) Bewitched by the rhetoric of the times, many on both sides of the faction fight lost sight of the 95 percent of U.S. students who did not consider themselves revolutionaries. Fortunately, the anti-war movement continued on without them.

SDS had been in trouble for some time. The isolation of the national office and national leadership of SDS from the chapters had been an acute problem for years. But now, for the first year since its founding, the number of SDS chapters had actually declined from about 350 in June 1968, to about 300 in June 1969. (Sale, p. 664) After June 1968 the new national leaders, who didn't necessarily agree about anything else, had become united in the view that Progressive Labor's growing influence in SDS, which they called a takeover threat, had to be fought "by any means necessary," as they said, imitating Malcolm X. As the struggle heated up, their argument became that they were better Communists than the PL people were. Since neither they nor PL had actually accomplished very much in the real world, much of the debate was about who had the "correct line." I thought that such theological discussions were a waste of time. At the time no one I knew in Progressive Labor thought that taking over SDS was even a good idea, much less a practical one.

For one brief moment at the very beginning of the convention I thought SDS might come out of this faction fight in one piece – when the chair asked us to rise for a minute of silence in memory of my friend Jeff Sharlet, editor of the newspaper *Vietnam GI*.

He had died two days before, at age twenty-seven, of cancer. I have a picture of Jeff in uniform when he was twenty-four, dark-haired, good-looking, tough, and smart. He had survived two tours of duty in Vietnam and two years of some of the most intense political work imaginable.

I had visited him in Florida for four days in the spring. When radiation and surgery had failed to stop the spread of cancer, he had gone to live with his mother in a small wood-frame house a few blocks from the beach. By the time I got there, he could barely walk around the house, much less to the beach. He did not acknowledge that he was dying, but it was clear to both of us that he was. He was very worried about the future of the movement. Neither one of us could accept the reality that we would have to carry on without him.

Now he was dead. For that minute of silence, everyone, including all the factions and the undecided, united in grief. But when the silence ended, the bickering and posturing began, and by the end of the day, the means for any rational sorting out of the factional differences had disappeared. That it had come to this was very sad for me. I could remember the days when people could go at each other tooth and nail in a late-night debate and yet still have fun together after the meeting was over.

By Thursday evening, the Revolutionary Youth Movement forces had already lost a few initial skirmishes. At that point, they prepared to play their best card. A leader from the Black Panther Party, allied with the RYM, came up to the podium wearing shades and surrounded by armed guards. At the outset, he pointed out that while the Panthers were out fighting the police to defend their communities, armchair Marxists like Progressive Labor "hadn't even shot rubber bands yet." (Sale, p. 566) People in the audience resonated to that message. The Panthers were, after all, brave comrades under the gun.

Then he started talking about women's liberation and went dramatically off message. "We believe in pussy power," he said to a stunned audience. Standing off to the side, at first I couldn't believe my ears. Many people started chanting, "Fight male chauvinism, fight male chauvinism." RYM's humiliations grew only worse when another Panther leader came to the podium and allowed as how the

strategic position of women in the movement is prone. The chants and scream-
ing reverberated off the cement walls of the coliseum, and the RYM forces
skulked off the stage. (Sale, p. 566)

For the Revolutionary Youth Movement, this was a disaster. Based on their
record of running the SDS national office for a year, not many people could be
persuaded that RYM had the correct line on everything. But RYM claimed their
allies the Panthers were the infallible guides on the path to revolution. The
problem for RYM now was that many women, and some men, were no longer
willing to put up with such blatant sexism, no matter how exalted the source. To
have their allies talking in such an obviously sexist way in public was an out-
standing setback for RYM.

At a distance, I would see Cathy Wilkerson and Kathy Boudin, who once
were so friendly and so engaging. Now they spoke woodenly, with no expression, and marched around in baggy khakis dressed like recent recruits to the
North Korean army. Frinde and I had known them fairly well before, or so we
thought. Now there was not even eye contact. What had happened to them? We
had no idea, but we were both pretty badly shaken by the change.

The Revolutionary Youth Movement got what it deserved, I thought. Their
whole outlook was colored by the very racism they claimed to combat. People of
color, who were viewed as stereotypes of ignorance and servility by traditional
racists, were portrayed by RYM as paragons of revolutionary virtue to the extent that this too became a racist stereotype. No longer negative stereotypes,
they remained stereotypes nonetheless, not real people. RYM had put the
Panthers front and center, hoping for an easy win. Now RYM was in deep shit,
where it belonged, I believed. The fact that the Panthers *were* under the gun,
and *did* need and deserve the support of people of goodwill all around the country, made RYM's attempt to use the Panthers for their own purposes all the
more reprehensible.

Six months later Fred Hampton, the leader of the Chicago Panthers, was
murdered at home in bed. An informant had told the Chicago police exactly
where his bed was. The police had fired a barrage of bullets through the wall
and killed him. He never had a chance, either to surrender or to defend
himself.

Incredibly, the next evening, Friday night, the Panthers came back to the convention. Desperate, RYM had persuaded them to return yet again to the cauldron of SDS internecine warfare. This time the leader of the Chicago Panthers read from the podium an ultimatum purporting to come from their national leadership:

> "We demand that... the Progressive Labor Party change its position
> on the right to self-determination and stand in concert with the op-
> pressed peoples of the world and begin to follow a true Marxist-
> Leninist ideology.... Students for a Democratic Society will be
> judged by the company they keep and the efficiency and effective-
> ness with which they deal with bourgeois factions in their organiza-
> tion." (Quoted in Sale, p. 569)

After the requisite chanting ("Power to the People," the Panther slogan, ver-sus "Power to the Workers," the PL slogan) and catcalls, Jeff Gordon, a national Progressive Labor student leader, came to the podium. Speaking slowly and calmly he said, "PL will not be intimidated out of SDS." He went on to affirm that we supported Third World liberation overseas, Black liberation in the United States, and the Black Panther Party. "But we reserve the right to offer comradely criticism to all our allies, including the Panthers," Jeff said. For once, I applauded. Most people in the hall did the same.

Progressive Labor temporarily stood on the high ground, and the Revolutionary Youth Movement was in the ditch. But by itself, PL and the Worker Student Alliance Caucus did not have close to a majority of votes at the convention, nor did RYM. To win, each side needed the support of the block of neutral swing voters. These swing voters appeared to be motivated by common sense rather than any particular factional program. For the moment, the center held.

The votes weren't there to expel Progressive Labor, but Bernardine Dohrn, the Revolutionary Youth Movement leader, was not to be denied the split. "We have to decide whether we want to stay in the same organization with people who deny rights of self-determination to the oppressed," she shouted into the microphone. (Sale, p. 570) Then she walked out.

When the RYM forces reconvened in the next room, their lack of unity was obvious – without PL around they fell to fighting among themselves. But PL was unable to exploit successfully the dissension on the other side. The walkout had stayed firm, despite the divisions within RYM. The RYM leaders, even the ones alienated by Bernardine and her group, were reluctant to come back because PL had attacked them so relentlessly and so personally.

One thing that the Worker Student Alliance Caucus and Progressive Labor did right, now that they were for the first time in the majority, was to proceed with the agenda of the convention in an orderly, democratic fashion. People who disagreed with PL were encouraged to speak out, and their views were incorporated in the final resolutions.

Late Saturday night the RYM forces returned to the main hall, five hundred or so strong, many more than they should have had. First, a file of women left their caucus room and lined up at the base of the stage, faces unsmiling. Then a file of men stood in front of the file of women with their arms folded across their chests, Panther style. (Sale, p. 573) Their huge production about security is so pathetic and ridiculous, I thought, since no one has any interest in beating them up.

Then Bernardine came out and delivered a long attack. At the end of her denunciation, she announced that those who did not accept her principles were no longer members of SDS. The audience began to laugh. Then she marched off the stage, proclaiming her allegiance to the correct line of a long list of Communist leaders whom she named, ending with Comrade Kim Il Sung of North Korea.

The next day, with RYM gone, the SDS convention elected officers. Soon afterwards, the SDS national office moved to Boston, where the Worker Student Alliance was strong, and began to pick up the pieces.

In retrospect the most important question was not whether this or that RYM leader was going to stay in SDS, but whether SDS remained an organization that ordinary students not involved with either PL or RYM might want to participate in and build. In June 1969, I was optimistic. The tragedy for SDS as it turned out was that in the end Progressive Labor didn't really value SDS as an independent national student organization anymore than the Revolutionary Youth Movement did.

Almost immediately after the SDS convention, RYM split into several factions, of which the Weathermen SDS, or Weathermen, became the most famous. At first Weathermen focused on recruiting working-class young people. They would show up at working-class high schools with provocative signs. Then to show how tough they were they often provoked fistfights with the young men they were trying to recruit. This campaign was a total failure. I remember a picture in the *Boston Globe* of "Rick," their New England organizer, and several other Weathermen being chased and beaten by students from Boston English High School after one of their raids. It's very hard to win people over to your side when you are looking down on them.

According to the Weathermen, to gain the respect of working-class young people, you had to fight them to show how tough you were. They assumed that working-class kids are violent by nature and the only way to win their respect is with violence.

This demeaning idea is still around, nurtured by countless TV shows and movies portraying teenagers, particularly teenagers of color, as naturally aggressive and violent. A more accurate way to look at working-class teenagers is that they are like the rest of us. They will fight, reluctantly, when they think they are being pushed up against the wall and there are no other options. Fights are more frequent in some working-class schools than they are in elite ones because the pressures are greater and the options fewer, not because the students there are naturally inclined towards violence.

A few years after these events in 1971, I taught for a decade in three primarily working-class schools. Over the course of my career as a teacher, I broke up several hundred fights. In my experience, one of the secrets to breaking up school fights is that with a few exceptions you rarely use force. Physical fights, between young men especially, are mainly theatrical events, at least at the beginning. Words have escalated, push has come to shove, and it's show time. The combatants don't really want to fight – but they don't see a way to stop it. This is where the teacher comes in.

A potential combatant needs to be able to say, "I'd a beat the crap out of him if that old Mr. Maher (or Ms. Jones) hadn't got in the way." So, when I step in between him and his opponent, he will act as if he wants to get past me and continue the fight. And I will act as if I am expending great strength and energy keeping them apart. Actually, neither one of us is working hard at all. We don't need to. The fight is over, and in a minute or two we will start trying to resolve the problem through discussion and negotiations.

In my ten years of breaking up fights, no student ever hit me, or even pushed me hard. After all, I was the peacemaker, and thus inviolable.

More Stupidity from the Weathermen

When I got to the meeting hall of the Huntington Avenue YMCA there were about a dozen Weathermen lined up at the door, some of whom were former Harvard students for whom I had always had friendly feelings.

The Weathermen SDS had called a meeting to recruit students to go to Chicago for their "Days of Rage," billed as four days of breaking windows and fighting the police. Since they used the name SDS, I felt obliged to go to their meeting to say that they weren't the real SDS, and that what they were proposing to do was just plain crazy. I had met twenty or so Worker Student Alliance people several blocks away. When we set out for the Y, I had walked as quickly as I could to get ahead of the rest, thinking that if I arrived at the door alone a physical confrontation would be less likely.

"How's it going, guys?" I said as I reached the door. Several Weathermen grabbed me and pulled me into the room; then they and several others formed a semi-circle around me and started throwing coordinated karate punches. I was totally caught of guard, but the shock disappeared in milliseconds. Keep on your feet and block the punches, I said to myself.

Things were actually going okay. Then I saw Rick, the regional traveler for the Weathermen SDS, sneaking around in back of me with a metal chair. That's serious, I thought. Suddenly Rick disappeared from view – a friend of mine had charged in and dropped him to the floor with a kick to the groin. The Weathermen backed away from me, regrouped, formed a line, and marched out the door chanting, "Ho, Ho, Ho Chi Minh, the NLF [National Liberation Front of South Vietnam] is gonna win."

I went to the bathroom and washed my face. I had a small cut and a few bruises. "So these are the people who are going to beat up the Chicago police!" I thought.

In the end, only several hundred demonstrators of the thousands trumpeted actually did turn up in Chicago. Before the demonstration, their former allies the Panthers pointed out that the whole thing was "Custerish" and their top leader Mark Rudd a "motherfucking masochist." (Sale, p. 602) Tom Hayden, on the other hand, offered his support saying, "Anything that intensifies our resistance to this war is in the service of humanity. The Weathermen are setting the terms for all of us now. Tear this monster down." (Ayers, p.169) At the event itself, the Weathermen ran through the streets at night, breaking some windows, and the police beat the crap out of them, as expected.

After the "Days of Rage" demonstrations in Chicago, Rick kept making the newspapers with one dumb action after another, at one point accused of beating up an elderly Harvard professor in a raid on the Center for International Studies. Then he disappeared from the front pages.

A few months after the incident at the YMCA, I decided to visit an old friend of mine dating back to my days in Washington. He had been sentenced to a year at the Billerica House of Correction for escorting a Harvard dean down the steps of University Hall the morning it was occupied by SDS. There had been no violence. Recently, he had helped organize a strike of inmates to protest conditions in the jail. He sent word asking me to drive down to Fall River to pick up the girlfriend of one of the other leaders of the inmate strike. Of course, I agreed.

Visitors and prisoners met under the supervision of guards but in a large open room holding about fifty people. Inmates and their visitors sat at tables and chairs and carried on their conversations in a relaxed atmosphere. My friend and I talked in a normal tone while the lovers talked softly to each other. My friend's friend had been there for some time. He was in for armed robbery. He seemed like a nice guy, but tough. Only rarely could his girlfriend get a ride to Billerica to visit him. When we had to leave, he told me how grateful he was that I had gone out of my way to bring her there.

As I got up to leave, I saw something surprising out of the corner of my eye – Rick in prison uniform sitting on the other side of the visitors' room, talking with someone. An evil thought crept into my mind. My friend's friend was my friend now. If I mentioned that Rick had tried to beat my brains out, it would have been all over for him. For my friend, beating up Rick was a piece of cake. Then I recoiled. Rick is a fool, I thought, but I don't want his blood on my hands. And I certainly don't want my friend's friend to get into trouble to settle an old score for me. I left without saying a word about Rick.

Some people don't appreciate just how lucky they have been. Rick should have known that my friend's friend was my friend now. But Rick was the classic big mouth. According to what I later heard, after I left he went up to my friend's friend.

"Do you know that guy Maher?"

"Sure."

"Well, you better watch out. He's a fucking cop."

"No shit! Thanks for letting me know."

That night someone threw Rick a blanket party. When he came to the wash-room to brush his teeth, someone threw a blanket over his head and several others kicked the shit out of him. The next day Rick was moved to another jail for his own protection.

Shortly after the "Days of Rage" disaster in Chicago, some of the Weathermen went underground and began a bombing campaign. Seeing SDS's name in the papers associated with terrorism added to my dislike of the Weathermen. Initially, they planned to target human beings, as Bill Ayers, a former leader of the Weathermen, admits in his memoir, *Fugitive Days*. In March 1970, three members of the Weather Underground were killed in an ac-cidental explosion in a New York City townhouse. Packed with screws and nails, the bomb they were building was an anti-personnel weapon to be used to kill and maim soldiers at a nearby army base in New Jersey. (Ayers, p. 272) That the three young people in the Weather Underground were killed is a cause of great sadness, especially for those who loved them, but had they carried out their mission it would have been a political and moral catastrophe.

What were they thinking? How could they consider killing the sons and daughters of the working class they were in principle so committed to reaching? Was it as an act of solidarity with the Viet Cong, who were killing U.S. soldiers and being killed by them, that such a course of action seemed just and moral? But the Viet Cong killed American soldiers because they had no other choice. To defend their country, they had to kill the invaders – that is the cruel logic of war. Americans in the anti-war movement had other options. We could talk to the soldiers and their families and support strikes and other actions in the military. We could educate, agitate, organize, and vote out of office the politicians who caused the war. We could limit the power of the rich contributors who had put these politicians into office. Why then should we try to harm the soldiers, most of whom were innocent of any crime? Physically attacking them would accomplish nothing beyond making it almost impossible for us to reach out to them and their families, and build a political force that could really end the war.

After the townhouse explosion left three members dead, the Weathermen decided that they should pull back from attacking human targets, and persuaded their allied organizations to do likewise. However, the Weathermen decided to continue the bombing campaign, focused on buildings, as part of their strategy of intimidating the U.S. rulers by "bringing the war home."

The U.S. government was already involved in at least three serious conflicts that it had provoked: with the Vietnamese, with Black Liberation organizations like the Panthers, and with our own soldiers. In all three cases, people were fighting back against U.S. government policies, often using force, because there was no alternative. For example, a week after the police killed the leader of the Chicago Panthers, the police attacked the Panther headquarters in Los Angeles. The L.A. Panthers survived because they were vigilant and were able to shoot it out with the police until the dawn came and the media arrived, providing some protection against the murderous attack. In the army, many soldiers faced hard choices when they were ordered to risk their lives in a war they no longer believed in. The number of officers killed by their own men bears witness to the intensity of the war within the army. (See Hedges, p. 85.)

Rich, attractive young people from well-connected families can get a lot of airtime if they want to, particularly if they're running around dramatically blowing up buildings to "bring the war home." But did the bombing campaign weaken the U.S. government's capacity to pursue the policies that led to these conflicts? Did it build support for the people who were actually in a real war with the U.S. government, because they had no other choice, like the Vietnamese, or the Panthers, or many of its own soldiers? If a news story compared the Viet Cong or the Panthers to the Weathermen, whose struggle suffered in the public eye? Violence is a terrible thing, to be used when all other alternatives have been exhausted. The gratuitous violence of the Weather Underground did not help the anti-war movement.

If only the Weather Underground had listened to the Viet Cong. When their delegation returned from a meeting with the Viet Cong in Cuba in 1969, Bill Ayers recounts in *Fugitive Days* that his girlfriend Diana told him "that the Vietnamese were only mildly interested in our willingness to die for the cause and much more animated about how we planned to reach our Republican parents, something that didn't interest us at all." (Ayers, p. 161) But reaching out to their Republican parents might have been produced something useful, while the bombing campaign was a disaster.

Life in the Party

Soon after I joined Progressive Labor, I was asked to participate in the leadership group, which then involved in a lengthy process of criticizing the New England PL leader, Jeremiah, to help him become a better person. The personal and organizational dynamics were very messy between Jeremiah and his wife. Without the support and validation that came from his relationship with her, a normal person, Jeremiah would have been considered too crazy to lead anything. But had she not been the boss's wife, no one would have picked her to lead the trade union work. Progressive Labor in New England was something of a family business, with a very dysfunctional family in charge. But the national leadership supported Jeremiah because he kept the money rolling in and the troops in line.

As 1970 began, I started to notice in PL a great deal of tension, a kind of desperation coming down from the top. I noticed this tension particularly in relation to PL's work with students, workers, and African Americans.

Although I had for a while wondered about just how much success Progressive Labor was having in recruiting working-class members, I had no idea just how serious the failure was. After a decade of intense activity around workers' rights and the war, this party of the working class had in fact almost no working-class members. The top leaders of PL had big ideas, but no base where their ideology told them they had to have one. They saw using student cadre to recruit campus workers to the party was their only chance to become an authentic working class party.

Shortly after the Weathermen and their allies left SDS, the SDS national office moved to Boston. The party leadership in New York came up with a new program for SDS, the Campus Worker Student Alliance. The problems with the leadership's strategy were obvious from the very beginning to Progressive Labor members working with students on college campuses. On campuses, the big issue was the war. The Campus Worker Student Alliance could work in some places as part of a larger program. But if it became the total SDS program, to the exclusion of campus issues and the war, students were going to take their energy elsewhere. The PL students in SDS saw the mood on the campuses and tried to respond with a balanced program. But the organizers doing the work were overruled. The party leaders wanted campus worker organizing campaigns right away; to them the war and other campus issues were a diversion.

Just back from a meeting of the national committee, Jeremiah attacked the New England leaders of PL's campus organizing. "The Campus Worker Student Alliance isn't the main thing, it's the only thing," he screamed in the course of a several-hour harangue. I found the bullying disturbing, but I didn't get involved, partly because I assumed everyone ultimately would respond intelligently to feedback from the campuses. I was wrong about the leaders responding, and very wrong to ignore the bullying. The leadership insisted, and the Campus Worker Student Alliance became the main program of SDS. It was a big bust.

(For unions then, the main focus was on maintaining their base in manufacturing and construction, not on organizing campus workers. Starting in the 1990s, when major unions became involved in organizing campus workers, student support has helped win some important victories.)

The largest campus uprisings in U.S. history occurred in late spring of 1970. On April 30, President Nixon announced that U.S. troops had invaded Cambodia. Three days later, a mass gathering at Yale called for a national student strike. On May 4, members of the Ohio National Guard fired into a group of unarmed students at Kent State University, killing four and wounding nine. Campuses all over the country then went wild. More than half the colleges and universities were at least touched by student protests, involving 60 percent of the student population in every state of the union. On May 14 police and Mississippi state troopers opened fire on an unarmed crowd of Black students at Jackson State College, killing two and injuring twelve. (Sale, pp. 635-638) Focused exclusively on the Campus Worker Student Alliance program, SDS played no role in organizing any aspect of the uprising. After Kent State, I began to appreciate how the party leadership had a genius for destroying opportunities and turning people off.

I do not believe that there was a Progressive Labor plan to take over SDS – with the departure of the Weathermen and their allies it fell into their laps. Then PL leaders had an opportunity to rebuild and influence SDS as a broad-based and powerful left-wing student organization. But once it was in their grasp, they could not let it develop according to its own needs. The top leadership of PL out of desperation saw SDS *only* as a vehicle to recruit workers to PL through the Campus Worker Student Alliance.

Within months, they broke the back of SDS. I saw it happen, and did nothing to stop it. Sitting on the sidelines while SDS was destroyed was a terrible mistake on my part.

Black workers, according to Progressive Labor, were the key revolutionary force in the United States. Underneath the rhetoric was the reality that Black communities in general and Black workers in particular were openly questioning the rules of the game. Black soldiers were also leading the struggle against the war in the army. PL's failure to recruit Black workers was an issue that the top leadership had to deal with, one way or another. Instead of looking critically at PL's programs they began to launch intemperate attacks on organizations like the Panthers, whom they considered rivals for the allegiance of Black revolutionaries.

For a while, I worked with the Black students in and around Progressive Labor, as part of the party's "Black Liberation Work." There were few such Black students, but they were bright and energetic. I thought they had a tremendous potential to help move the Black student and community organizing in Boston in a good direction. That meant working with existing organizations. But the party had a number of positions, completely condemning Black nationalism, for example, which if taken at their face value would have made work by PL in such organizations and campaigns almost impossible. Electing Black politicians in itself wasn't going to bring justice and equality to Black working-class communities, any more than electing Irish American politicians had brought justice to Irish American working-class communities. But inevitably many Black people were suspicious of white people and sought safety in the Black community, Black organizations, and Black-led campaigns, not surprising with the level of racism and racist violence in the United States so high. Saying that all nationalism was inherently bad was an interesting point to make in an academic debate, but as a guide to how you behaved and with whom you worked, it was useless.

I chose to believe that Progressive Labor's positions weren't to be taken literally. So, I encouraged the Black students in PL to work in coalitions and develop relationships with other Black activists. But the leadership of PL expected everyone to criticize nationalism at every opportunity, which made work with Black organizations almost impossible. The party leaders accused me of being "opportunistic," meaning I was willing to water down the party line to make it more palatable (which was true) and reassigned me to other work.

Soon enough I got to see how Jeremiah intended to make a name for Progressive Labor in the Black community. An African American woman had been accused unjustly of setting fire to a landlord's car, which had been found burning across the street from the Bromley Heath housing project in Boston. PL had brought people to the preliminary hearing before her trial began. Then

PL called for a rally of support in the courtyard of the housing project where she lived.

The Battle of Bromley Heath

When I arrived at the rally in Bromley Heath Housing Project, I saw we had a big problem. There was the woman we had come here to support, about twenty party members, two of whom were Black, and about twenty young Black men who were clearly angry that white people were there. While the white PLers stood around on one side of the courtyard, on the other side a furious argument was going on between the woman and the Black youth over whether white people belonged there. People were in each other's faces, and it was becoming more intense by the minute. She was mad. The young men were mad. Instead of building support for her, PL was isolating her – that alone was a good reason for her white supporters to get out of Bromley Heath. Then I could see the water rising behind the dam. It was time to go. But the top party leader at the event insisted cheerfully that the people from the project would soon see through nationalism and welcome our support.

Then the dam broke. The woman we had come to support was pushed to one side, and the young Black men, by now really worked up, charged straight at us. In the first sensible act of the day, the whites broke and ran. I assumed my accustomed role in the rear guard.

As I backpedaled down the street, I saw two dangers coming my way. One was a young man with a mean-looking knife. The other was a man in his thirties and forties with a three-foot-long board with a big nail sticking sharp side out at the end. The nail or the knife – I'll take the nail any day. So, I focused on fending off the young man with the knife, and took the nail in the right leg.

The man who hit me seemed like a regular working-class person. Seeing a confrontation between the youth of the project and unknown whites, he had come off his porch to protect his neighborhood. I wasn't angry with him, but I didn't stop to have a conversation. A few blocks further I jumped into a car and went to the emergency room.

Jeremiah, the New England leader, had cooked up the whole thing. He himself was off at some "command post," as he often was during dangerous confrontations. Afterwards there was no evaluation, any more than there had been a group discussion and planning before. When I asked him what he thought was going to happen when twenty white people showed up for a rally at Bromley Heath, he said that the attack by the local young people was unprecedented. "Black people have never attacked white people during riots," he told me. "What the hell do you know about riots," I thought, "and who are you to try to start one?"

Some of the young men who attacked us had said they were Panthers, not surprising when you remember the Panthers' popularity among young African Americans in the early 1970s. I was friendly with the Panther leaders. When I saw them afterwards they said they were sorry about the attack, but denied any involvement in the incident. I believed them. But the next *Challenge* blamed the whole incident on the Panthers, saying that they were "playing the role of cops." (*Challenge*, August 1970, p. 7)

A few days later, another Progressive Labor leader suggested that I head up a goon squad to ambush and beat up a group of Black teenagers – "to teach them a lesson." They had been harassing some white PLers who had moved into their apartment building. By then, I was very cautious in dealing with the leadership. I waited a full thirty seconds before I told him to go fuck himself. He left fast, and never spoke to me about it again.

XIII

Moving On

BEING AROUND SDS AND THE student movement had gotten pretty depressing for me. In the fall of 1969, I felt I needed to leave full-time movement work and go get a job, a real job. I hadn't had a paying job since working at MIT in 1965. Because Progressive Labor's strategy focused on organizing the industrial working class, I thought I should work in industry. I also began to realize that the group doing PL's factory work didn't know much about organizing workers. I knew that I wasn't going to be leading any strikes in the near future, but I wanted to work in a factory to see for myself and learn.

The Boston Woven Hose, a large factory in East Cambridge, made rubber products like garden hoses and Astroturf. The first time I walked into the plant I thought I had been transported back to the nineteenth century. Thick black dust covered everything. Grimy men in dusty uniforms scurried about with two wheelers or forklift trucks moving things from one largely empty room to another. Although the factory floor was freezing cold, huge machines in some lofts belched smoke and fire, and the men tending them were covered with sweat as well as grime. If I'd read an article in the left-wing press about a factory as dirty and dangerous as this one before I saw the Woven Hose, I wouldn't have believed it.

In the 1950s when it was the largest factory in Cambridge, the Woven Hose had employed 1,500 workers. When I was a Harvard undergraduate from 1956 to 1960, the factory whistle could be heard from one end of the city to the other. When I started working there in 1969, the plant employed only about 300 people, but the factory whistle still carried loud and clear to Inman Square, near where we lived on Prospect Street. At the 6:45 a.m. whistle, workers all over East Cambridge left their homes and headed for the Woven Hose to punch in at 7:00.

Since the Woven Hose was not looking to hire a Harvard graduate with a left-wing résumé, I had to conceal my past. I applied as a recent arrival from Houston, Texas, with factory experience. I still had a Southern accent. I had worked in a factory two summers when I was in high school. The summer I graduated from high school, I had worked in a copper mine. I already knew how to use a two-wheeler and a forklift truck to move things and how to pick up heavy loads without hurting my back. My story hung together. I even had a reference from Houston, a business associate of my father's, who didn't mind doing a little fibbing over the phone.

I was hired as a clerk in the receiving department, a soft job, compared to most other jobs in the plant. But it was a great job for someone who wanted to learn about factory life. I got to know the Teamsters who delivered the material to the plant from outside companies. Then I had to deliver all the small items, less than fifty pounds or so, to the right department. Pushing my two-wheeler stacked with packages all over the plant, I was able to see most everything and talk to most everybody. The only boring part was that I had to keep the files on everything that arrived.

After a few days on the job, I confirmed that the workers were unanimous in their belief that the boss was fucking them, "in the ear" and "up the ass," with low wages and horrible working conditions. But there were large and bitter disagreements about whether the workers as a group could do anything about this, and what the best course of action might be. There were those who thought you should suck up to the bosses and hope for the best, and those who thought you should fight them. Because an election for union president was coming up soon after I arrived, I quickly found out about the issues.

As the new guy I was courted. As a new guy just up from the South, I was especially courted by the union faction that felt that the only way to get ahead was for "us white folks" to stick together and trust management. Their man had run the union for many years. Now there was this other candidate. "How would you feel if a colored guy got elected to head the whole damn union?" a supporter of the current leadership asked me.

I was friendly and polite to everyone. But I made it my business to go see the insurgent candidate, "the colored guy." He said he was running for union president because he thought the union should fight to defend all the workers. He looked serious and determined. I walked away thinking I should do what I could to get him elected.

The division boss also courted me. One day he gave me a ride home after work. He let me know that he thought I had a lot of potential and that if I continued to work hard and kept my nose clean, there was a real future for me at the Boston Woven Hose. A few days later, he gave me some of his old clothes. I was actually touched by his charity, even though I knew that he wasn't motivated only by concern for my welfare.

I didn't intend to get into trouble with the bosses my first few months on the job, but damned if it didn't happen anyway. All union employees had the right to take a fifteen-minute coffee break in the morning. When time for the break came, the workers in the receiving department retired to the men's bathroom, the "shit house," to drink coffee, gossip, and complain. After a few weeks of taking my coffee with the other men in the "shit house," the foreman told me that he wanted me to take my coffee with him, in the office. I was polite, but no self-respecting socialist could let himself be separated from the workers in his department, especially when they were talking about the issues of the day. So, I continued to take my coffee in the shit house. Then one day the foreman told me I was being fired.

I went to see my friend, "the colored guy" who had just been elected union president. As usual, he was working his machine. He turned it off while I told him my story. He looked at me and said not to worry – maybe they would fire me, but the union would get me my job back. Then he turned on his machine again. I didn't exactly know what to make of this conversation.

At the hearing about my firing, there was the foreman, the boss of the division, and me. Obviously, I wasn't charged with spending my fifteen-minute coffee break in the shit house. Instead, the foreman, a beefy old Irish guy, a shameless liar, said that I was being fired because I didn't do the work.

"What work was it I didn't do?" I asked confidently. I'd been very careful to get my work done.

"Keeping the paper work in alphabetical order," he said. "Maybe you can't read too good."

"Wow," I thought, "a lot of good a Harvard education does me at the Woven Hose." I tried to defend myself, while concealing my background. He lied some more, and I was out the door.

I was discouraged when I left that day. I even went and got another job, in a non-union machine shop. But I was fired from that job after a week, for not making quota. But who knew the real reason? It looked like my luck was running out. Then I got a call from the Woven Hose – the union, United Rubber Workers Local # 69, had backed me up, and I was being rehired. When I came back the division boss, who had been so charitable with his old clothes before management figured out I wasn't trying out for their team and who had presided over the hearing, was suddenly my good friend again. Because of the "personality conflict" with the foreman, they didn't want me back in the receiving department. Instead, they offered me a better paying job in manufacturing. I would be working with a man named Lindsay running the gigantic machine that made rubber turf to surface playing fields. I said sure, and the division boss smiled and let me know that management thought I'd made a good decision.

Lindsay was from Jamaica. Plant gossip described him as a rabid Black nationalist who hated white people. But management couldn't get rid of him as long as he was the only one who knew how to run the synthetic turf machine that made the company's most profitable product.

Lindsay was not about to share his knowledge with someone he didn't trust. The last person to fill the assistant position was a white guy, a former Somerville police officer. One day when Lindsay was away, the huge machine had erupted, throwing molten rubber all over the enclosed space where it was located. The former police officer had run for his life, never to return. Rumor had it that

Lindsay had taken care of him because he didn't trust him. Since I was a white boy from the South, management probably figured that Lindsay would take care of me too, soon enough.

Lindsay did take care of me. He taught me the secrets of how to run the machine, and we became a team that management couldn't fire no matter what we did. What they didn't know was that Lindsay and I had been friends for months. A college SDS student who had worked there the summer before had given me Lindsay's name. Lindsay and I had had a few good conversations, and I had been over to his house in West Medford for a jerked-chicken dinner. A love for spicy food and left-wing politics brought us together.

Lindsay was a careful and witty observer of the world around him. He didn't hate white people out of some weird ideology. Based on experience, he just didn't trust most white people very much. Lindsay was not about to share his special knowledge with someone he didn't trust. But he had liked and trusted that SDS student, and he came to like and trust me. But he poked fun at my optimism about American workers, particularly white ones, who I believed would come to recognize their real interests by opposing capitalism. Lindsay recognized the injustice around him, but by now he was interested in survival, not changing the world.

Working as a receiving clerk wasn't too demanding, but the pay was terrible. It made sense only if you couldn't do anything else, or you had hopes of moving up into management. Running the synthetic turf machine was a well-paid job, but it was a challenge, which at first I enjoyed because I was young and strong. The machine was close to three stories tall, sticking up through a hole in the second-floor loft where we usually worked, loading in the raw materials and manipulating the controls. The labor was hard and the heat was amazing, up to 130 degrees. At lunchtime, I would go across the street to a shack that sold sandwiches and beer. Within minutes of returning to the machine, the beer I had drunk poured out onto my uniform as sweat. The lead-based dyes we sometimes poured into the mixture of raw materials would give us stomach cramps, which we treated by drinking small cartons of milk. When I got home, I would sit in a bathtub for half an hour to get the grime off. Then I would often eat a half-dozen baked potatoes at a sitting, to replace the energy I had burned up on the job.

I told Lindsay all about my background, as friends and comrades do. One day we were talking about boxing – rumor had it that Lindsay had been the middleweight champion of Jamaica. I confided in him that I too had been a middleweight champion – of my freshman class at Harvard. I was appropriately modest, and I had much to be modest about, since I had only had to fight one match to win the title.

Telling that story was a big mistake. After that whenever Lindsay was restless or bored, he would say, "Just a couple of rounds, John, Harvard versus Jamaica." I hated these matches, but I didn't feel I could turn him down. Lindsay was close to six feet tall, dark brown, and handsome, and he moved with the power and grace of a champion. In one round, Lindsay could land more punches than a dozen Weathermen. But Lindsay never hurt me bad. Since we had to shut down the machine during the match, the foreman would jump up and down with frustration. But he could count his lucky stars that Lindsay was pounding me, and not him, and I was the one taking home the bruises.

Once I settled down as Lindsay's assistant I could be as open about my politics as I wanted to be. Sometimes I sold *Challenge* at the factory gate in the morning. I participated in hundreds of political discussions all over the plant, learning about how people there viewed the world. We talked about the bosses whom everyone resented, the war which most opposed, and President Nixon, who was after all a Republican and no good for the working man in Massachusetts. We also talked about the possibility for big changes in who ran the show and how, which many thought was desirable, but few thought possible. While I didn't feel isolated, it was clear that the workers didn't really want to have anything to do with this Progressive Labor thing – too strident perhaps, too much certainty, not connected to institutions they respected, or just plain nuts. I didn't think that this lack of success reflected on me personally. The local PL people who had made a long-term commitment to factory work weren't doing any better in recruiting workers to the Progressive Labor Party.

I really liked the people at the Woven Hose, and I liked working there. I had learned a lot. But after about six months, I began to doubt whether organizing factory workers was where I could contribute to the movement.

I had begun to see the downside of factory work. I was thirty-two years old, and I could get the job done. But, I began to wonder, what about when I am forty-two, or fifty-two? What if I got hurt? Lindsay was a decade older than I was, but twice as strong and fit. His ambition was to get a job at the post office. He had seen the handwriting on the wall – no matter how strong and fit you were, this was a killer job.

I had another worry. How could I lead people if I had to conceal my background from them? I had come to the Woven Hose under false pretenses – I was not a working-class person just up from the South. Anyone who met my family, or friends, or neighbors would figure out soon enough that I was a Harvard-educated leftist. Neighbors in the working-class community where we lived knew who I was, either because I had told them or the FBI had. Some of my working-class friends and neighbors thought my story was a very strange one, but we could still be friends.

But playing a leadership role in the union at the plant was different from being liked in your neighborhood. Leaders have to be trusted. Could I ever be accepted and trusted for who I really am? Lindsay could accept me because he understood the political framework that made my working there a sensible choice despite the other options I had. But even he thought I was a little nuts. I didn't think the others would understand. Most workers thought that anyone who kept working in a factory like the Woven Hose one minute longer than they had to was a goddamn fool, or about to be promoted to management. Nuts or sell-outs could not be trusted. So, I decided to keep my class background under cover while I was at the Woven Hose, and seek out a more professional job where I could be open about where I had come from.

In June, Lindsay got his job at the post office and left immediately. Once he was gone, the place wasn't the same for me. I missed his quick wit and sense of humor. I probably even missed being punched around from time to time. Besides, I had decided that long term, factory work was not for me. I left soon afterwards.

The Woven Hose was a dangerous place to work, but for me it felt like a safe place compared to the political world outside. The murder of the leader of the

Chicago Panthers in December 1969 and the attempted murders of the L.A. Panthers a week later were a somber introduction to the New Year.

A few months later, two police officers in uniform and two in civilian clothes made a determined effort to take me off the streets. Back then, Boston neighborhoods were largely segregated. An African American comrade and I had been leafleting every Saturday for several weeks at a shopping area in a divided neighborhood in Dorchester, part of Boston, off Columbia Road, he on the Black side of the street and I on the white. One day while I was leafleting, a man came out of a bar and started an argument with me. At first I wasn't worried – I had defused dozens of confrontations like this one. But it quickly escalated. Suddenly he grabbed one end of the stack of flyers in my hand. I looked down at his hands and saw beneath them his black leather shoes – the guy's a cop and this is an ambush! I flipped the flyers into the air and turned and took off running. I was five steps away by the time the flyers hit the ground. My friend across the street saw another guy run out of the bar and two uniformed officers come out of an alleyway. They piled into a car and chased after me. But as soon as I had turned the corner and escaped their line of vision, I had jumped over a hedge and thrown myself flat on the ground, with my nose pressed against the dirt. I stayed there for some time listening to their car roaring around the neighborhood looking for me. Fast feet had saved me again.

In August 1970, I began taking education courses to become a teacher. A public school teacher with a Harvard degree was not that weird. My career as a 1960s organizer ended in August 1970, more than a decade after I graduated from Harvard College in 1960. However, one aspect of my involvement in the 1960s movements remained unresolved.

As I sat in class in education school nursing my leg wound from the Bromley Heath battle, I pondered my dilemma. On the one hand, I had fallen in with an organization led by fools. But if I walked out now I would be isolating myself from members whose work as teachers and welfare workers I respected. They were good people who were being used, who were trying like I was to find a way to be principled and effective. I felt we were on the same team. I also knew that what I wanted to do could not be done alone.

Many years after I left the Woven Hose, I met the union president on the street. He had just read an article about me in the *Boston Herald American* by Gordon Hall, the local expert on extremist groups whom I had debated in 1965. Hall had done a recap of my life's history, at least his version of it, "son of Houston oil millionaire, blah, blah, blah..." (My father maintained that the only thing he ever got out of an oil well was losses he could deduct from his tax bill.) "John," said the union president, "if I'd known your father was rich, I'd have got him to buy the place, and turn it into a public shit house." We chatted and agreed that it was a terrible fucking place, no doubt about it. He told me that very few workers were still there. The place was closing, and the union was negotiating severance packages for the workers.

In the 1980s, the whole factory was rebuilt as an entertainment center, with a cinema, a big parking garage, and restaurants. The grime is gone, and the terrible heat and cold. Now no one can tell how gray and filthy the beautiful exposed red brick once was. But the ushers, parking attendants, and wait staff don't have a union and don't make nearly the same money we did at the Woven Hose. I haven't heard a factory whistle in Cambridge for years.

Party's Over

After the summer of 1970, there was an uneasy truce between Jeremiah, the New England Progressive Labor leader, and me. I was given the responsibility of leading the professionals' club, which included professors and academics. This club was viewed as less central to the work of the party, as well as a better place to put a troublemaker. At the same time, I was asked to be a non-public member of the party. That was a big improvement for me because it meant I no longer had to stand out on street corners and sell *Challenge*.

Then one afternoon Jeremiah came by our apartment for a talk. After he sat down, he made a strange proposal. I should publicly resign from the party, he said, and return to Houston. In Houston I could use my family connections to enter the business and political elite of the city, providing valuable insights into the strategic thinking of the ruling class. What was unsaid was that I could also contribute greater financial support to the party.

"The Communist victory in China was made possible by agents who went underground in the 1920s, remaining secret sources of valuable information until the final victory of the revolution in 1949," Jeremiah said. "Then when socialism triumphed their great service could be recognized," he said with a smile signifying that my day too would come.

I smiled too, at the comparison between the Chinese Communist Party and Progressive Labor. "So they want me to become a cash cow," I thought, "out of the loop and in a place where my only source of information on the party's 'progress' would be little reports the leaders themselves give when they came to collect the money. Fat fucking chance!" My thoughts I kept to myself. But I made it clear I was building a life here, and not moving back to Houston, Texas.

In September 1971, I started teaching at the public high school in Somerville, a city just north of Cambridge. In 1971, it was still overwhelmingly working class. I taught world history to tenth graders. In October, my son Matthew was born. He was a lovely boy, but required three operations in the first six months of his life. Now I had a wife and two children who needed me. I became more careful about risking my life and wasting my time.

I had a great deal to say on the subject of world history, but I learned a hell of a lot more that first year than my students did. About two-thirds of the way through the school year, the head of the social studies department, who up until then had been supportive, suddenly turned hostile and harassing. I was acutely aware of the fact that I was an enthusiastic teacher with few skills. I was especially weak in classroom management – keeping order in the classroom.

One day the department head called me into his office and told me I would not be rehired for next year. Afterwards I wondered if it was the FBI or the problems I was having as a teacher. Or was it an underhanded effort by the school administration to cut back on the number of teachers without going through a formal lay-off process, which is what most of my colleagues at the high school thought when they heard it. Then he offered me a deal. If I resigned and went quietly, I would get a good recommendation. I told him I'd think about it. He gave me a recommendation, but I did not go quietly. I worked to improve my teaching, with the help of an experienced colleague. With the help of an extraordinarily brave and dedicated cohort of first-year social studies teachers, I made the case to the rest of the staff that I had not been treated fairly.

In the midst of this intense struggle, the party leadership suggested that I go public and tell the whole school, not just my close friends there, that I was in Progressive Labor. *Challenge* certainly would make this a great story, I thought. "Party member fights firing, rallies teachers against lay-offs, anti-Communist ploy crushed." But first, a reality check. I brought this proposal to my friends at the school, all of whom knew about my party affiliation. Their response was, "We're fighting to protect your rights, and our own. But we are first-year teachers, without seniority or tenure, your supervisor is a big shot in the teachers' association, and the Somerville Public Schools is not like SDS. If you go public, it'll get us all killed." I thought to myself, "What is more important, returning the loyalty of these people, or puffing up the reputation of the Progressive Labor Party?" The next day I told PL no way. I had established an important boundary.

I never did resign from the Somerville Public Schools, but I was not rehired. The following fall the Somerville Teachers' Association went out on strike, partly over the issues of harassment and fears of cutbacks in staff raised by my termination. One day I went to a meeting to wish the strikers well. They gave me a standing ovation. The strike was successful, and the teachers' association was restructured so that supervisors with the authority to hire and fire were excluded.

In the fall of 1972, I began teaching social studies at the Grover Cleveland Junior High School in Boston. That spring I ran for delegate representing the Boston Teachers Union (BTU) at the annual convention of the national union, the American Federation of Teachers. I didn't win outright. But after several of the winners were unable to go, I was moved up the list to replace them. When I arrived at the convention in June, I discovered that there were several open members of Progressive Labor there, as well as several non-public members like myself. The open members made big speeches over one issue or another, while the rest of us stayed in the background. The open members didn't know that we were party members also.

During the convention, public and non-public Progressive Labor members participated in meetings of the Rank and File Caucus. At one meeting, someone proposed that at the next meeting, the caucus endorse the idea of 30 hours work for 40 hours pay for teachers – "30 for 40" was the main campaign of PL's trade union program.

I didn't say anything at the meeting, but I was furious. Maybe "30 for 40" was a good idea for workers in heavy industry, but it offered teachers nothing. Progressive teachers wanted smaller class sizes, more paid time to prepare their lessons, better school facilities, and more parent involvement in the schools. What good was a 30-hour workweek if your classes were larger and you had no time during the school day to prepare for them? The second reason I was angry was that the whole vote would be a farce. Public and non-public members of Progressive Labor were in the caucus, and *no one else*. Thus its support for "30 for 40" would add nothing to the "30 for 40" campaign. It was an effort to manufacture an illusion of support that really wasn't there.

I made my case to the Progressive Labor leader at the convention. He came back and said that Wally wanted the endorsement anyway – Wally Linder was the national head of PL's trade union program and the editor of *Challenge*. I could imagine the article in *Challenge*, talking about how this vote in the Rank and File Caucus endorsing "30 for 40" showed that unaffiliated teachers were flocking to the party's banners. It would be a great morale booster for the party faithful.

I had decided not to provoke a confrontation at the convention. I voted the way I was told, but in my mind's eye a curtain had been pulled back revealing the Wizard of Oz behind it. Based on a little experience, but not much, Wally, Milt, and the other top Progressive Labor leaders had posed as the architects of what could become a powerful working-class movement. The membership was diligently trying to follow the blueprints for this grand edifice. In fact, the top leaders were barely qualified to supervise the construction of a small outhouse.

A few weeks before the start of the new school year, Wally's department sent me a box of materials to use in recruiting teachers in my union local to the Rank and File Caucus. No evaluation, no discussion of what had happened at the

American Federation of Teachers Convention, no strategic plan other than their say-so. I took the materials straight out to the trash, and I told the other teacher members that I was finished with the Progressive Labor Party.

Ironically, my trip to the convention came to the attention of the FBI. Unbeknownst to me they circulated a summary of my file to the leadership of the union. My conservative Irish American brothers on the Boston Teachers Union's Strategy Committee reasoned that because I was a commie, and commies were spies, it followed that I was probably a spy for the Boston School Committee. Go figure. When I turned up at the first meeting, they damn near lynched me. I couldn't believably say, "I'm finished with those PL fuckers," so I had to tough it through. A friend of mine who came with me to the meeting was so terrified he swore this was the first time we had met. At one particularly tense moment, I thought that they would come after me. If they did, I figured I could use a metal chair to take out the first two who moved and then crawl out the window and onto the roof to escape the rest. Fortunately, it didn't come to that. At first my career as a union activist seemed over, but the liberals led by Kathy Kelley stuck by me, and I was able to continue on. I joined thousands of Massachusetts teachers in loving Kathy ever since.

Leaving the World of Sects

Several weeks after my departure from Progressive Labor in the early fall of 1973, most people in the organization in New England revolted against the national leadership. I joined them in an effort to build a new organization more modest and more democratic than PL. But the same leadership and the same members ended up with the same result. One day a few months after the split I tried to have a friendly chat with Jeremiah about the need for democracy in the organization. The next day Jeremiah called me to a meeting. With all his manic energy he had organized the meeting well. The focus of the meeting was my errors and bad attitudes. Everyone there spoke against me. Sitting there silently I could imagine the little rehearsals before the meeting to make sure everyone said the right thing. I felt sorry for the people there whose fear and desire to please had so warped their judgment, but I had to admit that I too had contributed to the climate of bullying and ass-kissing that characterized PL. I had attacked people in meetings just to please the boss and ignored the gross breaches of democratic process that took place all the time. Now it was my turn to feel the lash.

I could have left in a huff, but decided to neither quit nor give way. I went about my business while waiting with an angry heart for my turn to come. Jeremiah was a sick puppy; the only normal thing about him was his wife and family. I knew that one day soon she would leave him. When she finally did, and revealed some of the insanity of their life together, I was able to tell the story behind Jeremiah's attack on me and my trial. The door opened a crack, and people could see they had been living in a dark little room taking orders from a lunatic who thrived at night. With great satisfaction I helped pitch Jeremiah out of the organization, but by then I was sick of the small dark room and most of the other people in it. Bored to death with the world of sects, I left the organization, and it collapsed soon afterwards.

❦ ❦ ❦

What I Learned About Political Sects, the Hard Way

- When dealing with people or organizations, never disregard your first instincts.
- Sects are good things to stay away from, or leave, if you've already gotten involved.
- Here are some warning signs that you may be dealing with a sect:
  - The leaders have special knowledge and understanding, which ordinary members can never hope to acquire.
  - The people who do the actual work in the organization are not listened to and respected.
  - Ordinary members are encouraged to suspend their moral as well as their political judgment.
  - Programs and leaders are evaluated at the leader's discretion.
  - Transparency in decision-making and other internal processes is discouraged.
  - The reputation of the organization is valued more highly than what it actually accomplishes.

XIV

The Aftermath of the Sixties

PROFESSOR SAMUEL HUNTINGTON OF HARVARD University disliked everything the New Left stood for. Writing in 1976 for the Trilateral Commission, a group of high-level establishment intellectuals and political leaders, he bemoaned the erosion of governmental and other forms of authority:

> "The essence of the democratic surge of the 1960s was a general challenge to existing systems of authority, public and private. In one form or another, this challenge manifested itself in the family, in the university, business, public, and private associations, politics, the government bureaucracy, and the military services. People no longer felt the same obligation to obey those whom they had previously considered superior to themselves in age, rank, status, expertise, character, or talents." (Quoted in Howard Zinn, *A People's History of the United States*, p. 559)

By 1970, the Student Nonviolent Coordinating Committee and Students for a Democratic Society were in decline, but the movements they had initiated continued to gain support. In the 1950s, most white Americans saw the segregation and subordination of Black people as the American way, the way things had always been. By 1970, integration had become the national ideal, even while neighborhoods remained in fact segregated and many white families took great care to ensure that their children continued to attend segregated schools.

Similarly, support for the anti-war movement continued to grow, involving millions of citizens and tens of thousands of soldiers. The last U.S. troops left Vietnam in 1973, and the American POWs were released at the same time. The South Vietnamese government continued on, too stubborn to negotiate but too weak to win. Despite the defeat of anti-war candidate George McGovern by Richard Nixon in 1972, the United States appeared to be moving towards a more peaceable relationship with the rest of the world. Richard Nixon was driven from power in 1974 as a result of his efforts to conceal the crimes of his presidential campaign organization. Finally, in 1975, the South Vietnamese army fled the battlefield and the regime collapsed. The whole U.S. cast of characters that had kept alive the illusion of an independent South Vietnam these many years had to run for the nearest exit. Thousands of frantic Vietnamese allies were left behind to fend for themselves.

I felt no sense of vindication, much less victory, as I saw on television the last Americans evacuated by helicopter from the roof of the U.S. Embassy. I had continued to speak out against the war after 1969, but my focus had shifted to issues other than the war, assuming that the war would soon be settled. But the U.S. part of the war had gone on for five years after polls had shown the public turning against it. So much bloodshed and destruction, for so many years, for nothing. I had been confident it would end soon when I moved on to other issues. Had I deserted the Vietnamese, and our own soldiers, I wondered?

The fall of Saigon to the North Vietnamese Army and Viet Cong on April 30, 1975, marked the end of U.S. intervention abroad, or so it seemed. The one consolation I could turn to was the thought that we Americans as a people had learned a lesson. The U.S. intervention in Vietnam had been sold to the American people as essential to the preservation of our freedom and liberty – better fight the Communists in the jungles of Vietnam than on the beaches of California. It was all a lie, but for years our people believed it. Now almost everyone I talked to seemed to be open to a different point of view. My feeling was confirmed by national polls. Two months after the final end of the war only 20 percent of the Americans polled thought that the collapse of the South

Vietnamese government was a threat to U.S. security. (Zinn, p. 556) The lies had lost their power. Perhaps we would all join hands now and say "never again!"

After the resignation of Richard Nixon, congressional committees began investigating the FBI and the CIA. The investigation of the CIA revealed its involvement in terrorism and secret operations of all kinds, straying far from its legal mission of gathering intelligence overseas. Some of the illegal CIA programs revealed included assassination plots against Fidel Castro and other heads of state; introducing the African swine-fever virus into Cuba; working to overthrow the democratically elected government of Chile; and extensive infiltration of the intellectual and academic community in the United States to generate propaganda for its own programs. The investigation of the FBI revealed a similar pattern of illegal actions such as forgeries, break-ins, and perhaps murder (in the case of Fred Hampton, leader of the Black Panthers in Chicago), designed to discredit and disrupt domestic opposition groups like SDS and the Black Panthers. (Zinn, p. 554-556)

The revelations were old news as far as I was concerned, although some of the gruesome details shocked me. It appeared that a broad section of the U.S. public had access to information that showed how under the cover of protecting national security the government had betrayed their interests and values. Now that this betrayal was widely known, I hoped, an aggressive foreign policy that trampled on the rights of other nations would be a tougher sell. Jimmy Carter, elected in 1976, seemed committed to keeping the country out of trouble.

In the 1970s, I felt I had found a stable and worthwhile career as a public school teacher. But teaching and keeping order in a middle school was harder than any job I had had before. Political life was also stressful, but I hung in there, reluctant to let go of the 1960s hope that from our efforts American society could be totally reconstructed.

Like many others shaped by the 1960s, I focused on smaller issues involving the lives of the people around me. In the 1977 teacher strike, whose main issue was smaller class size and a better education for Boston students, my school had 100 percent participation, due partly to my leadership and ties I had with the new African American teachers. The progressives had a thriving caucus, and even most of the conservatives in the union decided that even if I was a "fucking commie," I was "our fucking commie" and a good person to have on the team.

I was elected a union steward at my school and then elected head of the faculty senate. I organized a committee that brought the parents' perspective into union policy. I worked with parents, teachers, and aides in a caucus to fight for higher standards and parent involvement in the schools, as well as union support for affirmative action and school desegregation in Boston.

In the 1970s, some of the big issues brought up in the 1960s such as America's efforts at world domination seemed to recede into the background. Large numbers of 1960s students entered the workforce and the professions. Over the subsequent decades, the union leaders who supported the Cold War and accommodation with the major corporations were pushed aside. The civil rights, feminist, environmental, and peace movements that originated in the 1960s went on to become major if controversial forces in American society.

The left learned much in the 1960s, but so did the right. They learned from our successes as well as from their defeats. They learned how to organize.

Painful Transitions

My mother died on Christmas Eve, 1975. My brother Albert committed suicide a year later. Throughout all this, I remained busy and involved in organizing. I remained busy and involved, but became increasingly depressed and irritable. I wasn't much fun anymore. I drank too much, pitied myself, and blamed others. At first, going out drinking every Friday night with my colleagues seemed like the right thing for a political organizer to do. But getting loaded on Friday night, which I did all too often, was followed by the Saturday morning hangover, lethargy, and ill temper. I had detested my father's drinking, but occasionally I had to ask myself, had the acorn fallen that far from the tree?

Then my marriage fell apart. I had lost the love of the one I loved. At first, I didn't think I could survive. But with two children, life had to go on. Frinde and I decided to put our two children first, share custody, and continue to work together to be the best parents we could be, despite the breakup. I took stock and decided to cut back on the stress that seemed to dominate my life. With the help of Jonathan Kozol, I was able to transfer from the Grover Cleveland Middle

School to South Boston High School in 1979 and set up a reading and math literacy program there inspired by the work of Carol Chomsky and Paulo Freire. Southie was a rough school, the focal point of white resistance to desegregating the Boston Public Schools. But for me an occasional riot was a lot less stressful than the day-to-day torture of teaching in a middle school.

Finding Love Again

I began to date again after Frinde and I decided to separate. In the early spring of 1980 a matchmaking friend invited me to dinner. I met Ellen Sarkisian, gorgeous, strong, and athletic, with olive skin and dark eyes. She was bright, loving, and full of fun, and I started to fall in love all over again. For a time I kept my distance, determined to keep my options open, but I knew deep down that she was the one. Then in August 1980 we went on a great adventure together, and when we came back I knew that I wanted to live with her and no one else.

Ellen, my new love, had been an adult literacy teacher and had written a book on using games to teach English as a second language. We went to Nicaragua in August 1980 with other American educators and education writers on a group tour brought together by Jonathan Kozol to study that country's Literacy Crusade. If Nicaragua, one of the poorest countries on earth, was actually making progress on eliminating illiteracy, then perhaps U.S. visitors like us could learn things that could be applied to our own country, where illiteracy was a problem that refused to go away.

I will never forget one student in particular, who stopped by my classroom at South Boston High School in early spring of 1980. One of his teachers had suggested he come and see me, wondering if he had a "reading problem." He had recently played the last football game of his high school career. In three months, he would graduate from Southie. Since I was directing the reading and math literacy program at South Boston High School, it was my job to test him to see if he was among the 10 percent of the students there who were either totally illiterate or at least five years behind.

He was soft-spoken, respectful, and a good athlete. For almost twelve years he sat quietly in the back of the class while his teachers passed him along from grade to grade. Now he was sitting at a desk in front of me, able only to sign his name and read a stop sign. I looked him over. "He's young and strong but not much bigger than I am," I thought, "with no possibility of a career in professional sports. What kind of future will he have?" We worked together one on one for several months. Before he graduated, he fulfilled one of his greatest ambitions – he wrote a letter to his grandmother back in North Carolina. To this day, I weep when I think of how the schools failed him.

The Literacy Crusade

In Nicaragua I was drawn to a revolution that had been made by Marxists and Christians working together, and by a revolutionary government that was demonstrating a commitment to economic and social equality as well as respect for human rights. I had no idea that this trip would lead me back to the issue of U.S. government efforts to dominate and control other countries.

Under the Somoza dictatorship that had taken over the country with U.S. help in 1933, half the population of Nicaragua remained illiterate; literacy was prevalent only in the urban areas. After the revolution, the new government had closed the junior and senior high schools for five months and encouraged the students to be trained as literacy workers. Thousands of young people answered the call to make a difference for their country. High school students went to live with poor, illiterate families in the countryside to teach them how to read and write; younger students tutored the urban poor.

Ellen and I would never forget Nicaragua. The Literacy Crusade was visible everywhere. We could go anywhere we wanted, and we did. A huge earthquake had destroyed the center of the capital, Managua, in 1973. In Managua, the poor majority lived in two-room cinder block houses along narrow roads or unpaved paths. In the countryside, the houses of the poor were even more ramshackle. Wherever we went we saw blackboards displayed outside or on the wall of the front room with the day's lesson there for all to see.

Everything about the Literacy Crusade conveyed creative energy and thrift. The workbooks were beautifully designed but printed on the cheapest newsprint. Bottle caps had the letters of the alphabet printed on the bottom – instead of tossing them in the trash, learners composed words with them. Illiterate adults proudly showed their lessons to the foreign visitor. Hands gnarled by the sun and hard labor struggled to form letters without breaking the pencil.

The crusade was not only visible but also transparent. "We don't have the resources to end poverty in this country, but we are doing what we can to bring literacy and power to the poor," the Jesuit priest in charge of the Literacy Crusade told us. Then he went on to describe the issues the crusade had to address to really succeed. "What level of skills do the new readers need to be able to continue reading on their own, what needs to be done after the crusade to keep hundreds of thousands of new readers from slipping back into illiteracy?" he asked. The Literacy Crusade was the real thing.

The humanity of the revolution was visible everywhere – in government policies, poetry, song, and public art. Typically, the losers in a civil war are executed. But one of the first acts of the new Nicaraguan government was to abolish the death penalty. At the end of the crusade we joined over three hundred thousand people, one-tenth of the total population of the country, who had come together in the plaza in front of the main cathedral in Managua to welcome the young literacy workers back to their homes. To protect the returning students from road accidents, the government decreed that no alcohol could be sold or consumed from the day before the welcome home through the day after. This revolution cared about its young people. I couldn't even get a cold beer.

A Warning from Daniel Ortega

When our group had arrived in Managua, we asked for a meeting with Daniel Ortega, leader of the Sandinistas, a revolutionary organization named for Augustus Cesar Sandino, a Nicaraguan leader who had fought against the U.S. occupation of Nicaragua in the 1920s and early 1930s and who was murdered by the Somoza dictatorship in 1933. Ortega was also the coordinator of the five-person Revolutionary Directorate and at that time provisional head of state. He was elected president of Nicaragua four years later.

One evening, to our great surprise, we were told to be at the Government House the next morning at 8:45 a.m. for a nine o'clock meeting with Commandante Ortega. "Why would so busy a leader take the time to see us?" I wondered. The next morning we entered the Government House, a modest two-story building that had survived the earthquake, and were ushered upstairs to a conference room where a translator was waiting. At nine o'clock sharp, Ortega, dressed in a simple khaki uniform with black trim walked into the conference room. He was alone, no bodyguards, no flunkies. He offered us coffee, thanked us for coming to visit his country, and then got down to business.

"Many of the soldiers of the Somoza dictatorship's National Guard have fled across the border to Honduras," he said, "and occasionally these counterrevolutionaries make raids back across the border. As you know, they murdered four literacy workers recently in the border region. It is our opinion that if Ronald Reagan is elected president he will rearm the National Guard and send them back to Nicaragua. This will mean a second civil war here with enormous bloodshed and suffering for the Nicaraguan people. I urge you to do everything in your power to prevent this from happening." After he delivered his message, Ortega stayed for a few minutes to answer questions. Then he was gone.

I was stunned. The call was clear but I did nothing. At the time I felt there was almost nothing I could do to affect the outcome of the national election, and anyway like many New Leftists, I looked down on electoral politics.

In 1981 Ronald Reagan was elected, and the tragedy of Nicaragua unfolded. As Daniel Ortega had predicted, the second war began, this time with the United States supporting the overthrow of the legitimate, internationally recognized government of Nicaragua. The restrictions on U.S. intervention abroad that had come about because of popular revulsion against the Vietnam War went out the window one by one. I realized that inaction in the face of the rollback of everything I had fought for was a big mistake.

In June 1981, I left a job I loved at South Boston High School, hoping that perhaps I could do something to help end U.S. government support for the Contra, the counter-revolutionaries trying to overthrow the Nicaraguan government. In August 1982, I went to work at Oxfam America, an international relief and development agency based in Boston, Massachusetts. If we could find ways for the poor Nicaraguan farmers to tell their stories to people here, I believed that the U.S. public would turn against this intervention.

My personal life was a much happier story. Ellen and I had become inseparable after our trip to Nicaragua. In April 1982, she and I were married in the

Unitarian Church in Harvard Square with Matthew and Sarah in attendance. In June 1984, Ellen and I adopted a lovely little two-year-old boy from El Salvador, Gregory Gerson Alano Maher. My home life was filled with joy.

Looking at Ourselves from Mali and the Muslim World

I traveled in the summer of 1986 to Mali, a predominately Muslim country whose political history I had studied in Paris twenty-five years before. My mission was to bring financial aid from Oxfam America to a group of former slaves who had escaped from their nomadic Taureg masters during the Great Drought of the mid-1970s. Now they wanted to settle down and become farmers.

One day at a bend in the River Niger between the towns of Mopti and Timbuktu, a group of men invited me to join them for the noonday meal. In this harsh land just below the Sahara Desert, my survival depended on the kindness of strangers. As we knelt down in a circle beside the river, my companions put their swords and daggers to one side. Then a large bowl was placed in the middle of our group, with rice heaped along the edge and fish stew in the center. Mentally, I rehearsed my Malian table manners: keep your left hand away from the common bowl, scoop up a handful of rice in your right hand, roll it into a ball, and dip the ball into the fish stew. I was hungry and ready to eat.

Then someone asked me a question that took away my appetite. "Comrade, I heard on the radio this morning that your government bombed the house of Muammar Qaddafi [leader of Libya] near Tripoli and killed some of his children. What do you think about that?"

I felt a dozen pair of dark eyes fix on me. "My answer better be good," I said to myself as I collected my thoughts in French. "I'd hate like hell to die here for the sins of Ronald Reagan." Out loud, I said, "I care nothing for Qaddafi. He is a dictator who oppresses his own people. But nothing he has done can justify bombing his house and killing his children, who are innocents. I am ashamed because of the actions of my government." My companions looked at one another and nodded, then turned to the lunch. My appetite returned. This incident was not big news in the United States. But it was the top story that day in this remote place on the edge of the Sahara, and throughout the Muslim world.

In 1989 I left Oxfam America, and a year later I joined the staff of Neighbor to Neighbor, which was working to change U.S. policy supporting the repressive, right-wing government of El Salvador.

XV

Neighbor to Neighbor Massachusetts: Let the People Decide

IN 1991 NEIGHBOR TO NEIGHBOR decided that in addition to our work on Central America we would campaign for affordable health insurance for everyone (called then "single payer," now "Medicare for all"). I led the Neighbor to Neighbor campaign in Massachusetts. In 1993, national health care reform was defeated, a political disaster. We had to figure out how to do better. Neighbor to Neighbor Massachusetts concluded that without more working-class participation in the political process, basic reforms like universal access to health care don't have a chance. From now on, any campaign we worked on had to increase their participation.

A year later Newt Gingrich overreached and gave us the issue: the new Republican majority in Congress decided to try to cut back funding for Medicare and Medicaid. This direct attack on working people spurred our organizing in Massachusetts, led by Dan Gilbarg in Fall River and Harris Gruman on the North Shore. In 1996, the two community-based political organizations we helped build played an important role in defeating two Republicans and electing to Congress two very progressive Democrats, Jim McGovern and John Tierney. To this day Tierney and McGovern work closely with the Neighbor to Neighbor chapters in their districts to defend working people's interests in domestic and foreign policy.

These two victories gave credibility to the idea that a successful mobilization of low-income voters could swing an election. But what should our next step be? There were no obvious targets for us in Congress – after all we had just defeated the last two Republicans, and Massachusetts had one of the most progressive congressional delegations in the country. But a Republican governor and a conservative Democratic Speaker of the House dominated state government. Who controlled state government was key because under the Reagan administration so much power over domestic programs had devolved from the federal government to the states.

Developing a Statewide Strategy

In mid-August of 1997, Jim Marzilli, a leader of the Progressive Caucus in the Massachusetts Legislature, invited the staff of Neighbor to Neighbor to his house for a barbecue. About a dozen of the twenty-five or so members of the Progressive Caucus were there too. The day had been hot, but large trees shaded Jim's back deck. The Boston skyline was way off in the distance. Our plates were heaping with barbecue, and we were well into our second beer when Jim got down to business:

> "We vote for economic justice even though most of us represent well-off districts. The Speaker makes us pay big time for stepping out of line. The people who supposedly represent low-income people vote the other way, but nothing happens to them. If you people [meaning us] can't find some way to hold these other reps accountable to the needs of their constituents, then I'm outta here."

The other members of the Progressive Caucus nodded in agreement, and I started sweating. Without them in the Legislature, overcoming the conservative grip on the State House was a pipe dream.

To understand this paradox of a progressive congressional delegation and a right-wing state government, Harris Gruman had led the staff of Neighbor to Neighbor Massachusetts in a strategic planning process. We had to figure out what to do, where, and why so we could put our very limited resources where they could make a difference. We researched the demographics of each state representative district, looking at the percentage of voting age working-class people, the percentage of voting age people of color, and the percentage of eligible voters who did not vote in the last election. We also looked at the voting record of the incumbents, particularly their performance on issues of vital importance to working-class families.

To have a progressive majority (eighty-one plus votes) in the Massachusetts House of Representatives, we needed the additional votes of forty-five state legislators with districts where a substantial percentage of low-income working-class, and/or minority voters lived, but who were currently voting against their constituents' interests in terms of working-family issues like jobs, wages, education, and affordable housing and health care. These legislators were reelected every year because far fewer people voted in state contests than in national ones – a small group of family and friends could win for them year after year. However, if these forty-five legislators could be persuaded, pressured, or replaced, there would be a progressive majority in the state Legislature in Massachusetts. If low-income people voted in these districts, they could determine the outcome. Our plan was to get these low-income people organized and voting their own interests.

Fortunately, these forty-five districts were concentrated in six urban areas. The largest concentration of target state legislators was in Worcester, the second largest city in Massachusetts. We decided to start organizing there.

One day shortly after the barbecue at Jim Marzilli's home, Harris Gruman and I drove out to our first meeting with the leaders of the Worcester Labor Council – a tough bunch, not generally welcoming of outsiders, particularly liberals. We were anxious and aware of coming from "liberal" Boston, fifty miles away.

Voter turnout in the housing developments and other low-income and immigrant neighborhoods in Worchester was miserable. The Lakeside Housing Development, with hundreds of potential voters, had only fifteen votes in a previous election. Only a few dozen people voted in Great Brook Valley, with thousands of residents. Anti-union, anti-working-class state legislators were immune to pressure. When we said that those were the neighborhoods where we wanted to organize, the leaders of the Labor Council offered their full support. N2N-MA was off and running.

Great Brook Valley, with several thousand residents, was the first place we began to organize. When the residents we had brought together invited the state representative to come to a community meeting, he swaggered in late, dressed in blue jeans and a tee shirt, grabbed the microphone from our organizer, and told his Latino constituents he didn't care what they thought, and didn't have to, because they didn't vote. Then he swaggered out again.

What Victory Feels Like

Low-income voters typically associate politics with powerlessness, isolation, and defeat. This legacy of defeat can be overcome with building power, unity, and victories based on strategies that work, demonstrating that political participation is worth the effort.

Election Day, 2000, 7:40 in the evening. The shadows from the trees covered the low, brick buildings of Lincoln Village, a working-class housing development in Worcester. I am driving up and down the gentle hills, stopping at voters' houses to offer rides to the polls. The sun had set a couple of hours before, and the polls would close in twenty minutes. Victory is so close I can taste it. But there is time to get one more voter to the polls.

Ahead of me, I see a woman pull into her driveway. I check the address on my list of voters committed to our candidate for state representative. She is one of ours. That her name isn't crossed off means she hasn't voted yet. As soon as she and her daughter get out of the car, I call to her, "The polls are about to close. Let me give you a ride."

"But there's nobody home to watch my daughter."

"Bring her along," I said.

We go to the polls. Afterwards I drop them back at their apartment. It's over. I drive back to the Neighbor to Neighbor campaign office wedged into a volunteer's apartment in another housing development.

Victory did not seem so close earlier in the day when I was trouble-shooting. In the morning our opponent, a state representative and Assistant Speaker of the Massachusetts House, was yelling at our volunteers when they brought

Latino citizens to vote. He succeeded in intimidating the staff at a key polling station. Despite what the regulations clearly say, they ruled that voters could not bring the person of their choice inside with them to translate the ballot. I had to call on the lead lawyer at the Massachusetts secretary of state's office, which supervises elections, and get her to straighten them out.

Then in the early afternoon, the unions deployed at the polls big strong guys with signs on big thick sticks. No more intimidation by the state rep and his pals. No more need for a troubleshooter. When I had left the office to drive supporters to the polls, I looked at the list for Lincoln Village. The crossed-off names told me most of the work had already been done. Six months of going door to door building support for our candidate had paid off. I felt better than Sitting Bull after the Battle of the Little Big Horn.

When the votes were counted our labor/community/Irish/Latino coalition had defeated a key ally of the House Speaker. The vote was 71 percent to 29 percent, the largest margin of victory against a member of the House leadership in state history. Voter turnout was up 1,000 percent in low-income communities in Worcester where we had worked, like Lincoln Village and Great Brook Valley. Dozens of immigrants who had never participated before in the continental U.S. worked on the campaign. What a party we had, hosted by U.S. Representative Jim McGovern. Latinos learned to drink Guinness, and Irish Americans learned to dance!

How We Got There

In Worcester, we began to develop our approach to organizing. We decided that people would become members of N2N-MA by taking action. We first come to potential voters not with candidates to support, but with issues where their participation right now could make a difference. In our first campaign N2N-MA volunteers would say:

"You said that affordable child care is important to you. Soon the state House of Representatives will be voting on a bill to increase funding for child care by $100 million. Your representative says he doesn't know how he'll vote on this bill. He needs calls from registered voters in his district to help him make up his mind."

"But I'm not registered."

"No problem. I can register you now."

"I don't have a phone."

"No problem. Use my cell."

In two minutes, the resident has taken two actions, registering to vote and making a phone to the legislator. After a key vote was taken at the State House, we made sure to inform the residents about whether their representative in the Legislature supported their interests or not. Emphasizing accountability around the issues meant that when election time came, our members had the facts and knew whom to vote for.

Developing New Leaders

Earlier in its development when it was focused on Central America or health care reform, Neighbor to Neighbor had successfully recruited and mobilized middle-class political activists. In districts where members of Congress were persuadable, Neighbor to Neighbor sent organizers to help local activists mobilize constituent pressure to change their votes. Later, Neighbor to Neighbor initiated a boycott of Folgers Coffee that played an important role in pressuring the Salvadoran coffee barons to agree to peace. Now with the new strategy based on building power in working-class communities, the biggest challenge for me was learning how to recruit and train activists from these communities to become organizers and leaders.

Leaders from the neighborhoods had to lead the fight, but to succeed we had to go beyond the gatekeepers and develop new organizations and new leaders around issues the residents thought were important. Once we decided that working-class participation was key, community outreach – knocking on doors – was the only way to go. As director, I had to set the example – and resist the temptation to shoot the breeze in comfortable Boston conference rooms. Organizers who didn't want to knock on doors had to seek employment elsewhere.

Neighbor to Neighbor had always been an organization aiming for measurable results: signatures gathered, phone calls made, votes changed, elections won. Now we had to add leadership development as a prime objective. Every person who signed our petitions needed to be treated like a potential volunteer. We needed to treat every volunteer like a potential leader. The top leaders of the organization had to monitor the development of potential leaders regularly to ensure that they were in fact learning to be leaders.

I tried to develop personal relationships with all the potential leaders. One day before a local election I went out door to door with Luz Ramirez in the Lakeside Housing Development where she lived. She would pound on the metal door of each apartment we came to. When the door opened she would explain, "Do you want politicians to pay attention to us and our community? If you do, you have to vote tomorrow. We have to get involved in politics if we are to go forward."

Luz had worked as a volunteer in a local social service agency at Lakeside. She knew her neighborhood had problems that could not be addressed unless the government took her community's needs seriously. She decided to volunteer also with Neighbor to Neighbor. Luz was not political in the traditional sense of following elections, but she cared deeply about what happened to her community. "This woman has it in her to become an organizer," I thought. "She is concerned about the community. She understands how important political participation is. And she is fearless."

The challenge was to ensure that the middle-class organizers we had, who were preoccupied with many pressing tasks, followed up regularly with Luz and volunteers like her. Monitoring the progress of our organizers-in-training became an essential part of each staff meeting – "Tell me about Luz, tell me about Ana," a Dominican-born activist who had participated in a youth group supporting my hero Colonel Caamano Deno back in the 1960s.

Attention to developing leaders takes time. In the short term, putting serious resources into developing local volunteers as leaders meant fewer signatures or fewer phone calls to legislators. But having organizers from the community gave us the legitimacy, strength, and staying power we need for long-term success. Our summer intern program that once trained college students to become organizers was transformed into a paid apprenticeship program open only to working-class people from the communities where we were organizing.

There were many rivers to cross. Often people from working-class communities have been taught to defer to the outside experts or to the middle-class people they know. Our methodology was to favor the people who actually did the work. But women, typically most concerned about community issues and most likely to do the actual work of building a community organization, have been taught that when it comes to big political decisions they should defer to men. Our organizing had to deal with these stereotypes and prejudices to ensure that people from the community, particularly women, took their rightful place as organizers and leaders of N2N-MA.

I knew I needed to learn new skills, but where? Younger organizers like Allison Kennedy, twenty-three years old and a recent graduate of Providence College when she started working at N2N-MA, were committed to the leadership development process and had a better understanding of it than I did. For us to succeed in developing new leaders I had to follow her lead.

Under the leadership of young organizers like Allison, our community meetings became more disciplined, more closely tied to the grassroots action our strategy required. Every person who came to a meeting had to leave with something meaningful and specific to do. Skills needed to be shared and developed. Experienced people needed to delegate responsibilities and then follow up to make sure new leaders succeeded. College-educated organizers had to learn not to talk so much. Better decisions got made when the insights of everyone, above all people from the community, were incorporated into the plan. To get people to participate, we began to use brief brainstorms to lay out the options, and then break down into sub-groups to formulate or evaluate different aspects of the campaign.

Allison insisted that each meeting be evaluated. In five minutes, we could go around the room with each participant saying one good point about the meeting and one thing that could be improved. This way everyone learns how to lead an effective meeting. Because we took the time to evaluate meetings, our meetings got more inclusive and more productive as time went on. Rotating the job of running meetings encouraged more experienced people to train others in the skills of building an agenda and leading a discussion. Also rotating visible leadership responsibilities increased inclusiveness and unity by breaking down gender, race, and other stereotypes about who can lead.

For us it became crucial that the volunteers as well as the organizers know if we are meeting our objectives, and what is working and what is not. In evaluations, points are made in an objective manner that strengthens the program and builds the group rather than blames the volunteer: "how can we do better" rather than "here's what you did wrong." Staff evaluations likewise also try to identify the things a person does well, and the areas where he or she needs improvement.

All staff and interns are regularly evaluated by the people they work with, including of course the director, who is evaluated by the whole staff. One day Ellen came downtown to the N2N office to have lunch, but I had left so that staff could say without inhibition what they thought about how I was doing my job. In walked Ellen, followed by an awkward silence. The staff was gathered around a paper taped to the wall with "John" at the top and two long columns underneath labeled "rules" (good) and "sucks" (not so good). Asked if she had anything to add, Ellen made contributions to both sides of the ledger. Tough love is essential to strong organizations and strong marriages.

What We Have Become

A key event in 2000 marked the transformation of N2N-MA: Luz Ramirez and Ana de la Cruz, volunteers from Worcester, completed the new organizer-training program and became full-time organizers. To complete the transformation, in 2001 a new board of directors made up of working-class activists elected by the chapters and affiliates took over the leadership of the entire organization. All board members must have direct life experience with working-family issues and live in a working-class community in Massachusetts.

Now fifteen years old, Neighbor to Neighbor Massachusetts is a vehicle for neighborhood organizing to build collective consciousness and political power. Thousands of people across Massachusetts knock on their neighbors' door, listen to the challenges they face, and encourage them to take action with their fellow community members to change things. Through its organizing, communities that were previously excluded from the political process and public debate are now at its forefront, and have profoundly changed our state's politics.

Since N2N-MA was founded in 1996, Massachusetts has led the country in key policy changes including health care reform, corporate tax reform, marriage equality, environmental reform, and most recently, comprehensive criminal justice reform. At the same time, we elected a majority progressive congressional delegation, continuously voted to the left of the rest of the nation in federal elections, and elected our first African American governor.

Because of our work, issues that once divided working-class communities in Massachusetts have become less important. A significant number of the board members and activists are evangelical Christians. What could be a more natural way to affirm family values than volunteering for an organization like N2N-MA, dedicated to defending and enhancing the lives of working families? N2N-MA does not try to change people's personal beliefs on questions like abortion and gay marriage. But the organization does take a stand against discrimination of any kind. Being part of a diverse organization working year-round to support working families also encourages a culture of respect and tolerance around issues where not everyone has to see things the same way. Empowered working-class activists, including evangelical Christians, have no problem choosing between a candidate running against abortion and gay marriage and one running for the things working families need to survive. When a question was put on the ballot to overturn the Massachusetts Supreme Court's ruling in favor of gay marriage, Neighbor to Neighbor said, "Vote no."

N2N-MA is the voice of its low-income members in the communities where we organize. According to the late Senator Paul Wellstone, our supporter and friend, Neighbor to Neighbor Massachusetts and its allies had proved we could combine three things progressives need to become relevant in American politics: "a vision to inspire working people, grassroots organizing, and winning elections."

For me Neighbor to Neighbor Massachusetts became a "beloved community," a community bound together by common purpose, love, and trust like some projects in the 1960s were – SDS in the mid-1960s, Vietnam Summer, and the Boston Draft Resistance Group. I also feel that the faith in ordinary people and the belief in democracy and participation that drew me initially in the movement in the 1960s have been vindicated yet again by the work that N2N-MA has done.

In 2001 I decided to move on to work more on how to integrate opposition to the drive to empire into a broader, nationwide, working-family agenda. Harris Gruman, organizer, strategist, and architect of N2N-MA's electoral successes since 1995, was selected by the staff and board to succeed me. Juan Leyton became the director in 2009. I have remained on as a volunteer. La lucha continua.

❦ ❦ ❦

What I Learned about Building Working-Class Political Participation and Power at N2N-MA

- Organizing to build power in working-class communities is a year-round process that involves not only elections but also holding elected officials accountable to serving the needs of their constituents.

- Power is exercised by electing and defeating candidates. But building power for the long term begins with building an organization that fights for the things people need to survive and prosper.

- Campaigns can focus on a single issue, but the organization must have a multi-issue strategy that reflects all the things that working-class people need.

- Organizing for power needs to focus on districts, issues, and candidates where victory is possible.

- Given limited resources, organizing for power requires a strategy based on a study of politics and demographics to determine where victories can be won, and around what issues.

- Organizing for power in low-income communities must be combined with coalition work with unions, seniors, and middle-class people who share the same interests and outlook. Such a coalition can organize an effective legislative campaign to pressure elected officials, as well as work to defeat those who don't cooperate.

- For long-term success, organizations must be rooted in and accountable to the communities where they organize.
- Organizing is not the same as mobilizing, where a leader or leadership group makes all the key decisions. Successful organizing in working-class communities means developing leaders from the community who are accountable to the community.

XVI

A Way Forward

FUNDAMENTAL CHANGE WON'T COME TO the United States without the active support of the working-class majority, those who have the most to gain from such change. I've known this for a long time, even if I haven't always acted on it. That's why I went to New Bedford to work on the Hughes campaign in 1962, that's why I helped put together Vietnam Summer in 1967, that's why I helped develop Neighbor to Neighbor Massachusetts, and that's why I remain active today, as a Neighbor to Neighbor volunteer and as an activist in a campaign to make large cuts in the military spending.

Class matters everywhere; the United States is no exception. In *The Working Class Majority: America's Best Kept Secret*, Michael Zweig looks at the class structure of the United States from the point of view of the power and authority different groups have at work. A relative handful of people have a great deal of power and authority over what happens in the workplace, while a much larger number have almost no power and no authority, unless they are organized into a union. The first group are the capitalist class, the second the working class.

"The great majority of Americans form the working class. They are the skilled and unskilled, in manufacturing and in services, men and women of all races, nationalities, and religions. They drive trucks, write routine computer code, operate machinery, wait tables, sort and deliver the mail, work on assembly lines, stand all day as bank tellers, perform thousands of jobs in every sector of the economy. For all their differences, working-class people share a common place in production, where they have relatively little control over the pace and content of their work, and aren't anybody's boss. They produce the wealth of nations, but receive from that wealth only what they can buy with the wages their employers pay them." (Zweig, p. 3)

Looking at U.S. Department of Labor data about the number of people in hundreds of different occupations, Zweig concludes that 62 percent of the workforce is working class, with about 30 percent in the middle-class category that includes professional people, small business owners, and managers and supervisors who have authority over those at work. (Zweig, pp. 4 and 28-29)

But "working class" has practically disappeared from the American political vocabulary. Do the overwhelming majority of Americans think of themselves as middle class, even if they aren't? Actually, most Americans will only describe themselves as middle class if the choices are limited to lower, upper, and middle. But given the option of describing themselves as working class or middle class, most working-class people will choose working class. (Zweig, p. 58) Polls show American workers understand where they stand relative to others.

Obviously, the social structure of the United States is dynamic and changing. For example, manufacturing jobs in the United States have declined dramatically, and fewer members of the working class have a job that supports a family. The intermediary institutions like the Main Street of local banks and family-owned business are disappearing. The government, and the economy, education system, culture, news, and entertainment are all dominated now by large for-profit corporations in a way they were not even two decades ago. Through TV, Facebook, and Twitter the large corporations are also moving into a role in mediating relations between people the way cafés and bowling alleys, for example, did a generation ago. But because Wall Street is triumphant and corporate power is so omnipresent, fewer people actually benefit from the way things are done now. A step towards change is demanding accountability from the institutions that are supposed to serve us.

Build Political Participation and Accountability

Government policy is a major determinant of how well working-class and middle-class people live. Government sets the rules that make it easy or difficult to organize a union, and what issues the unions can bargain over. Government spending on schools, health care, housing, transportation, and childcare – the "social wage" set through the political processes – is vital to people in the working class as well as to the middle class. The political process also determines foreign policy, military policy, and trade policy so crucial to working-class survival and the health of the nation as a whole.

If the majority is working class, and sees itself that way, why does the working class appear to have so little influence over government policy? Part of the answer lies in the absence of strong working-class participation in the political process.

Political participation in general is low in the United States, much less than in other democratic countries. Post-World War II voter turnout peaked in the 1950s, and then it began to slide. Between 1964 and 1980 voter turnout dropped 8 percent, from 63 percent to 55 percent. Voter turnout by primarily working-class groups declined 16 percent, or twice as much, over the same period. (Frances Fox Piven and Richard A. Cloward, *Why Americans Still Don't Vote: And Why Politicians Want It That Way*, p. 123) Only 55.3 percent of eligible Americans voted in 2004, 56.8 percent in 2008, the Obama election year, which was still far less than the 63.1 percent who voted in 1960. In non-presidential election years, voter turnout has been below 40 percent since 1974.

Many factors help explain low voter participation in the United States, including a political process heavily influenced by big money interests and the "winner take all" structure of the Electoral College, encouraging only people in the swing states to turn out for presidential elections. But working-class turnout, particularly potential voters in non-union households, is much lower than even the low U.S. average.

The decline in working-class participation reflects the decline in union membership, the collapse of urban political organizations that used to get working-class voters to the polls, and political defeats that demoralized many low-income and minority voters.

The decline in the strength of the labor movement is associated with declining working-class political participation. In the 1950s, 35 percent of the workforce was unionized, while today only 13 percent belong to unions. Only about 40 percent of the working poor (the low income 25 percent of the workforce, almost all without union protection) vote, vs. 76 percent of the investor class. (Michelle Conlin and Aaron Bernstein, "Working... and Poor," *Business Week*, May 31, 2004) In many low-income/immigrant communities, voter participation of citizens is far below 20 percent, particularly in local and state elections.

Anti-union laws and administrative procedures have played a major role in sapping union strength, but racism inside the labor movement has been a major factor as well. Since the 1950s, mass production industries employing typically white male workers have declined absolutely in numbers of workers and relative to other sectors, while a new working class concentrated in the service sector, resting heavily on women and minorities, has emerged. The white male leadership of the labor movement has been slow to adapt to this new reality.

Racism has been used to divide the working class in other ways. Low-wage workers who rely on public assistance to survive are demonized as an "underclass," removing the poor from the mainstream of American life and values. But in any given year, the great majority of people receiving welfare did so for a short period. (Zweig, p. 81) But from Ronald Reagan's "welfare queens" to Bill Clinton's "ending welfare as we know it," low-income workers have been subjected to unending abuse and demoralizing defeats. Thanks to these policies, the U.S. has the highest child poverty rate in the industrialized world.

Racism was also an obstacle to incorporating Black and Latino citizens into the political machines that had brought previous generations of working-class voters to the polls. White flight from urban areas finished off these once powerful institutions. Racism against immigrants is also currently being exploited by politicians seeking to fan the fires of fear in the post 9/11 world.

Low-income people in the United States lead very demanding lives, "where one missed bus, one stalled engine, one sick kid means the difference between keeping a job and getting fired, between subsistence and setting off the financial tremors of turned-off telephones and $1,000 emergency-room bills that can bury them in a mountain of subprime debt." (Conlin and Bernstein) Low-income working people have lots to do. To many of them, voting seems hardly worth the trouble if you're going to get screwed anyway. And they are really getting screwed.

Declining working-class voter participation potentially condemns the progressive movement to irrelevancy. In some parts of the country working-class voters have abandoned the Democratic Party to vote for Republican conservatives running on "family values" issues like anti-abortion and anti-gay marriage. But are working-class people really becoming more conservative, or are conservatives filling a political vacuum left when the Democratic Party abandoned working families? Thomas Frank describes the "criminally stupid strategy" of the current leadership of the Democratic Party that has led to this debacle.

> "The Democratic Leadership Council (DLC), the organization that produced such figures as Bill Clinton, Al Gore, Joe Lieberman, and Terry McAuliffe, has long been pushing the party to forget blue-collar voters and concentrate instead on recruiting affluent, white-collar professionals who are liberal on social issues. The larger interests that the DLC wants desperately to court are corporations, capable of generating campaign contributions far out-weighing anything raised by organized labor. The way to collect the votes and – more importantly – the money of these coveted constituencies, 'New Democrats' think, is to stand rock-solid on, say, the pro-choice position while making endless concessions on economic issues, on welfare, NAFTA, Social Security, labor law, privatization, deregulation, and the rest of it." (Thomas Frank, *What's the Matter with Kansas?*, p. 243)

Fundamentalist Christianity is not new to farmers and workers in Kansas, nor is economic hardship. What is new is that today in some places only the Christian Right and now the Tea Party speak to their discontents. When Democrats abandon working families, the right wing thrives.

Progressives in the Age of Obama

A Democratic victory in our precinct of Cambridge, Massachusetts, where we live, can be taken for granted. But Ellen, my wife, grew up in Lancaster, Pennsylvania, a traditionally conservative town in a swing state. We spent weeks working for Obama in Lancaster in 2008, knocking on doors first for the primary in the spring and then for the general election in November. We loved the work. It was like a Neighbor to Neighbor-led campaign, systematic, well organized, and focused on getting low-income people to the polls. On Election Day the voters came out.

Talking to low-income whites, African Americans, and Latinos in Lancaster gave new meaning to the word "hope." Their openness and enthusiasm conveyed hope for a well-paying job, hope for affordable health care, hope that their children might have more opportunities for a better life. I had hopes too, that Obama's commitment to change and a better life for working families in the United States would lead him to reexamine the previous administrations' commitment to world domination.

But I seriously underestimated the importance of Obama's ties to Wall Street, ties which were probably necessary for him to get the nomination. In the end I think we all got screwed. Sadly, the Democratic administration under President Obama embraced the empire – huge "defense" budgets and continued war in Afghanistan while the educational system and infrastructure upon which our prosperity depends falls apart for lack of funds. Not surprisingly, Obama's indifference to the needs of working people regarding jobs and housing has had political consequences as well. Twenty-nine million people who voted for Obama in 2008 did not vote for the Democrats in the congressional elections in 2010. The Republican decline in 2010 was fifteen million votes, much less, allowing the Republicans to take control of the House of Representatives. My guess is that working-class alienation and despair accentuated the normal mid-term election decline in Democratic voters. Unless progressives can provide a real alternative to the administration's policies, I expect a significant part of the potential Democratic base to stay home in 2012.

The structure of U.S. imperial power now extends to every corner of the globe. In 2001, the United States military expenditures were 37 percent of the *total* worldwide. (Chalmers Johnson, *The Sorrows of Empire: Militarism, Secrecy, and the End of the Republic*, p. 63) Now the U.S. spends close to 50 percent of the total spent on the military worldwide. According to the Report of the Sustainable Defense Task Force, "In 1986, U.S. military spending was only 60 percent as high as its potential adversaries (taken as a group). Today America spends more than two-and-one-half times as much as the *potential* adversary states, including Russia and China."

During the 1960s anti-war activists like myself denounced U.S. imperialism, and the other side hotly denied this accusation. Now things are out in the open, as Secretary of State Hillary Clinton made it perfectly clear: "Now there should be no mistake. Of course this administration is also committed to maintaining the greatest military in the history of the world...." (A Conversation with U.S. Secretary of State Hillary Rodham Clinton, Council on Foreign Relations, September 8, 2010, Washington, D.C.)

The American people are coming to know what Chalmers Johnson calls "the sorrows of empire." Drive to empire kills our people, undermines the system of international law and cooperation on which our safety really depends, destroys our own democracy and constitutional government, and turns much of the world against us. In addition, the enormous financial resources required to defend the empire devour the resources needed to protect the homeland and provide a decent life for most Americans.

What I see today is middle-class and working-class Americans being squeezed from all sides. Imperialism makes the world a more dangerous place for Americans. Military spending goes in large measure to develop and protect the empire, and line the pockets of the military contractors, not to protect Americans at home. But the rich can afford to fly in private jets, live in gated communities, and hire private security personnel to protect them. The working class and the middle class get to take their chances.

In addition to making the world more dangerous for Americans, military expenditures are leading to an enormous budget deficit. The rich who benefit from the empire get their taxes cut, which makes an enormous budget deficit even larger. The budget deficit then is used as a justification to withhold public funds from education, health care, housing, and retirement benefits that working-class and middle-class Americans need to survive. With fewer opportunities at home, working-class young people join the military hoping to better themselves. Then they are sent overseas, to fight and perhaps to die in a war from which they have nothing to gain.

I believe that the United States is following the seventy or so previous global empires on the well-trodden path to disaster. While progressives are coming to grips with this reality, many conservatives now recognize also that the empire is destroying the republic. For humanity to survive and move forward the drive to empire must be curtailed. As Jonathan Schell warned in the middle of the last decade:

> "... [T]he American imperial solution has interposed a huge unnecessary roadblock between the world and the Himalayan mountain range of urgent tasks that it must accomplish no matter who is in charge: saving the planet from overheating; inventing a humane, just, orderly, democratic, accountable global economy; redressing mounting global inequality and poverty; responding to human rights emergencies, including genocide; and, of course, stopping proliferation as well as rolling back existing arsenals of nuclear arms." (Jonathan Schell, "The Empire Backfires," *The Nation*, March 29, 2004, p. 16)

The world is already facing huge problems that our nation could help solve if we became global citizens and forced our leaders to abandon the arrogant notion that they are uniquely qualified to direct other nations in the managing of their own affairs.

An enormous responsibility rests on the shoulders of progressives in America. Today the costs of our present and future wars are threatening the foundations of our economy and society. Those who have little are being asked to make even greater sacrifices. Income inequality is at its highest level since 1929. The richest are hardly taxed at all. The Obama administration is utterly failing to protect working-class interests while pouring resources into the war in Afghanistan and the "defense" budget. No serious protections exist against job loss and foreclosure. With level funding of discretionary domestic programs at the federal level and the huge state deficits promises for major improvement in the educational system and infrastructure are a cruel joke.

Even health care reform, the signature accomplishment of the Obama administration, is on the ropes. In response to the fiscal crisis, states have begun to cut Medicaid, a central piece of the health care reform and crucial piece of the safety net for seniors and low-income people. Cutting the funding means the most vulnerable will suffer. What's next?

If progressives do not put forward a comprehensive alternative to these disastrous policies, if we abandon the working families, we risk the total isolation of the left, the disintegration of the center, and the triumph of the right. This would be a catastrophe. Humanity has a huge stake in our success. Redirecting our country away from empire will require an enormous mobilization of people and resources, reaching out to working-class, middle-class, and immigrant communities, seniors and youth, soldiers and their families. We must learn from the 1960s if we are to complete the work begun then.

In the 1960s, my generation faced an undemocratic social order at home and an imperialist war overseas. In the course of the struggles of the 1960s we learned some useful lessons – grassroots power can confront undemocratic institutions and win, and that wars will end when the soldiers fighting them, and their families, realize that the war has nothing to do with protecting the homeland. The struggles of the 1960s got us out of Vietnam and outlawed some of the most visible forms of racism, but we neither stopped the drive to empire nor constructed a real democracy at home. We did not find ways to bring significant numbers of working-class people into our movement. Those failures haunt us today.

Now we face a tremendous task in an environment different from the 1960s. We must understand how to respond to the obstacles and opportunities of this environment. Where is the youth movement of the 1960s, with its massive anti-war demonstrations? Then there was the draft, which spread the risk of death in Vietnam more equally over most youth, and was a major recruiter for the anti-war movement. Today the draft is gone and no longer do young men in general fear they might die in an unjust and unwinnable war. Because service in the armed forces is now voluntary, progressives must reach out to soldiers and their families to help overcome their isolation and the sense that because they volunteered they can't complain. Currently for many, the alternative to military service is a bleak job market or higher education that ties them to a mountain of debt. Young people's voices need to be heard when they demand quality education for all.

In the 1960s America was at the peak of its economic power. The war took vital resources away from the early reform efforts of the Johnson administration, but continued prosperity fostered the illusion that we could have both guns and butter, at least for a while. While working people tended to oppose the Vietnam War, their economic survival was not at stake. Today our well-being as a society is on the line and the survival of institutions on which working people rely depends on cutting the defense budget and implementing a fairer tax system. I have been working for some time on campaigns to make big reductions in the bloated "defense" budget, and end the attempted occupations of Iraq and Afghanistan.

In the 1960s a much higher percentage of the workforce was in unions, but the union leaders were more often than not pro-war. Today's union leaders are far more progressive, but unions represent a much smaller percentage of the workforce. In these terrible economic times people – blue collar, white collar, whatever – need unions more than ever. Over the last three decades, living standards for the average American have declined as people work longer for less. Unions are critical for the direct action we need now, strikes and demonstrations, as well as getting working-class voters to the polls. But without broad and well-organized political support, unions will not be able to overcome the legal and institutional obstacles that keep them weak. Supporting the right to unionize is essential if progressives want to win.

Involving working-class people and embracing working-class issues remains the central challenge of the progressive movement. Progressives must relearn how to build a people's movement from the grassroots up. Two imperatives dominate this generation: getting the working class back into the political process, and building an independent political force including liberals, conservatives, and progressives committed to dismantling the empire. Neither effort will succeed without the other.

Single-issue politics, where each issue is separate from all the others, has been a problem for American progressives forever. But now that the empire has bled us dry, one issue ties all the others together – where the money will come from to rebuild our country and provide for the needs of working families. Working-class and middle-class people produce the wealth of this country, and they have had less and less say about how that wealth is used. If my work at Neighbor to Neighbor taught me one thing it is that if we focus on the needs of working families, people can put aside strongly held differences on potentially divisive social issues and work for the common good. Progressives today have an unprecedented opportunity to bring people together and build a nationwide movement united for change. We must not let that opportunity pass us by.

BIBLIOGRAPHY

Books

Adelson, Alan. *SDS: A Profile*. New York: Charles Scribner's Sons, 1972.

Ali, Tariq. *Bush in Babylon: The Recolonisation of Iraq*. New York: Verso, 2003.

_____. *Street Fighting Years: An Autobiography of the Sixties*. London: Verso, 2005.

Anders, Evan. *Boss Rule in South Texas*. Austin: University of Texas Press, 1987.

Anonymous. *Imperial Hubris: How the West Is Losing the War on Terror*. Dulles, VA: Brassey's, Inc., 2004.

Appy, Christian G. *Working Class War: American Combat Soldiers and Vietnam*. Chapel Hill: University of North Carolina Press, 1993.

Arnove, Anthony. Iraq: *The Logic of Withdrawal*. New York: The New Press, 2006.

Ayers, Bill. *Fugitive Days: A Memoir*. New York: Penguin Books, 2003.

Barfield, Thomas. *Afghanistan: A Cultural and Political History*. Princeton University Press, 2010.

Becker, Jean-Jacques. *Histoire politique de la France depuis 1945*. Paris: Armand Colin, 2000.

Branch, Taylor. *At Canaan's Edge: America in the King Years 1965-1968*. New York: Simon & Schuster, 2006.

Brecher, Jeremy, et al., editors. *In the Name of Democracy: American War Crimes in Iraq and Beyond*. New York: Metropolitan Books, 2005.

Brunet, Jean-Paul. *Charonne: Lumières sur une Tragédie*. Paris: Flammarion, 2003.

Carter, Jimmy. *Our Endangered Values: America's Moral Crisis*. New York: Simon & Schuster, 2005.

Charters, Ann, ed. *The Portable Sixties Reader*. New York: Penguin Books, 2003.

Chomsky, Noam. *Failed States: The Abuse of Power and the Assault on Democracy.* New York: Metropolitan Books, 2006.

_____. *Hegemony or Survival: America's Quest for Global Dominance.* New York: Metropolitan Books, 2003.

_____. *Imperial Ambitions: Conversations on the Post-9/11 World.* New York: Metropolitan Books, 2005.

Cunningham, Bill. *Which People's Republic?* Seven Cats Press, 1999.

Curry, Constance et al. *Deep in Our Hearts: Nine White Women in the Freedom Movement.* Athens, Georgia: University of Georgia press, 2000.

Dedijer, Vladimir. *The Battle Stalin Lost: Memoirs of Yugoslavia 1948-1953.* New York: The Viking Press, 1971.

_____. *The Beloved Land.* New York: Simon and Schuster, 1961.

Edwards, Emily with photographs by Manuel Alvarez Bravo. *Painted Walls of Mexico: From Prehistoric Times until Today.* Austin: University of Texas Press, 1966.

Engel, Richard. *A Fist in the Hornet's Nest: On the Ground in Baghdad Before, During & After the War.* New York: Hyperion, 2004.

Evans, Sara. *Personal Politics: The Roots of Women's Liberation in the Civil Rights Movement & the New Left.* New York: Vintage Books, 1980.

Frank. Thomas. *What's the Matter with Kansas? How Conservatives Won the Heart of America.* New York: Metropolitan Books, 2004.

Ferguson, Niall. Colossus: *The Price of America's Empire.* New York: The Penguin Press, 2004.

French, Howard W. *A Continent for the Taking: The Tragedy and Hope of Africa.* New York: Alfred A. Knopf, 2004.

Garvey, Helen. *Rebels with a Cause: A Collective Memoir of the Hopes, Rebellions, and Repressions of the 1960s.* Los Gatos: Shire Press, 2007.

Gettleman, Marvin E. *Vietnam: History, Documents, and Opinions.* New York: New American Library, 1970.

Gitlin, Todd. *The Sixties: Years of Hope, Days of Rage.* New York: Bantam Books, 1989.

Goldstein, Gordon M. *Lessons in Disaster: McGeorge Bundy and the Path to War in Vietnam.* New York: Henry Holt, 2008.

Greider, William. *One World, Ready or Not: the Manic Logic of Global Capitalism.* New York: Simon and Schuster, 1997.

Grossman, Jerome. *The Relentless Liberal.* New York: Vantage Press, 1996.

Hayden, Tom. *Reunion: A Memoir.* New York: Random House, 1988.

Hedges, Chris. *What Every Person Should Know About War*. New York: Free Press, 2003.

Hirsh, Arthur. *The French New Left: An Intellectual History from Sartre to Gorz*. Boston: South End Press, 1981.

Isserman, Maurice and Michael Kazin. *America Divided: The Civil War of the 1960s*. New York: Oxford University Press, 2004.

Johnson, Chalmers. *The Sorrows of Empire: Militarism, Secrecy, and the End of the Republic*. New York: Metropolitan Books, 2004.

Johnson, Chris and Jolyon Leslie. *Afghanistan: The Mirage of Peace*. Zed Books, 2008.

Karnow, Stanley. *Vietnam: A History*. New York: Penguin Books, 1997.

Keniston, Kenneth. *Young Radicals: Notes on Committed Youth*. New York: Harcourt, Brace & World, 1968.

Kennedy, Paul. *The Rise and Fall of the Great Powers*. Vintage Books, 1989.

Kinzer, Stephen. *All the Shah's Men*. Hoboken: Wiley, 2003.

Klare, Michael T. *Blood and Oil: The Dangers and Consequences of America's Growing Dependency on Imported Petroleum*. New York: Metropolitan Books, 2004.

Kozol, Jonathan. *The Shame of the Nation: The Restoration of Apartheid Schooling in America*. New York: Crown Publishers, 2005.

Kupchan, Charles A. *The End of the American Era: U.S. Foreign Policy and the Geopolitics of the Twenty-First Century*. New York: Vintage Books, 2002.

Kurlansky, Mark. *1968: The Year That Rocked the World*. New York: Ballantine Books, 2004.

Lasater, Dale. *Falfurrias: Ed C. Lasater and the Development of South Texas*. College Station: Texas A&M University Press, 1985.

Mann, James. *Rise of the Vulcans: The History of Bush's War Cabinet*. New York: Viking, 2004.

McDermott, John F. M. *Restoring Democracy to America: How to Free Markets and Politics from the Corporate Culture of Business and Government*. The Pennsylvania State University Press, 2010.

Miller, James. *Democracy is in the Streets: From Port Huron to the Siege of Chicago*. New York: Simon & Schuster, 1987.

Moses, Robert P. and Charles E. Cobb, Jr. *Radical Equations: Math Literacy and Civil Rights*. Boston: Beacon Press, 2001.

The New York Times. *Class Matters*. New York: Henry Holt, 2004.

Orwell, George. *The Orwell Reader*. New York: Harcourt Brace Jovanovich, Inc., 1956.

Piven, Frances Fox and Richard A. Cloward. *Why Americans Don't Vote*. New York: Pantheon Books, 1989.

_____. *Why Americans Still Don't Vote: And Why Politicians Want It That Way*. Boston: Beacon Press, 2000.

Preble, Christopher A. *The Power Problem: How American Military Dominance Makes Us Less Safe, Less Prosperous, and Less Free*. Cornell University Press, 2009.

Progressive Labor Party. *Revolution Today*. Jericho, NY: Exposition Press. 1970.

Richardson, Louise. *What Terrorists Want: Understanding the Enemy, Containing the Threat*. New York: Random House, 2006.

Ricks, Thomas E. *Fiasco: The American Military Adventure in Iraq*. New York: The Penguin Press, 2006.

Roy, Arundhati. *An Ordinary Person's Guide to Empire*. Cambridge, Massachusetts: South End Press, 2004.

Sale, Kirkpatrick. *SDS*. New York: Random House, 1972.

Schell, Jonathan. *The Unconquerable World: Power, Nonviolence, and the Will of the People*. New York: Metropolitan Books, 2003.

Schirmer, Daniel B. *Republic or Empire: American Resistance to the Philippine War*. Cambridge, Massachusetts: Schenkman Publishing Company, 1972.

Silvers, Robert B. and Robert Epstein. *Striking Terror: America's New War*. New York: New York Review of Books, 2002.

Stiglitz, Joseph E. *Globalization and its Discontents*. New York: W. W. Norton & Company, 2003.

Sutcliffe, Bob. *100 Ways of Seeing an Unequal World*. New York: Zed Books Ltd, 2001.

Szulc, Tad. *Dominican Diary*. New York: Delacorte Press, 1965.

Truong, Nhu Tang. *A Vietcong Memoir: An Inside Account of the Vietnam War and Its Aftermath*. New York: Vintage Books, 1985.

Teixeira, Ruy and Joel Rogers. *America's Forgotten Majority: Why the White Working Class Still Matters*. New York: Basic Books, 2000.

Wellstone, Paul David. *The Conscience of a Liberal: Reclaiming the Compassionate Agenda*. New York: Random House, 2001.

Weiner, Tim. *Legacy of Ashes: The History of the CIA*. New York: Doubleday, 2007.

Wright, Lawrence. *The Looming Tower: Al-Qaeda and the Road to 9/11*. New York: Alfred A. Knopf, 2006.

Zinn, Howard. *A People's History of the United States, 1492-Present*. New York: HarperCollins Publishers, 1999.

Zweig, Michael. *The Working Class Majority: America's Best Kept Secret*. Ithaca, NY: Cornell University Press, 2000.

Articles and Reports

Afghanistan Study Group. *A New Way Forward: Rethinking U.S. Strategy in Afghanistan*. August 16, 2010.

Anonymous. "CIA Insider Says U.S. Fighting Wrong War." Interview with Andrea Mitchell, NBC News, Wednesday, June 23, 2004, distributed by *Truthout*, June 25, 2004.

Booth, Paul. "National Secretary's Report." *New Left Notes*, April 1, 1966, p. 1

Cambridge Chronicle. "City's Elderly Face Rent Crisis: Plan Convention." August 1, 1968, pp. 5-6.

Cambridge Chronicle. "Senator Donahue Announces He Will File Local Option Rent Control Legislation." October 2, 1969. p.10.

Danner, Mark. "Taking Stock of the Forever War." *The New York Times Magazine*, September 11, 2005.

Dedijer, Vladimir. "Mr. Dedijer's Personal Statement." *The Times*, Wednesday, December 22, 1954.

_____. "A Letter to Jean-Paul Sartre: The American Left Carries the Hope of the World." *New York Times*, February 4, 1971, p. 35.

Dehghanpisheh, Babak and Larry Kaplow "As Sunnis Flee, Shiites Now Dominate Baghdad." *Newsweek*, September 10. 2007.

Engelhardt, Tom. "George Orwell ... meet Franz Kafka." *TomDispatch*, June 13, 2004.

Filkins, Dexter. "Votes Counted. Deals Made. Chaos Wins." *The New York Times Week in Review*, April 30, 2006.

Galbraith, Peter. "Iraq: Bush's Islamic Republic." *New York Review of Books*, August 11, 2005.

Hall, Gordon. "Boston's Radical Student Left: The Story behind Those Vietnam Demonstrations." *Boston Sunday Herald*, May 23, 1965.

Hedges, Chris and Al-Arian, Laila. "The Other War." *The Nation*, July 30, 2007.

Hiro, Dilip. "How the Bush Administration's Iraqi Oil Grab Went Awry: Greenspan's Oil Claim in Context." *TomDispatch*, September 25, 2007.

Howe, Irving. "New Styles in Leftism." *Dissent*, fall 1965.

Johnson, Chalmers. "Our First Victory Was Zapatero." *TomDispatch*, June 11, 2004

Lewis, Anthony. "Making Torture Legal." *New York Review of Books,* July 15, 2004.

Maher, John. "Beyond the anti-war movement to other problems." *Vietnam Summer News,* August 25, 1967.

———. "Communists in SDS." *New Left Notes,* August 24, 1966.

———. "New Politics Convention." *Ramparts,* October, 1967.

Moot, John R. "CCA Gives Rent Control Stand." *Cambridge Chronicle,* October 9, 69, p. 10.

Morgan, Dan. "Congress Backs Pentagon Budget Heavy on Future Weapons." *Washington Post,* June 11. 2004. Cited in Truthout, June 12, 2004.

Parenti, Christian. "Afghan Wonderland." *Middle East Report,* Summer, 2006, pp. 12-17.

Rosenthal, Stephen J. *Vietnam Study Guide and Annotated Bibliography.* Students for a Democratic Society.

Schell, Jonathan. "The Empire Backfires." *The Nation,* March 29, 2004.

Sustainable Defense Task Force. "Debt, Deficits, & Defense: A Way Forward." June, 2010.

The Task Force for a Responsible Withdrawal from Iraq. *Quickly, Carefully, and Generously: The Necessary Steps for a Responsible Withdrawal from Iraq.* Commonwealth Institute, 2010.

Vietnam Summer News. "Profs distribute protest 'commencement program.'" June 23, 1967.

Webb, Lee D. "Viet Summer shows what can be done." *Vietnam Summer News,* August 25, 1967, p.7

Unpublished Materials

Adams, Thomas Boylston. "A Policy for all Americans."

Alperovitz, Gar et al. *A PROPOSAL FOR A VIETNAM SUMMER.*

Bello, Walden. "The Crisis of the Globalist Project & the New Economics of George W. Bush." Paper prepared for the McPlanet Conference, Berlin, June 27, 2002.

Chomsky, Noam. "The Responsibility of Intellectuals." Text of a talk given at the Harvard Hillel Foundation, March, 1966.

H-R May 2 Committee. "The Significance of the White Paper." 1965.

Jehlen, Alan. "WE ALL HATE TO STUDY."

———. "William Pepper's Lonely Heart's Club Band."

———. Editor. Vietnam Summer Work List Mailings.

Maher, John and Rev. Patrick O'Connor. Correspondence and letters to the editor from each printed in the *Boston Globe*, December 1965 and January 1966.

Maher, John. "Citizens Committees and the Student Movement Against the War." Manuscript.

_____. "Imperialism and Fundamental Social Change." Paper prepared for Seminar on Fundamental Change in America, fall 1967.

National Conference for New Politics. "The Convention." *New Politics News*, August 28, 1967.

Perry, Amy. "Harvard/Radcliffe Students for a Democratic Society 1960-1972: The Origin, Growth and Demise of a Movement for Social Change." Harvard University undergraduate thesis, March 20, 1986.

Potter, Paul and Hal Benenson. "A Critique of Radical Perspectives on the Campus."

Thorne, Barrie. "Resisting the Draft: An Ethnography of the Draft Resistance Movement." PhD Dissertation, Brandeis University, 1971.

Vietnam Summer. "King Calls for Anti-War Referenda." Undated press release.

Vietnam Summer. *Project Profiles*.

Vietnam Summer Revolutionary Workers Committee. "Manifesto."

Vietnam Summer Teacher Student Project. "Teachers Against the War." Newsletter, August 17, 1967.